CRASHING

CATHEDRALS

EDMUND WHITE

BY THE BOOK

EDITED BY TOM CARDAMONE

ITNA PRESS
Los Angeles, CA
www.itnapress.com

Originally published in New York, NY by Itna Press in 2019.

Quotations from Edmund White's work are used with the author's permission.

Previously published essays include:

Tom Cardamone, "*The Unpunished Vice* by Edmund White," Lambda Literary, 2018

Wayne Hoffman, "On Its 40th Anniversary, Revisiting the Powerful Communal Vision of *The Joy of Gay Sex*," Slate, 2017

Robert Glück, *A Boy's Own Story*, Review of Contemporary Fiction, Vol. 16, Issue 3, September 1996

Allan Gurganus, *A Boy's Own Story*, Introduction, Modern Library, 2002

Leo Racicot, "The Faber Book of Gay Short Fiction," *Gayletter*, Issue #5, 2017

Sarah Schulman, "Genet as Feasting with Panthers (And Palestine): Edmund White's *Jean Genet*," sessumsmagazine.com, 2017

Tim Teeman, "Terre Haut," excerpted from his book, *In Bed With Gore Vidal: Hustlers, Hollywood, and the Private World of an American Master*, Riverdale Ave Books/Magnus, 2013

William Sterling Walker, "*The Flaneur*, as Sentimental Ex-Patriot," Chelsea Station, 2016

Donald Weise, "*Sacred Monsters*, as Snapshots from an Editor: Working with Edmund White," Lambda Literary, 2016

Cover art courtesy of Lincoln Perry Copyright © 2024
Cover design courtesy of Chris Stoddard Copyright © 2024

Tom Cardamone, Editor – 2nd ed.
ISBN 979-8-9882829-3-8

Library of Congress Control Number: 2023952548

To Edmund White

CONTENTS

INTRODUCTION

A STEAMY YET airless August day—I flew down the subway's stairs, slipping past befuddled tourists and tired office workers to effortlessly slide between the closing doors of a Manhattan bound A train. This successful subterranean ballet, a moment of pride among New Yorkers, is more luck than skill. Still, doubling down on my self-satisfaction, I took the last available seat next to a middle-aged man (always forgetting that I, too, am now middle-aged, expecting that I'll only think of myself as middle-aged once I reach old age). He was well-ensconced in *City Boy*, Edmund White's memoir of his initial years in New York. Always titillated when I spy someone reading something other than a tattered (or worse, highlighted) Bible in public, I was about to remark that I had literally just finished the book, but hesitated as talking to strangers on the subway is such a crapshoot, though I have had some marvelous conversations, a good number had fallen flat or turned remarkably weird (I once warned a women that an emboldened rat was inching close to her sandaled feet and she thanked me, and then proceeded to nod vigorously, saying "thank you" over and over for what felt like twenty minutes while we both waited for the next train). So, I settled in and wondered: *what other books by Edmund White had the man read and when had he read them?* At what stages in his life did he turn to one of White's novels, pick up a biography or collection of essays? I ran my fingers across my mental bookshelf as well, cataloging for the first time all the various times I had read Edmund White.

My initial exposure to White's work was shortly after coming out of the closet. I had sold everything I had to move from

Florida to New York to deliberately burn through the last of my twenties. Nights were spent stalking the streets of Chelsea and navigating the still burgeoning club scene—days I drifted through odd temp jobs and scouring the stacks of the main Brooklyn library for gay stories, to decode this exhilaration. I started and stopped a number of flat, disappointing titles until I stumbled across *A Boy's Own Story*. I can say with great clarity that I recall reading the majority of this short novel *standing up* in the stacks—so electrifying were the deeply recognizable yet never before vocalized stations of our journey. A few years on, having moved from excited reader of queer destinies to a fledgling writer of one, the first collection of gay short stories I read was White's stunning *Skinned Alive*. Later, laid off and living cheap in yet-to-be gentrified East Harlem, I dedicated a goodly slice of a lazy summer to reading the rest of White's autobiographical trilogy, being so struck by the concluding volume, *The Farewell Symphony*, that I often recommend it as one of *the* great New York City novels. And then I got another job (sigh), within walking distance of the Strand Bookstore. Lunchtimes were spent haunting particular stacks wherein I came across White's illuminating *The Burning Library*. Afterwards, once I had devoured all of Genet's work (bought for me en masse by a straight friend who rolled his eyes with exaggerated exasperation upon learning that I'd not yet read him) and hungry for more, I turned to White's seminal biography.

This mental inventory continued after I exited the train—I don't remember where I was going that day, only that I questioned why some author's oeuvres had burned brightly in my life—Mishima's ornate, compartmentalized homosexuality (but what a jewelry box!), the historical romances of Mary Renault, the dark cool of Dennis Cooper—just to name a few of the writers whose work I devoured quickly, wholly—why was Edmund White there throughout?

Edmund White has produced a body of work that spans decades, recording the most tumultuous times in modern gay history—the argument could be made the birth of gay history. His writings, frequently drawn from his own life, capture the dawn of a new civil rights movement and the following plague that consumed his circle of lovers and friends. *The* novel, *A Boy's Own*

Story, is a modern classic—the first book within the aforementioned trilogy, itself among the penultimate books of gay letters, which runs from Stonewall to AIDS. Known equally for his prodigious nonfiction output, White's work encompasses biography and autobiography, essays on diverse topics: sex, travel, literature—stories of literary friendships and midnight encounters found only by living in New York and Paris.

Edmund White's perseverance and art have created an unparalleled legacy, winning him awards and international acclaim. He is the only living gay writer to have a biography written about him (*The Burning World*, Stephen Barber). Additionally, Keith Fleming, his nephew, produced a memoir, *The Boy with the Thorn in His Side*, chronicling White's stewardship during his troubled teens, as well as a book about White's childhood (*Original Youth*). (White states in an interview in *The Review of Contemporary Fiction* that he took on *The Joy of Gay Sex* primarily to support Fleming.) Such preeminence has many starting points. Several of his titles taken on their own would have guaranteed literary prominence, but the permanent impact of *A Boy's Own Story* is unparalleled. In his introduction to the Modern Library edition (reprinted here), Allan Gurganus finds "the heroic solace in one's own self-admitted self-administered condemnation." The casual perversity of the wholesome title, this almost flippant laying claim to a slice of Americana at the dawn of Reaganism, both solidified and catapulted a career that has, in turn, given us an artistic touchstone to find such solace *outside* ourselves. The path is now lit. Doubly fascinating, given the timing of publication, is that this book doesn't concern itself with coming out, but is, rather, a type of going inward. *A Boy's Own Story* is about being, complicated by sexuality, and is less a classic of queer genre and simply one in general. With apolitical impudence, equality trumps assimilation.

That would have been the pinnacle of any career, but then a decade later came *Genet: A Biography*. Newly HIV positive, living in Paris with few friends and unsure of the language, White was asked by his publisher if he knew anyone who could write the biography of the recently deceased author. Surprised that there wasn't already a book in English, he took the project on. In *My Lives: An Autobiography*, White reports that within Jean-Paul Sartre's *Saint Genet* "the hard biographical facts. . .could be reduced to a thirty-page summary. All of its hundreds of other pages were filled with speculation, brilliant but controvertible." He then records an almost decade-long literary journey: tracking down letters, publications, friends and acquaintances across France and around the world—as the outsider-pretending-to-be-an-insider of *A Boy's Own Story* writes the definitive book on the definitive outsider of the 20th century.

Several years ago I edited an anthology, *The Lost Library: Gay Fiction Rediscovered*, wherein I asked writers I knew or had read to write about a favored, meaningful out-of-print gay novel or short story collection. Those writers that joined the project were then asked to refer another writer. This was an education. And this was a deliberate act of remembrance: so many authors I'd meet would recount a gay book they treasured, only to end with a poignant, offhand-oft-repeated comment "if you can find it. It's been out of print for years." And the books covered spanned a century, touching many continents and cultures. The stories were quite diverse (and it turned out I had previously only read one of the books, so I often missed my subway stop, engrossed in one of these nearly forgotten novels or short story collections). I felt like a literary archeologist. Years later, my internal accounting of White's work inspired me to reconnect with several of the contributors to *The Lost Library*. Philip Clark, Jerry Rosco, Ian Rafael Titus, and Rick Whitaker were all excited to tackle a favorite White title. I then reached out to authors I'd recently read, reviewed or interviewed, like Kathe Koja and David McConnell. I shared a stage with Charlie Vázquez at a Housing Works Gay Pride Reading. He asked me what I was working on and we immediately fell into a conversation about how much *The Burning Library* had meant to us. Poet Philip F. Clark was queued up behind me for cocktails at the Lambda Literary Awards (where I'd just taken a selfie with the cowboy from the Village People) and our chat of course led to Ed, who was honoring John Irving that night. Everyone I connected with was enthusiastic and I was deeply grateful. Where *The Lost Library* was an act of discovery and remembrance, this forming and then-untitled collection felt downright celebratory. And everyone, throughout this gathering of voices, was calling him "Ed." With a sociable ease, with a warm, firm claiming of friendship we were toasting one of our own. I realized that not only are we charged with recording our own history, but that we are here to honor *our* history makers.

On that note, I was introduced to more folk in Ed's circle, his bibliographer, reviewers, writers who'd written about him previously, friends and colleagues who valued his work. His husband, Michael Carroll, made several introductions and wrote a powerful memory piece while excerpting juxtaposed passages from *Skinned Alive*. Sheila Kohler, Ed's former Columbia student, writing about his Proust biography, notes that Proust "(w)as the novelist who believed that life presents the author with only one book to write: one's own life translated." How easily we could claim White as *our* Proust. But this is a man who firmly attached the word "Joy" to "Gay" and "Sex" in 1977 and in doing so wrote a permission slip for thousands upon thousands of men to own and enjoy their bodies and minds. And when the crisis hit, he was a founding member of the GMHC. Proust expertly observed society. White rolled up his sleeves and joined in. The traversing and recording of Gay America in *States of Desire* opened up a fabulous tableau of a dynamic culture in transition; and in doing so the ever erudite Ed preserved for us a historical document that is de Tocquevillian in scope. As Colm Toibin notes in his essay on *The Married Man*, "Edmund White manages in the most subtle way to make the most personal book into the most political."

It was in misremembering a passage from the Fleming memoir that this long untitled-project was finally named:

My uncle's reading voice took some getting used to, being higher and more prissily precise than his everyday voice. And if he happened to be in the midst of a particularly beautiful passage, his voice could get so reverent and soft that it wasn't always completely intelligible above the surging arias of Bizet's Pearl Fishers playing on the stereo. With his raised eyebrows and gently blinking eyes, he made me think of those older choir boys standing a head taller behind the younger boys. These beautiful passages in Nocturnes featured lots of what my mother referred to as "those flights of poetry Eddie's always sailing off into— flights she said she skipped when reading his stuff so as to get back to the story. But though these flights usually sailed over my head, my uncle, sensing sometimes that I might not have got it, would look up and explain, for instance, that the "ruined cathedral" was based on an abandoned warehouse along the Hudson where he went cruising sometimes, and that he had in mind a gigantic bird when he wrote "Soaring above me hung the pitched roof, wings on the downstroke… "

Edmund White crashes through the cathedrals of art, history, politics, culture, and memory. As these waves withdraw and reform, raw truths are exposed. The best writing is particular, splintered, and in spurning and being spurned, shows us the oceanic in ourselves just before it is drawn back into the whole.

Thank you, Edmund White.
Thank you, Ed.
Thank you for taking so many journeys, from the most harrowing through to the more immediate and valuable currents of love.
Thank you for sharing your expeditions of the heart with all of us.

Tom Cardamone
New York, NY
2019

"'Not at all,' the woman tells him firmly. 'That would have been vulgar. Color isn't vulgar in life because everything happens so quickly in life, but in a picture it—'"

—from *Forgetting Elena*

FORGETTING ELENA

DAVID McCONNELL

BOOKS STARTED TO frustrate me at age nine or ten, I think. They were served up with foil Newberry medals stuck to heavy-weight unglazed paper dust jackets. The teacher's pet of art forms, as they still are, books were riddled with false-seeming virtue and as clever as oatmeal. Even holding one felt weird and old-fashioned.

But I was a lonely child and the company of writers, faraway or dead, brilliant, and largely male, I admit, was the society that formed me. I would have chosen music, if not for the dangerous-seeming sensuality, the inarticulateness. So from the start I was a writer who didn't like the contemporary culture of books and writing. I say I *was* a writer and not that I aspired to be one, because the notion of identity I decided upon at the start was that it was something handed to you, a kind of fatality independent of any action in the world. In fact it speaks to the incredible power of pure language that a kid who spent as much time watching TV as I did, was actually formed by the books he "let in" from time to time.

Why, for someone with a personality deformed in just this way, was Edmund White the only living writer worth thinking about? This seemed an obvious truth to me right from the start. In retrospect I'm fascinated that even an ostensibly slight book like *Forgetting Elena* could have been so extremely important to me. And if I now understand why people were always rolling their eyes or frowning in alarm when I shrugged off my friends' enthusiasms for, say, Ashbery or Merrill, and talked, "Edmund, Edmund, Edmund" with Kool-Aid conviction, I still think it's important to take the strange youth I was seriously. Maybe I had a point, though I never deigned to explain it to anyone. Like everything else I considered worthwhile, it simply *was*.

The story used to go around New York that after a gifted young man wrote a book, *Forgetting Elena*, the poet Richard Howard straightened its collar as a fond parent would for a son going off on a date with a debutante. (I've also heard claims that editor Patrick Merla contributed something, but his hand isn't visible.) *Forgetting Elena* does have an elbow grease polish that doesn't feel quite like Edmund and which soon, thankfully, disappears from his work. Maybe that's Howard.

Edmund himself tells of (and has written about) a related incident. Howard once took the young writer to see the already illustrious poet James Merrill to whom Edmund read from the manuscript of *Forgetting Elena*. Merrill had nothing whatever to say about the reading. His non-response was understandably crushing and is curious in someone generally kind and well-mannered. Years later Edmund, who had doggedly persisted his way to the pinnacle of American letters and was now friends with Merrill, asked him about the incident. As Edmund tells it, Merrill was urbanely reassuring and said that he'd certainly just been drunk that evening. In Edmund's telling the story warns against reading your worst fears into an inscrutable person. But I've heard it whispered that Merrill really didn't like *Forgetting Elena*. For the purposes of my design here, Merrill, the old, the sophisticated, the lionized, hated *Forgetting Elena* for some reason, and his reaction is equal in importance and opposite to that of an obscure, angry, self-convinced, very young man, myself.

Art, it seemed to me back then, in every familiar form, was over. One by one, each art, in relation to its own tradition, had split into an intellectually compelling, but difficult, branch and a popular but rote, folk branch. One was too dry and the other too vapid. This was a simplistic view, but there is obviously something to it. In terms of the novel, things looked bleak. Since age nine or ten or whatever it was, I couldn't read any of them—even hold one—without screwing my face up at the hackneyed tropes of narration or at the deadly experimentalism. Like a lot of people at the time, even more now, I often took refuge in the escapism trash offered—the now ubiquitous "folk novel" (my term) or "genre" or "YA" (theirs). Some practitioners were more skillful than others, and it was fun to pretend they were almost good: Stanislaw Lem, Stephen King, the Anne Rice of *Interview with the Vampire*, Philip K. Dick. Turning from them to a book by Claude Simon, for example, caused the mind to stall. Simon's work wasn't even in the same category. His pleasures were the pleasures of a fantastic day job. Reading him was work, as the know-nothings complained, but work in the best sense. Unfortunately everybody (except for me) already had a day job.

Many people (and not just gay men) recognized their lives when they first read *A Boy's Own Story*. That was a big part of its importance. For me, the book was overwhelming mainly as an artistic discovery. That's what I told myself at the time. I think, in fact, the gay content also meant the world to me, and I simply chose to focus on the art.

I received my copy of the book as a kind of party favor after spending the night with Chris Cox in his old Chelsea Hotel studio. The novel was dedicated to him, and he had a half-emptied box of the hardbacks next to his bed. I was shocked that a book born of sex would turn out to be so important to me. After reading just the first page, I think, I closed the book for a long moment, "realizing" that Edmund was the only living writer worth thinking about.

The present, living world is crucial to understanding Edmund's work in a way that's less true with other writers. In the case of a roman à clef like *Forgetting Elena*, or a memoir, like *A Boy's Own Story*, an actual key to the whole thing existed, real people you could meet. With *The Joy of Gay Sex*, you could put the book into practice in the real world. Edmund himself boasted of experimenting with every position he wrote about in the guide. The biography of Genet was obviously real world history. But what part of the real world could possibly inform the elements of fantasy and confection in *Forgetting Elena*, *Caracole* and others?

After I read *A Boy's Own Story* I thought, "Aha, non-fiction is what gives this art its urgency and dispels the formulaic." That was wrong. Normal non-fiction is exceedingly formulaic. Read any journalist. *Forgetting Elena* had a real world key—gay circles on Fire Island circa 1972 (and it is sometimes crazily specific in detail. "The deck forms an L on two sides of the glass-enclosed dancing floor." That's the Blue Whale during low tea). But *Forgetting Elena* reads as a novel, a fantasy even. Irked by the demotion, Edmund once mocked a bookstore that shelved the novel in "Science Fiction" along with King and Dick.

Over the years I've become convinced that the real world counterpart for the streak of fantasy in Edmund's work is art itself, the creative act. *Forgetting Elena* is an anticipatory poetics, as important for understanding everything else he writes as *The Joy of Gay Sex* clearly is for a writer whose cardinal subject is sex.

And this is why I bring up that story about reading the manuscript to Merrill. At the very heart of *Forgetting Elena*, a portrayal or embodiment of artistic careerism, is a manuscript, a memoir by a woman we will learn is Elena herself. The novel takes place in an atmosphere of withering refinement in a community of, basically, sophisticated poets (of Merrills and Merrill wannabes). Elena's manuscript first appears when she diffidently reads an excerpt. Her polite listeners dissemble how her work repels them. (Ironically, excerpts from the memoir are the only sentences in the entire book with the feeling and directness a normal reader would expect. The rest of *Forgetting Elena* seems designed for scientists, other writers or those who may be brilliantly immature in other ways.) Elena breaks off her reading abruptly, and her manuscript spends the rest of the novel in a box of some horn-like material—until the very end when it is finally read through (we get another feeling excerpt) as a kind of ceremony of farewell by her forgetful brother/lover/prince whose alternate self Elena is best understood to be. In fact, an easy way to wade into the sense of the novel from the shallow end is to think of her as the narrator's sincere self. The title becomes *Forgetting My Sincere Self*, also the subject of some of Merrill's best poems.

The questions remain, why did the book mean so much to me, and why did, at least for the purposes of this argument, Merrill hate it? Why did another monster aesthete, one whom Merrill adored, Vladimir Nabokov, after first declining to blurb the book, later mention Edmund as the American writer he most admired? (Considering how the blurb marketplace operates, Nabokov may not have had time to read the book at first. His wife Véra committed passages of it to memory.)

Forgetting Elena can be looked at as more exercise than art. A written-out cadenza. A Mendelsohnian song without words paradoxically composed of nothing but words. A certain kind of writer—not all—and a certain kind of young person—also not all—will find it intoxicating.

Schematically, the novel, like almost all books by young writers, is a variety of education story. A young man discovers his place in the world and, at the moment of his greatest triumph, he rejects the woman who has helped and consoled him. This stark plot is almost entirely obscured by peculiarly intense writing. And the incidents of which the plot is built are as uncertain as clouds of silt carried in a river. The narrator wakes in the book's first sentence with a fascinating form of amnesia which, while leaving untouched or even enhancing his intellect, sensitivity and linguistic prowess, strips him of all recognition of the familiar and of the past. At first he doesn't even know what his own body feels like. A great, bizarre passage describes how the sensation of sweat trickling across his torso makes him feel as if his body were surrealistically deformed (like a figure in Dalí's "Persistence of Memory"), upper and lower bulbs linked by a fleshy filament. He doesn't know his name or what he looks like or what he has done in the past or where he is or the identities of the people around him. This—the book's central conceit—is like putting a Darwin in the place of a newborn, or Aristotle on Mars.

The novel describes a strange island society. At first the narrator assumes himself to be a low-ranking member of an older man's household—Herbert, who, it emerges, has led a coup of sorts against the *ancien régime* of a woman named Doris. She lives in retirement with some of her partisans in a house next door. (A view into Herbert's bathroom window means they can study its inmates' most private moments, which, in a society this layered, turn out to be only a little revealing). The community resembles E.F. Benson's village of Tilling, but if petty politics and obsessive attention to social minutiae are taken seriously to comic effect there, here all, especially the amusing, the inconsequential, the light, is deadly serious. A closer analogue, probably a direct inspiration, is Heian court society as described in Sei Shonagon's *Pillow Book*. The islanders frequently stop everything to christen some infinitesimal incident (watching a house fire becomes "The Fire Viewing") or to commemorate it in spontaneous verse, often written, like Sei Shonagon's morning after letters, on special paper with special colored inks selected with an exhausting consciousness of effect. The society is rule-bound. Its repressed energy, masked by idle creativity, serves ambition for ambition's own sake. Readers register, without being able to name it—because the cynicism is structural, never expressed—an extremely cynical view of a society of artists.

Herbert's circle is a bit more egalitarian, slightly more "Protestant," Doris's more aristocratic, more formal. But both groups are too refined to permit breathing without thinking. While everyone else knows who the narrator is and what his role is to be in the near future, he himself must piece it together with the coy help of Elena and her attendant Maria. These two women don't seem to fit into either camp, though Elena was once connected to Doris's old guard—whose name emerges: the Valentines. The narrator, after spending most of the book in humble agonies of anxiety and bemusement, finally grasps that he is a great Valentine himself, in fact, the ex-Prince Royal, son of the island's former ruler. His John-John Kennedy-like public role is still of huge symbolic importance on the island, and the responsibility of that role dooms his almost recovered love affair with Elena. The whole book builds toward a heartless ritual burial in which the narrator ceremonially dispenses with Elena and returns to his amnesiac state.

I was once told who "Herbert" was based on, but I can't remember now. I imagine him as a sort of Sandy McClatchy, prim and self-serious. A further real life key, aggressive in its baldness, is the name "Valentine," which is Edmund's middle name. Love, to which Valentine might allude, is talked about a great deal in the book, but, except in Elena's feelings for the narrator, it is chillingly absent. Doris speaking of Elena: "'She's a bewitching woman, fascinating, quite fascinating, of course... But she is not a realist. This is not the best of all possible worlds, but we must live in it...'" The demystified absence of love in the book, when it later turns from cold to forlorn, to yearning, becomes the poignant ground note of all of Edmund's best work. For him love is as problematic as God was for Updike (an unexpected fixation, like Newton's on alchemy, and one I frowned over, until I decided the obsession itself was compelling even if its object wasn't).

I haven't even mentioned the closetedness which for some people is the most notable thing about *Forgetting Elena*. After all, this is a novel about a gay world—or a gay novel—dressed (sort of, grudgingly) as straight. Is it also about closetedness? Many intellectuals at the time—this is hard to imagine but true—believed real art could never explicitly deal with homosexuality. The poor gay artists had no alternative but to inflate whatever they might come up with by generalizing it. That's what Proust did. More to the point, that's what Ashbery and Merrill were doing. One critic claimed that the artistic strength of *Forgetting Elena* lay in the very fact that it was closeted. For him Edmund failed as an artist the moment he started writing, with fluorescent clarity, about men having sex with other men. Presumably the critic asked himself, "where's the art in that?"—as if the business of literary art is to cover bits of the world with words. Language can fog up over time. The opacity can even be pretty, but it begins to miss the truth. A certain kind of good writing is simply cleaning the panes as a thoughtful glazier's job involves a rag and spit. Strangely, there was an element of cultural or self-fulfilling (same thing) truth in that critic's view, and it may have felt to Edmund at the time—as it certainly looked to some people, especially an older generation—that Edmund was, as they say, committing career suicide by writing about king dick. The closetedness and the careerism in *Forgetting Elena*, a debut that operates as a swan song for certain kinds of personal aspiration and old ways of looking at art, may come from a single source.

Is there no content at all? Stripped of emotion, love hollowed out of it, a rattle with bone dry artistic ambition, what is the novel even about? For me it comes back to art, since the all-consuming sex that is Edmund's true subject—biological, "low" and so novel that it's slimed with blood, bawling and naked of meaning—doesn't appear yet.

But, am I really talking about Edmund White, the ever-genial raconteur, the helpful blurber, the fretful but ambitious chef, the airily brilliant, over-eating, tireless, magnificently well-read but non-confrontational (even a touch slavish at times) author so many people know and love—and even condescend to!—in New

York, Paris, London and so on? Why would a nobody, a book-irritated loner (me) look for an artistic lesson from a man who seems to embody the sissified formality, the glamorous, the *mere*, exclusivity of dead art (gay socialite, Princeton professor, *Académie Française*, American Academy of Arts and Letters)? More importantly, why would the king of that world, James Merrill (Awards, awards, awards, lord of Yale Younger Poets, stayed-in-James's-Venice apartment, masterpiece-writer, American Academy of Arts and Letters ((*superior echelon*))), "hate" the same man's first book?

Merrill wasn't wrong, of course. He was a great poet of love. On one level, it's plain how *Forgetting Elena* might have upset him. He would have been self-consciously alarmed to see youthful energy devoted to surfaces and loveless coldness. But a worse fear might have been lurking. What if youth *is* surfaces and loveless coldness? What if love, art, *Romeo and Juliet*, and the whole grand (Merrill's) tradition of feelings and meanings is over? Maybe the lesser artist, a non-poet, a guy who has committed career suicide, a scattered littérateur who churns out sex guides, works for Time-Life, dips into biography, memoir, writes ceaseless articles, *a man who never revises his work*—maybe he's the one who speaks more urgently to the times or to the future. Artistically, Merrill was the Real Thing, but he may have divined from Henry James's story of that name that a certain kind of authenticity is redundant.

Edmund and Merrill both had a lifestyle quirk that was generational and gay in origin. Back then, you kept your real, grown-up public life quite separate from your erotic life of sexy, inarticulate hustlers. The glaring class discrimination involved in living this way is incredibly upsetting to people nowadays.

Historically, a compartmentalized life isn't unique to gay men or white men or even to men. Many artists and non-artists do something similar. It may be a masculinizing habit or a habit of success. Or of fame? By "fame" I don't mean celebrity or the recognition of achievement. I'm using "fame" in its most current, or next, sense: the fevered personality type that must experience relationships in huge quantities. (The unknown flatter themselves that there's a difference of quality in these relationships as well, but that's probably not true. Anyway interior experiences are impossible to compare.)

Unlike Merrill, Edmund took the clean-public/dirty-private model of life as matter-of-fact fodder for his art. When he did that he ceased to have a life separate from his art. And his art stopped looking so much like... well, art.

When I went to Paris to meet Edmund at the peak of his fame as "Mr. Gay Literature" (an irritated straight friend's term), I almost immediately realized—an observation as secretive and calculating (as self-revealing, fantastical and wrong in many ways) as any made by the narrator of *Forgetting Elena*—that Edmund was operating in two worlds. In one lived the famous people (famous in both old and new senses), the accomplished and those on the road to accomplishment. The other was a sort of terrarium of feelings where "loves," "crises," "personal disasters" could play out harmlessly in miniature and be drawn upon by the artist. In my fevered fantasy, this secondary world was populated by lesser beings, people who didn't count, who wouldn't make a mark on history, people whom time would kill off utterly, who would be forgotten, like Elena. My pattern-mad theorizing became so crazed that I noted to myself how these mostly young men were physically smaller than Edmund. What unfairness or cruelty did that represent? Of course, it was France, so a doll-like stature was common, but I also knew that Merrill's equivalent invisibles, David Jackson, Strato, Peter Hooten, my friends Charles Barber and Jerl Surratt, were all quite large. Hmmm! This was the nonsense of ingrown ambition. It is very close to the gorgeous delirium described in *Forgetting Elena*. "In the morning's strong crosslight leaves ring like bells without clappers. A jangle of bird calls attempts, ineffectually, to mimic the silent cacophony of pealing foliage and to transpose the ultrasonic music into songs within the range of merely human ears."

Some of the pleasure of *Forgetting Elena* is insidery in a way that has nothing to do with its keys. Any good writer will experience pure delight seeing never-before-noted particulars of the real world turned into words for the first time. In Canto Four of Nabokov's "Pale Fire" "Shade" writes about this when describing his morning shaving routine!

My Adam's apple is a prickly pear:
Now I shall speak of evil and despair
As none has spoken. Five, six, seven, eight,

> Nine strokes are not enough. Ten. I palpate
> Through strawberry-and-cream the gory mess…

This kind of originality looks insignificant to most people, but it is the fundamental work of writing, of language, and closely allied to metaphor, the basic unit of human meaning, which most people, even most writers, also think of as mere ornament. Writing like this is enjoyed most intensely by the learned young for whom the world really is fresh. Indulging too much can come across as immature, however. Merrill is quite as good as anyone with a metaphor, but we don't think of him as an amoral reporter of the sensory world the way we do with Nabokov and Edmund.

I used to get upset when I read Nabokov. Indeed, the self-annihilating domination I felt with certain books has always made me a nervous reader. Nabokov was the worst. He really didn't seem to care what he was doing to one's young mind.

Moral offensiveness, traditionally a boyish addiction, is one of the strangest and most important aspects of Edmund's work. How could a forelock-tugging sweetheart turn into his society's savage *guillotineur* on the page? (A transformation not unlike discovering one's inner Prince.) Frankly, though I felt vulnerable to Nabokov's aristocratic contempt, I felt naturally allied to Edmund's American-inflected up-from-below version.

To the barricades! Susan Sontag is a fraud. Richard Sennett is a fool. Edmund's brilliant portraits can be breath-taking character assassinations. They have the non-art, real world muscle of gossip. As humane as they are poisonous, the portraits combine the serene, almost official, technique of Ingres with the revolutionary fire of Goya.

The revolution in question, a revolution against New York artistic circles and everything they stand for—the same revolution foreseen in *Forgetting Elena*—played out in much of Edmund's work, even as his career prospered by every conventional New York measure. This is a paradox built into art as we experience it today. It's quite familiar from the world of visual arts. We shiver with pleasure at stories of Pollack pissing into bourgeois fireplaces. What was rare about Edmund's case, thrilling to me, appalling to Merrill, was that he felt compelled to piss into the intellectual fireplace. Even more important, he did so without ever rejecting conventional intellectual and artistic standards. So, not a revolution, but a coup. And, as if his art were as harmless as a dove's, it all sounded like cooing.

Anything that prompts both visceral love and visceral hatred, as I'm claiming *Forgetting Elena* can, probably also flags a great cultural fault or coming danger. Layered affectation and indirection were thick in the air back then. If Edmund, like Warhol, modestly acted like a fake-it-till-you-make-it artist, while secretly believing he was a king, even Merrill sometimes satirized himself as a literary grunt who was just affecting the yawning airs of a Huysmans. But for Merrill belief in art was everything. He was a priest who clung to his belief. Edmund strikes me as an unexpectedly deep natural artist for whom belief in art doesn't matter in the least. To him, Huysmans and grunt, careerist and Kafka, Homer and magazine hack, are all mysteriously equal.

The danger of Edmund's position (apart from it being so subtly expressed that most people assume he's saying the opposite of what he means!) is that it's perilously close to being anti-art. This is the last thing anyone would think to say of him. I'm pretty sure he would object himself. He's quietly reverent of art in so many ways and one of the few people I know who fairly values the "high" of what used to be called high art.

An anti-art twitching of the whisker is sometimes more noticeable in his admirers than it is in him. Wide-eyed partisans like my younger self. Or the many people nowadays too impatient to study and digest the full traditions of arts that feel dead—ballet, opera, the novel—but too in love with the idea of tradition to embrace video games, graphic novels, King, Dick—at least until they've steeped for a few more centuries. This is a conservative aesthetic. It can quickly turn intolerant, even alarming. Memory flashes on *A Clockwork Orange* (the movie) when Alex slaps his Droog for disrespecting Beethoven. That's the kind of oxymoronic reverence Edmund and Merrill would both reject. The kind I should be ashamed for enjoying. But an involuntary hint of "anti" can be seen even in Edmund's younger self. In *Forgetting Elena*, for example.

Maybe he had to wrestle with "anti" a little, as I've had to wrestle with it a lot—since nine or ten! The savagery which ruined many of his friendships and for which he was famous, mellows in his later work, is sometimes even replaced by a windy considerateness more appropriate for blurbs than art. And, insofar as such an amiable man can get cranky, he now gets cranky about "tall poppy syndrome," a term borrowed from English-speaking Oceania. The term may be new, but what it denotes—the human urge to cut down to size anyone who stands out, who's exceptional, attention-seeking, contrarian—is eternal and lies at the heart of the famous Anglo-American loathing (not too strong a word) for the artistic spirit.

Merrill's joblessness and elevated east coast origin protected him somewhat. Growing up in the Midwest, having to earn money frenetically all his life, Edmund was far more vulnerable. What I, also a Mid-westerner, saw as Edmund's miraculous first achievement, was transmuting Midwestern hostility to art, by way of the anti-art poetics hinted at in *Forgetting Elena*, into a new, everyday form of art too sinewy to scythe. If art, as I feared and supposed, was a defunct religion, his books suggested a way of starting over without having to go all the way back to the beginning.

"Sex is one of life's chief pleasures."

—from *The Joy of Sex*

THE JOY OF SEX

WAYNE HOFFMAN

WHEN I STARTED college at Tufts University in 1987, my active sex life was a mere two months old and included just two partners. Early in my first semester, in the tiny library in our campus gay group's cramped office on the third floor of an unmarked clapboard house, off campus in suburban Somerville, Massachusetts, I found *The Joy of Gay Sex*, which Edmund White co-authored with Dr. Charles Silverstein a decade earlier, in 1977. Too nervous to take it back to my dorm, I sat on a rump-sprung sofa behind the office's closed doors and nervously flipped through the pages. Although the book was only ten years old, it already seemed like a document from a distant age.

AIDS had hit the headlines several years earlier, when I was starting junior high, so I'd never thought or even fantasized about sex in a way that didn't involve risk—constantly looming, often unknowable, potentially fatal. But because *The Joy of Gay Sex* was published before the epidemic began, it didn't contain any of the specific information about HIV or condoms or safe sex I urgently needed to overcome my ignorance and anxiety in such a toxic time.

Despite such unavoidable omissions, and the ways in which it failed to offer many practical tips that might have applied to my own sex life at the time, the book nonetheless communicated a simple message that made an enormous impact on me as a horny but terrified teenager: that sex, including (or perhaps especially) gay sex, was about *joy*. This theme—daring in the seventies, downright revolutionary in the eighties—flows implicitly through the book's frank and shame-free prose, and surfaces explicitly at several points in case readers might otherwise miss it, starting in the introduction, when the authors state flat out: "Sex is one of life's chief pleasures."

As a sixteen-year old who'd followed my first, quite tame sexual experience that summer by dragging my then-boyfriend to a clinic for an HIV test—the two-week waiting period for results turning into an extended panic attack—I had never framed my desires in such unambiguously upbeat terms. It took a while to get past the fear, the second-guessing, the sense of doom with every encounter, but reading *The Joy of Gay Sex* helped me focus on the sheer bliss of it all, the ecstatic thrill of sex. And that allowed me to grow into the safer, saner, happier gay man I am today.

Rereading the first edition of the book now, more than forty years after its publication, I am still impressed by its sex-positive tone—no less radical today. But now that my active sex life stretches back decades and includes, well, far more than two partners, I'm surprised to find, while the book deeply influenced how I continue to feel about my sexuality broadly speaking, it doesn't particularly connect to the actual sex I've had since I read it in college.

"The gay sexual repertoire may thrill you or repel you or just bewilder you," White and Silverstein explain. And true enough, the acts that they catalogued in alphabetical order in *The Joy of Gay Sex* seem reasonably wide-ranging. Some are things the authors clearly enjoyed, like rimming ("a prime taste treat") and threesomes ("a way for lovers to add spice to home cooking"); others they included despite apparent disdain, such as fisting ("extremely dangerous") or water sports ("what is the appeal of piss?"). But it's immediately clear that these menu items are thrown in as optional sides for the single main dish of gay male sex—fucking. White and Silverstein can't stop waxing lyrical about the many positions in which one man can fuck another, each getting its own rapturous section with a catchy name: Bottoms Up, Crab, Doggy

Style, Face to Face, Scissors, Side by Side, Stand Up and Take a Bow, Topping It Off. Even the vaguely titled First Time is not about the first time a man has any kind of sex with another man, but specifically the first time a man gets fucked—as if bottoming were the *sine qua non* of gay sex, the thing that *defines* a gay man's "first time," the only act that really *counts*. Considering how frequently gay men's sex lives are presented elsewhere in the book as distinct from straights' (and how gay sexuality, in the authors' estimation, threatens the very foundations of straight society), putting so much emphasis on fucking as the central act, the one all other acts ultimately lead to or else conspicuously avoid, seems awfully heteronormative. (And I felt that way even before I learned that word in a queer studies class at Tufts.)

For a cocksucker like me who's never evinced any particular interest in fucking, White and Silverstein have little to say. The entry on Blow Jobs gets less than one page—less space than they devote to Camping (as in humor, not as in tents)—and even that brief bit describes the act that has driven my erotic desires since my memory began as merely "a prelude to the full symphony of intercourse." Their tips on technique are cursory and unremarkable: "Use your hand as an extension to your mouth." (I got more detailed advice from my sister's *Cosmopolitan*.) Oral sex warrants just one more entry: Sixty-nining. And here, too, the authors sound bored and confused: "Few people have much to say in favor of sixty-nining save as a variant to more usual fare, or as a first or second course in a long erotic supper." Never the last course, or even the whole meal?

I try to imagine how I might have written this book differently. In my head I tally how many positions for oral sex I can conjure, and what catchy names I might give them: Open Wide and Say Aaaah, Kneeling at the Altar, Hang Your Head, Lie Back and Think of England. Would entries like those have spoken more directly to my younger self? At 16, I had just discovered my nipples; White and Silverstein were mum on the subject. There's also no mention of phone sex, which consumed so much of my cash in college, ten-cents-a-minute (twenty-cents-for-the-first) at a time. Or personal ads, the old-fashioned kind in the classified section of the newspaper, which is how I met my first boyfriend, as well as the man who'd eventually become my husband.

Yet while it's easy enough to list the things that are "missing" from *The Joy of Gay Sex*, I can also name many things I'm glad White and Silverstein included. The book serves, in part, as a quite specific how-to guide for certain situations that otherwise might be baffling at first glance, including bathhouses ("for sheer efficiency, the baths can't be bettered"), public bathrooms ("the etiquette of tearoom sex is elaborate and codified"), and cruise bars ("the signals are as elaborate and subtle as the movements in the Japanese kabuki"). Here, the authors are at their most practical; I wish more men today would read their simple instructions, and carry them on crib notes in their pockets. It would save so much time and aggravation.

The book is even more essential for discussing subjects that some might (wrongly) consider separate from sex: alcohol, drugs, depression, emotional problems, guilt—issues that Silverstein, a psychologist and sex therapist who had been instrumental in getting the American Psychiatric Association to remove homosexuality from its list of mental illnesses in 1973, had surely seen his patients wrestle with. Coming out gets a hefty ten pages, and gay liberation and politics are presented as inherently connected to desire.

But most of all, *The Joy of Gay Sex* remains important as an antidote to shame; the authors discuss risks, downsides, dysfunction, illness—but never in a way intended to stop readers from exploring and enjoying their sexuality. No judgments when discussing orgies—only the comment that "organizing them is the hardest part." A thorough dismissal of the entire concept of promiscuity: "It is a word that makes little sense in gay life." And a clear stance on fidelity and monogamy—"they are not necessarily the same thing"—that many gay men would be wise to remember in this age of same-sex marriage (and divorce).

There's a sense of excitement that pervades the book, as the writers envision (and help delineate) a sexual community of like-minded souls—one with a shared past, present, and future. The authors' history of homosexuality and modern gay identity, described so eloquently in the introduction, is truly stirring. "Modern gay life has no antecedents," the authors write, as they leap through pre-modern precursors by touching on everyone from Plato to Oscar Wilde. Then, drawing on examples from Michel Foucault to Batman and Robin in their discourse on contemporary sexual politics and masculinity, they boldly proclaim: "The modern homosexual is free to become the man he wants to be."

AIDS was unknown in 1977, so of course it's not in the book—although it does cover *other* venereal diseases. (Gonorrhea, the first edition explained, was "the major health problem of male homosexuals.") The authors were criticized nonetheless when the epidemic struck a few years later. "The idea that we'd erred somehow in not foreseeing an unprecedented disease no scientist in the world had predicted strikes me as bizarre and unfair," White recounts in his 2009 memoir *City Boy*. "The publisher certainly made a mistake, however, in not withdrawing the book immediately and replacing it with an AIDS-conscious edition." The authors believed that a revised edition would not only be more useful in the bedroom, but might actually save lives, as Silverstein recalls in his 2011 memoir *For the Ferryman*: "By the late 1980s, the AIDS epidemic had already killed tens of thousands of gay men. The original *Joy of Gay Sex* was out of print and I thought that a new edition…might influence young gay men to avoid unsafe sex." Due to issues with the publisher, however, a revised edition would ultimately take fifteen years to be published.

When *The New Joy of Gay Sex* finally came out in 1992—including entries about HIV and safer sex, not to mention nipples and phone sex—Felice Picano took over as Silverstein's co-author, but White wrote the preface for the new edition. By this point, he was already a prominent gay author, having published *A Boy's Own Story* and *The Beautiful Room is Empty*, as well as *States of Desire*. But that hadn't been the case when he wrote *The Joy of Gay Sex* in 1977; at that point, he had just one novel (*Forgetting Elena*) to his credit, and coming out as a gay writer bore its own risks. As he reveals in the preface to *The New Joy of Gay Sex*, he had considered using a pen name before ultimately rejecting that notion—in keeping with the liberated spirit of the book: "I discovered that signing it was the most liberating act of my life, the first time I identified myself as a proud homosexual. At the time I was sort of whistling in the dark, but I was the first to be convinced by the cheerful, confident tone of our own words."

White was being modest. He didn't merely identify himself as gay by putting his real name on *The Joy of Gay Sex* in 1977. He outed himself as a *sexually active* gay man. "An endless round of one-night stands or short affairs can provide a gay man in a big city with constant novelty and excitement and introduce him to a wide variety of erotic delights," the original introduction explains, before adding a more personal aside: "And these delights can be deeply rewarding." Lest there be any question about which author was speaking, the volume's dedication says it all: "To all my tricks, from Ed."

Readers never knew how difficult it had been for White to appear so carefree and comfortable, until he reflected on co-authoring *The Joy of Gay Sex* years later in *City Boy:* "My own problems in dealing with being gay were crippling——I'd devoted decades in therapy to coping with them and as a teenager had often been suicidal. But in our sex manual I decided to take a jaunty, relaxed tone, to 'act ahead of my emotions,' as a friend undergoing therapy put it."

By deliberately presenting himself utterly at ease with sex in general, and his own sex life in particular, White helped me (and, I'm sure, thousands of others) separate desire from shame. He presented a gay world with a shared sense of history and politics as well as eroticism, a community that was fundamentally decent and responsible as well as playful. He may not have truly believed it himself in 1977, but he helped me believe it as I came out a decade later. And I still believe it today.

"I longed away my childhood, resisted my youth, regretted the rest, and in that history appear, here and there, my protestations of good will and my pleas for redemption any serious historian knows to ignore."

—from *Nocturnes for the King of Naples*

NOCTURNES FOR THE

KING OF NAPLES

NICHOLAS RADEL

I READ *NOCTURNES for the King of Naples* two times in the decade after its publication in 1978: first, in the early 1980s, shortly after it appeared in paperback, when I was in graduate school in Bloomington, Indiana; and, second, in the mid-80s, after AIDS, and after I had accepted a job in the South, at a small university in an even smaller town. Both times and places were, for me, highly politically charged, which may explain why I still see the novel as being both compelling for its unparalleled artistry and significant for its political and cultural insight. It's an odd perspective no doubt, for a number of years ago an otherwise admiring Richard McCann seemed to declare *Nocturnes* politically null and void. In "Years Later, By the Pool," McCann wrote that the novel "felt like writing, *real writing*, at a time when North American gay writing was defined by Gordon Merrick's *One for the Gods*, perhaps, or by Patricia Nell Warren's *The Front Runner*." But AIDS changed everything, even White, who, as we all know, moved in the early 80s toward a more accessible, sociological style of fiction that McCann speculates may have been more appropriate to gay writing after AIDS: "I doubt that Edmund White would now write *Nocturnes for the King of Naples*, even if he were able."

Although White has been well-beloved by many readers, especially from my generation of gay men, McCann isn't alone in questioning the political relevance of White's early novels and his work in general. Recently, a younger crowd of gay and lesbian political critics and queer Johnny-come-latelies have associated his writing (surprisingly and wrongly) with the bland drive toward assimilation that scuttled the radical gay movement after the worst of the AIDS crisis. So driven is David Halperin to dissociate ongoing, powerful queer subcultural identifications from dominant, assimilationist gay culture in the post-Stonewall era that in his otherwise bold and stimulating book, *How to Be Gay*, he remarks rather too glibly, "Why would we want Edmund White, when we still have *The Golden Girls*?" Well (to provide one answer), I've always imagined there was room for Edmund White and *The Golden Girls*—and I don't consider myself a gay-marriage-advocating, "if-only-we-would-act-normal" kind of assimilationist homo! Indeed when even queer theorists turn intellectual somersaults (as did Richard Thompson Ford in an essay a few years back) to embrace both their queerness and (in Ford's case) heterosexual marriage, one is encouraged to wonder what such either/or kind of thinking actually accomplishes, for Halperin or queer thought itself (which was supposed to have freed us from rigid binaries).

My reading of Edmund White suggests how important he is to the political and sociological issues of his time, which continues to be our own. When I first read *Nocturnes*, life seemed like a paradise of queer possibilities. Bloomington was a charmed place to be young and gay. As I recall (and memory is a dedicated liar) I spent days discussing—freely, openly, at a table in the student union full of unassimilated faeries who would do Halperin proud—the ways gay sex was creating a new pan-sexual ethic, the pitfalls and pleasures of cruising toilets, one particular trumpet player whose very appealing lips were imagined to be as useful as they were beautiful, and—in those days before *The Golden Girls*—*Mary Hartman, Mary Hartman!* My nights were spent dancing at Bullwinkle's, a gay bar in the center of town, in a building that had once been the Elk's Club. How queer is that?

In those early post-Stonewall days, gay life was a new beginning. I was mesmerized by the portrait the narrator of *Nocturnes* draws of his free and unconventional older lover, whom he had left to his regret and whom he addresses throughout the novel only as "you." I longed to know this mysterious, absent man and his intellectual friends, to be invited on his travels, and sit at his dinner parties. I would learn later that this older lover was based in part on the novelist himself, that White was using his own experience to shape a new model for gay living in a time before any of us really knew what that might mean. And even though it would take me a long time to understand that this was only a partial, white, middle-class version of gay life in America, I took the narrator at face value (and continue to do so) when he writes about his lover that "the old law was being lifted by you, word by word, the prohibitions broken, and some festivals dropped from the calendar." The novel's address to "you" transferred all these potentialities to me, its reader, making it possible for me to be part of the new gay world order being built all around me. *Nocturnes* held forth for the future that world promised. To be sure, it is narrated by a man who comes to understand the value of such promise only too late. But his failure was a clear warning, a cautionary tale about what one might become if one neglected to embrace what being gay was offering in that brilliant time and place.

Nocturnes has always seemed to me to be not only about a particular relationship but in some ways desire—gay desire—itself. In my loneliness, I often recall the narrator's lines to his lost lover: "I've searched for you and not found you, attempted to forget you and found you everywhere, in foreign children, in my own childhood memories, in the bodies of hundreds of men I've ransacked, tearing them open as though surely this one must be concealing the contraband goods, only to throw them aside, meaningless raffia, and I've watched my own face age as I waited for your return, fearing I would no longer attract you should I ever see you again. . ." Who is this "you" if not evanescent desire (always, Jacques Lacan assures us, a yearning for what is not there)? In "Baroque Inventions" the poet J. D. McClatchy rightly suggests that the novel represents "the Psyche's reminiscence of Eros."

Of course, AIDS did change things. I re-read *Nocturnes* in the mid-80s in desperation, trying to get back in touch with its hope. Living in Greenville, South Carolina, in a time and place where people had almost nothing positive to say about being gay and in the presence of a disease that, as White memorably put it in *The Farewell Symphony*, "seemed all of a piece with the hate promulgated by know-nothing American fundamentalists," I needed to hear again the ecstatic voice of gay desire that infused the novel's every sentence. Reading it then, in a bleak time and place, called me to loves irretrievably lost. This time around I came to identify (as did McCann) with its loveless narrator, and I came to feel the truth of the words he speaks about himself, words written before AIDS but that could have been on the lips of every gay man I knew in the late 1980s—"In those days I was not yet the ghost that I've become." Even so, *Nocturnes* never backtracked on gay love and desire, which always echo in the narrator's recall of his lost lover.

In *Nocturnes* White brilliantly anatomizes what he calls the "hydraulics of passion" and no gay writer before or since (at least in my opinion) has done so more perspicuously. How much he warns us—in the voice of his troubled narrator—about idealizing love as if it were divinity. Because the narrator leaves his lover in search of an ideal, what he imagines will be a god-like replacement, this once vibrant young man misses out on life and dwindles into ghostliness. It's telling that in his narrator's worshipful embrace of one of his many lovers, Craig, White references the scene in Shakespeare's *A Midsummer Night's Dream* when Bottom makes love to Titania—a supernatural figure, a faery—and awakes to find himself an ass. White warns us about the consequences of disconnecting love and desire from mature self-sufficiency, which, the narrator childishly suggests, "may inspire admiration but not love." How, I wonder, do these prognostications and warnings fail to be political—both before AIDS (when gay men and lesbians were only with difficulty finding a psychic space within which to love themselves) and after (when that same self-love sustained us all)?

Nocturnes seems like the first AIDS novel—not in the literal sense that it responded specifically to the disease, for how can anyone have expected that ungentlemanly caller before he came knocking? But its voice, which Karen Smythe in *Figuring Grief* identifies as that of the "elegist" mourning the loss of his dead friend and lover, would become a familiar literary trope only a few short years after its publication. And *Nocturnes* did something the best AIDS literature, when it began to appear, would also do. It gave me, and I think others, a justification for walking around self-defeating habits of mind that were present before and newly energized by HIV. The hardest thing for me to tease out during those terrible years was the connection between a sex that was sustaining and murderous. *Nocturnes* didn't tell us how to do so, but it advocated faith in self-sufficiency as well as practical and practiced sexual objectives. And it helped teach me, at least, that no matter how virally sullied we might become, we were not dirt.

White's hapless narrator, a man who gets so much wrong, was and remains a model for what not to do if one wants to live. The depth of his despair inspired me to see differently in those years, when I lived in the South and in proximity to disease, both of which wanted me dead. (AIDS has relented somewhat—I'm not sure about the South, or much of it.) *Nocturnes* taught me (long before Michael Warner used the phrase as the title of his book) "the trouble with normal." In my early years in Greenville, South Carolina, I eked out a bare social life among the few men I knew willing to socialize with other gay people in public. These were kind men in an inhospitable land. Still, there was always one—an earnest young man in a white shirt and tie, good looking, needing to be kissed—who, when the talk turned to politics, lectured us (that assemblage of people who merely dared to be gay and unashamed). "If only we would just act normal..." he always began. What? Would we be embraced by heterosexuals whose blessing, it was assumed, we wanted or needed? His passionate desire to be like the straight people around us worried me—he seemed so much like White's narrator who, given opportunity and a possibly great future, could still be caught out expressing the cloying wish to leave his lover, to be taken "home to a bungalow in a development" by "Mom," "Dad," "the kids and the collie." If, slowly, almost imperceptibly, the narrator comes to see his folly, if, hesitantly, he moves toward self-understanding (if not self-justification), the novel itself holds out for the new and the unknown, the future the narrator spends his time rejecting. It taught me to hold out as well.

Perhaps I make too much of it. Maybe *Nocturnes for the King of Naples* is just a particularly beautiful novel. I certainly came to admire its aesthetic brilliance when I was writing *Understanding Edmund White*. One can easily see in the novel's title an apt reference to music, and White's style, like sounds in a musical nocturne, is brooding, melancholic, and moody. Moreover, like the colors in that series of paintings J. M. Whistler called "nocturnes," individual sentences and fragments of language in *Nocturnes for the King of Naples* reveal gradations of perception that emerge as coherent thought or sensation primarily in comparison and counterpoint.

When the novel begins, the narrator runs into someone he recognizes as an old admirer of his lost love. "We smile," he says, "and begin to talk about you." "You," the lost love, is a specific man with a past (if no present). But innumerable sentences addressed to or written about him throughout the novel transform this "you" into a variant signifier. As I've already suggested, he—that is "you"—reflects the evanescence of desire. He is also a god who withdraws his favor: "Now that I am ready you have hidden your face." Or he is the reader: "And what was I feeling, you ask, as I nestled against Linda...?" And, one more thing, "you" stands for the persistence of love itself, which the narrator discerns in everyone he desires: "As I looked at the other passengers, I could easily pick out those expressionless, intriguing beauties I address as *you*, those same faces, dark or fair, brooding or elated, whom I'd always believed I could love, even if I'd seen them only for a moment..." We discern in these sentences subtle but significant variations on the narrator's longing and sense of insufficiency, a variety that gestures toward both metaphysical and meta-textual understandings of this complex novel. With *Nocturnes* one doesn't comprehend meaning through the usual elements of plot and setting, but the careful analysis of word, tone, and syntax.

Re-reading *Nocturnes* in the 21st century, when age had placed me at a distance from the potent threats of earlier gay American history, also allowed me to see how the novel revises our understanding of what that literary form can do. At once prose poem and memoir, *Nocturnes* fractures the traditional novel's confidence in the individual subject. Its main character emerges only in the dialectic of his own speaking voice and the imagined "you" he addresses. *Nocturnes*, in fact, made clear and steered clear of the self-possessed speaking subject of the novel as we had known it until the sixties by opting for a narrative that abandons teleology. It calls forth its subject (in the sense of its topic), that is, the "you" always addressed and spoken to, in words, and thereby reveals its subject (in the sense of the individual assumed to have agency, the person who speaks) as the textual remainder of his own speech about another. Perhaps the achievement of *Nocturnes* is, then, purely literary, intellectual, or aesthetic.

But I don't think so. Its artistry underlines its political and historical observation. The narrator's act of writing, which produces the novel itself, dramatizes a creative response to the predicaments of living that is one of the permanent promises of gay life, so it reveals the novel as a performance, a performative act, linking White to the emerging chorus of thinkers at the time of its writing who were questioning the Western idea of an Enlightened Subject or Self. As a result, the very form of *Nocturnes* gives it great power to advocate for change. It doesn't tell us how to be gay but how not to be (it is White's most judgmental work). It recalls us to a primal scene of loss in many gay lives, which are almost always constituted as a rupture from what one knew or expected as a child. In this, it has much in common with White's first novel, *Forgetting Elena*. But whereas the narrator of that novel coped with this trauma by cultivating an amnesia leading toward the tabula rasa of his mind at the end, *Nocturnes'* narrator attempts tragically to regain meaning and feeling out of the detritus of the past. He just can't stop depending on a time that was, a deeply painful family life, and a fatefully-unwise decision to leave a man who perhaps loved him more than anyone ever would again. So, he ends up trapped, identifying with the photograph of a soldier from the civil war, a young man forever locked in a static image—just as he is forever inscribed in the narrative he addresses to a lover who is dead and can no longer hear.

Nocturnes is literally an elegy for a lost lover, but also a lament for a future that will never be, the narrator's future and potentially our own (should we forget the novel's lessons). What remains astonishing is that White brought us to mourn the possible loss of a gay future before it had even happened for most of us. He alerted us to loss and warned us about rejecting what could be. Surviving AIDS (and we *have* survived) suggests we didn't forget. So, it is not clear to me that the political and social utility of one of White's most difficult novels was obviated by the plague years. On the contrary, those years corroborated its greatest insight: we survive not by looking toward the past but by creating and embracing a future in which we can only live.

"His was the consummate Texas rap, complete with the expression, at the moment of climax, 'I'm fixin' to come.'"

—from *States of Desire*

STATES OF DESIRE

JERRY ROSCO

BEFORE EDMUND WHITE moved to Paris I was invited to
tag along to meet him at his apartment in New York's East Village
and then go out to Indian dinner. I followed a new friend, Canadian poet and writer Ian Young, up the stairs of the historic
Colonnade Row building at 434 Lafayette Street, just across the
street from the Public Theater. At that time White was well
known as the co-author—with Dr. Charles Silverstein—of *The Joy
of Gay Sex*. Even though that book sold ten times as many copies,
it was his lush first two novels that had impressed me.

Back then White was lean and struck me as shy but intelligent
and intense. I won't trust my memory much (I was a mere child
at the time) but there was one thing I remember clearly. Like most
writers White kept his latest published work in sight. There on the
coffee table, as we had a conversation in the living room area, was
a copy of *Christopher Street* magazine. The magazine printed chapters from his forthcoming *States of Desire: Travels in Gay America* in
four issues, and this one contained "The Pacific Northwest: Portland and Seattle." I remember because that issue also included an
overly ambitious, Thomas Wolfe-type story on which I'd worked
long and hard.

I recall that after *States of Desire* was published I co-hosted a
party for White at the Bond Street loft where I still live. Ian Young
suggested it because I had the largest space around. Ian was

already a solid literary guy, but back then I was more into the wild punk and hardcore scene. I was an immature host and my raucous rock friends far outnumbered the literary types. Included were such rock stars as Patrick Mack of The Stimulators and Ritchie Detrick of The Nuns. I knew my rock pals were perfectly happy smoking pot and listening to The Ramones at full volume. Actually I think Ed White enjoyed the scene but I forgot that he and other writers might actually like to hold conversations. Finally, the distinguished photographer Arthur Tress insisted that I lower the blasting rock music. "It isn't right," Tress scolded me, "it isn't fair." He was right and I lowered the volume so my more civilized guests could talk about another breakthrough art form: gay literature.

Now, after Ed White's colorful years in Paris, and after all his wonderful novels and nonfiction books, it is only right that his early travel book is back in print, as *States of Desire Revisited* (University of Wisconsin Press).

Of course, this is more than a travel book. Or perhaps it's more correct to say that it is the kind of travel book that retains its value and gives glory to the genre. Who better than Edmund White to describe people and places in a way that's as vivid today as it was in 1980? The Trojan Horse that was AIDS struck our consciousness in 1981, which means the disaster was secretly already underway. Like a flashbulb photo in time, this book captures our world as it was just before our worst nightmare. Or as White says in his introduction to the new edition, the book gives us our "past world preserved in amber."

The new introduction provides a sweeping overview of how much the gay world has changed—and looks forward from today's standpoint. The early gay rights leaders, White says, adopted strategies and actions from the civil rights movement. When the tragedy of AIDS struck, he himself was involved in creating Gay Men's Health Crisis. While national gay rights legislation never got anywhere, it was GMHC and Act-Up that changed the gay movement into something that rocked popular culture, here and in other countries. The fight for gay marriage which seemed so hopeless twenty years ago has now evolved into a culture-changing force, faster than even its proponents could imagine. Likewise there has been the overturning of the Defense of Marriage Act, and Don't Ask Don't Tell in the military. Still, White warns, gays worldwide face homophobia and violence in Russia, the Muslim world, and Africa. There is a long way to go, but today a growing part of the world accepts gay people as a minority.

Political advances aside, what is surprising on a rereading or a first reading of *States of Desire* is how contemporary so much of it seems. Superficial things change, such as the monetary cost of everything, which comes up so often. But places don't change much, and neither do the people in those places. Regions that are progressive, or libertarian, tend to stay that way. And regions that once had anti-gay teacher legislation followed that with anti-gay marriage laws a decade later, and so-called "religious protection" laws a decade after that.

In his travels, White's observations and commentary describe the various cities with accuracy, insight, and humor. But it is his conversations with everyone, from wealthy businessmen to young and older couples, bar kids, preachers, and rent boys that make this book feel so vivid and current. Part of it is his skill for description, but it's also his sensitivity and compassion for these lives. In each city, White usually set up a meeting with an acquaintance or friend of an acquaintance, and worked his way into the community from there. "In this book," he says, "I am trying to describe the styles of life that are unique to a city, not those that could be lived in any city equally well." Here are brief glimpses at the stops in his journey.

Los Angeles residents will readily agree with White's view that the movie industry dominates the city. Less obvious is his comment that gays in LA, while always claiming to be laid back, are in fact hard working and driven by career and social life. A pair of LA lovers I know grinned when asked about that, as if the city's secret had been revealed. One jumps from one electronics sales job to a more lucrative one, and the other quit his boring, safe office job in order to buy and flip houses in Palm Springs. White states that wealthy men keep young men more openly in LA than in any other city, except perhaps Paris. What of all the body consciousness, the pool parties? "Hedonism," he says, "is the governing principle of gay Los Angeles. With the collapse of traditional values, hedonism seems as workable as any other available code." And yet, he notes, LA gays take care of their own, with a community center and services that are the most active and civic minded in the country.

In San Francisco, White managed to meet and talk with a wide range of people, from wealthy David Goodstein, publisher of *The Advocate* and a force behind assimilationist politics, to the much more radical and sexually liberated Castro Street types. He found that while the local economy always seems difficult, there is the beauty of the city and of nature, and it is easier to be openly gay here than anywhere else. People piece together jobs and relationships that work for them. "San Francisco is probably the best place in the world in which to come out," he writes, "because it presents to the newcomer a large, thriving and varied panorama of gay life—a sense of choices, quite a few of them attractive."

Portland, White found, represented the old Northwest. It really was laid back, and gay friendly. Like the self-made men he met there, it was unpretentious, individualistic, virtuous, but with a lack of style. In other words, "conventional style and progressive thinking."

In contrast, he found Seattle to be a city with style, from its many art galleries to its thoughtful urban planning. He took away many attractive visual memories and even got lucky with a tall, Nordic twenty-something who helped show him around town. The young man had helped in the fight to defeat the anti-gay Initiative 13. Even in more homophobic times, voters here refused to discriminate in housing and employment. Seattle earned its reputation as a city that works, a city that's rational—and also has the lowest church attendance in the country.

Santa Fe was a short stopover for White but he managed to stay with an old friend, and learned a lot from a Chicano college student, a young professor, and a mature Native American man who served as a female substitute for straight Indian men when their wives were sick or unavailable. Among gays, he found, the Caucasians were connected to the Santa Fe art community, the Chicanos to their separate world, and likewise the Native Americans.

Flying into Salt Lake City, White no doubt felt an ominous warning as he observed the blank-eyed young Mormon missionary sitting next to him. What he learned in coming days is how much the Mormons control Salt Lake City and much of Utah. At that time church income from four million members and many businesses and properties was said to be one billion dollars a year. The film *8: The Mormon Proposition* reveals how Mormon millions got that anti-gay amendment passed in California in 2008. Today someone I know on fellowship at the University of Utah, Salt Lake City, says that while the university is public, the control by the Mormons is indirect but insidious. A content clause in the syllabus states that if students find content offensive, professors have to assign other content. In the public arena, it's very hard for a business to get a liquor license and the giant Mormon-owned mall downtown is completely closed on Sundays. A thirty-something straight friend of mine quit the religion because of its homophobia and other intolerance. He says the church is obscenely wealthy and that the overwhelming majority of government leaders in Utah are practicing Mormons. And, he adds, they own a high holding company called Deseret Management Corporation which owns two major newspapers, radio and television stations.

During his stay in Salt Lake City, White encounters a young man who was forced out of a good and important job because he was gay. His only backup plan was to help start a disco. White remarks: "When people complain about the energy and ingenuity gays devote to silly pursuits, they should be reminded that so many serious ones are closed to us." In many places this is still true today. Before leaving town, he hears more troubling and frightening tales by other damaged people, and finally in a bar meets a middle-aged redhead with haunted eyes who turns out to be stark raving mad.

"After Salt Lake City, Denver seemed an abrupt reentry into the 20th century." While Colorado Springs has a redneck reputation, White found gay life in Denver like that on the two coasts, except smaller and a little more conservative. Back then, most of the drugs in the United States flowed through Colorado. Today the state is one of the leading producers of medical marijuana. The people White met were all interesting and the sexual diversity was over the top. A twenty-year-old bisexual took him for a long drive in the mountains and explained that he'd had sex with hundreds of women but he also liked sex with men. A middle-aged man with a construction company invited him to dinner at his beautiful house and revealed that he had a male lover but that he'd previously been married to a woman and had six sons—four gay and two straight! (White: "I felt far from Salt Lake.")

Arriving in Houston "in malarial heat" was surreal. The city was overcrowded with conventions and White found himself in a part of the city with no sidewalks, in a third rate hotel filled with Jehovah's Witnesses there for a convention, Arab oilmen, and prostitutes and johns. Aside from his humorous descriptions, White's interviews capture the human intimacy with strangers that we all experience in travel. He makes his way to a leather bar where he meets a twenty-two-year-old who was experimenting with a moustache "which looked like a caterpillar paralyzed by stage fright," a mixed-up kid trying to be flamboyant and butch at the same time. The product of a closeted gay father, deceased, and a homophobic mother who threw him out, the boy's contradictions seemed like a metaphor for Texas. At another bar he meets a computer programmer who was a Navy veteran, a boxer and weightlifter, and who, at fourteen, had been thrown out by his parents. Taking an extra interest in Texas because he has relatives there, White interviews other men and attends a gay activists meeting where the main concern is fag-bashing and police entrapment and brutality. Even among gays with their complicated stories, he decides, redneck culture emerges. He calls the Texas cowboy "the gaudy stereotype of American machismo."

"Dallas is more sure of itself than Houston, more rigid and smug," he asserts. He arrives on the seventeenth day of 100-plus degree heat. In the bigger and richer city, he interviews a very successful decorator, formerly married to a woman, and several young professionals. He proclaims Baptists as "the storm troopers of the anti-gay offensive." But he compliments Southern manners and warns that stereotypes of Texans are often unfair. He sees the state as complex and in flux. No doubt, that's still true.

Interviews were essential to these city profiles, but White found, "In Kansas City I met more rejections and incomprehension than anywhere else in my travels." Instead of the more balanced gay relationships he found in larger cities, here men were in older / younger pairs, role-playing the heterosexual model. Gays themselves believed that gay bars are all there is to gay life. There was police entrapment. One man said he became an activist after being entrapped. A lesbian activist said she'd like to return to her home in San Francisco but too much work needed to be done. Maybe courageous activists have made a difference over the decades, but at the time White's opinion was that "Kansas City is the Fifties in deep freeze."

Cincinnati was loaded with meaning for White. He'd been a child there, and later summered there until he moved to New York. His father, homophobic, racist and anti-Semitic, still lived there, and White would see him for the last time. His thoughts about this, and his youthful memories are revealed here in depth.

At the bars he meets a teen high school football star who says his teammates would kill him if they knew; a thirty-two-year-old masochist who was actually in a happy relationship; and others who were friendly and sweet despite being marred by prejudice.

"After Cincinnati," White says, "Chicago comes as a relief to the gay traveler." Large, sophisticated, comfortable and cultured, it brought back different youthful memories from when he lived there with his divorced mother. In the same square where as a boy he hired hustlers a few years older than himself, he finds and chats with the latest crop of rent boys. Among the pleasures of the bars and baths, he also revisits the downtown beachfront on Lake Michigan, and the gay cruising area. In conversations he is reminded that, as the heart of the Midwest, Chicago is tolerant but conservative.

In Minneapolis, White is met at the airport by a friend of an acquaintance and before he knows it he is surrounded by a clique of men of a certain age who see themselves as the movers and shakers in town. In reality they are like the overwrought crowd in *The Boys in the Band*, though much nicer. Soon enough he meets a variety of much more up-to-date gay men. However, two of his best conversations are with lesbians—a therapist at the Minneapolis G+L Center, and an activist in twin city St. Paul, where the community is still reeling because a gay protection law had been rescinded. Seeing similarities with Chicago, White decides, "The Midwest is not as faddish and rootless as the West Coast, nor as class conscious and pretentious as the East Coast." For some it can be a trap. But for many, especially couples, the conservative Midwest offers stability.

In Miami, White notes that "show" drag persists more seriously and stubbornly in the South than in other places. The more oppressive the culture, the less gay visibility in everyday life, and drag is only for bars and private parties. There's a different edge to drag in the big northern cities.

It was easy to understand the success of homophobe Anita Bryant. Most Miami gays were in the closet and considered local gay activist Bob Kunst a troublemaker. A local survey showed that 90 percent of straights said they had never met a gay person—gays wouldn't come out, so they didn't exist. White manages good interviews with a wealthy retired man in Coconut Grove, a Cubano in Miami, and a porn magazine editor. He escapes to Fort Lauderdale where the Marlin Beach Hotel pool, bar and disco are guarded at night by security men against the hoard of drug-addled hustlers... unless a boy arrives with a guest. White has a conversation with a man in his forties who keeps a boy. And he resists the dubious charms of a handsome hustler. All his life, he says, he has hired rent boys, but he doesn't like the seedy situation where johns are addicted to hustlers and hustlers are addicted to drugs.

In mellow Key West (which White still visits) he describes sunset at the Front Street pier. He visits bars which men of, yes, a certain age will remember. Delmonico's Bar opened to a backyard garden, a discrete full acre of trees, bushes and winding paths. I remember being young there myself, with an even younger lover. We had taken a small plane from Miami over coral-colored waters into Key West, and discovered our favorite gay resort ever—tropical beauty, a lazy atmosphere, friendly restaurants and bars. At Delmonico's after sunset, we sipped tropical drinks and looked out at the overgrown garden and trees. On the bar's oversize video screen the lush porn film "Class Reunion" showed many beautiful men having sex around a pool. In that soft summer night, a bar patron near us turned and said, "Isn't this perfect?"

Not so ideal is life in the Bible Belt. In Memphis, Tennessee, White hears stories of repression and police entrapment. A comical young couple invite him to their apartment and a friend comes by with a copy of *The Joy of Gay Sex* to be signed. Then it's off to two parties where there are plenty of interesting people to meet, including one who is a member of the Metropolitan Community Church. White noticed that one young man who had the nerve to come out to his strict, Church of Christ parents was the one person who seemed to have the most self-respect and confidence.

A highlight of White's visit to New Orleans is a long visit and talk with painter and photographer George Dureau and those pages are a bonus to readers of this book. There are several other interviews with locals, including one who compares New Orleans to Venice (the mix of cultures, great food, tourists, a permissive brand of Catholicism, and poverty mixing with opulence). However, a gay activist complains that gays are tolerated but not respected. Since Hurricane Katrina, some of the low income parishes outside the Quarter have been restored. New Orleans is like a pirate hideaway for those on a low budget. A few years ago I was able to rescue someone from my past, with a plane flight from the deep snow of Colorado to a boarding house room in NOLA.

The so-called "New York of the South," Atlanta seemed fairly civilized to White, and benign to gays. Yet he found it telling that one man said he and all his friends might march in the annual Pride Parade—"but of course we'd have to wear masks." A black and white couple were White's hosts in Atlanta and the black man, Ted, was affable, religious, and a positive, nurturing force in the community. A week after Edmund left Atlanta, he was saddened to hear that Ted, only 41, died of a heart attack.

When White first gets to New York, he allows himself one of his favorite indulgences as a writer: exaggeration. Perhaps for fun, he mentions odd characters and bizarre groups that are too strange by half. But then he discusses sweeping topics—decadence, fantasy, camp, the direction of gay liberation, the analysis of desire, and gay sensibility. It is as though he sees New York as the cultural leader and intellectual platform of gay America. He says, "All over the country I saw a replication of New York in recent, if not current, New York style." White knows that life in New York is difficult, but that there is more to life than comfort. "Occupying the center is the great consolation of New York gays. In return for the costliness and inconvenience, the squalor and discomfort in our lives, we get to participate in whatever is the latest."

Since this book first appeared, new gay neighborhoods have emerged. In Manhattan, Christopher Street remains but lost out to the boom years in Chelsea—and now Chelsea is overshadowed by Hell's Kitchen in the midtown west side, which alone has fifteen bars. In Brooklyn, gays are a big part of hip Williamsburg.

And in Queens, Hispanic gays have a strong presence in Jackson Heights.

White affectionately describes the summer resort of Fire Island, the long narrow island on the Atlantic off Long Island, the scene of his first novel, with the lavish Pines for the A-gays, and Cherry Grove for the rest of us. Referring to the Pines, White writes, "Perhaps the most overwhelming moment on Fire Island is the afternoon tea dance at the Botel. On two spacious decks the best-looking men in the city are assembled." Among the men standing around and drinking and talking will be a disco owner, a movie star, models, fashion designers, doctors, lawyers. All are assembled outdoors where a long row of yachts are moored, while indoors others are dancing. Cherry Grove may be less impressive, and less mannered, but it has its moments. One of the best places to watch the sunset is from the top deck of the gaudy, ornate 1950s Belvedere guesthouse, where Rock Hudson once stayed. One evening I was reading *The Gay Metropolis* at the top of the Belvedere, and when I turned a page author Charles Kaiser described being at the top of the Grove's Belvedere "when the sunset was pink, and it lasted for three hours."

Admittedly painting with a broad brush, White believes that Boston is the center of gay radicalism and that Washington, DC is the center of conventional lesbian and gay politics, the assimilationists. That view of DC is still on target. In Boston the days of radical publications like *Fag Rag* and the NAMBLA (North American Man Boy Love Association) *Bulletin* have been gone for decades. Still, Boston has more variety of political thought than the DC jacket and tie crowd. As White says, Boston is the place to find intelligent, educated gays who are interested in politics, the arts, and social issues. He examines sensational man / boy legal cases of the time, and reveals his own memories as an underage boy seeking adult males, and includes a candid and moving conversation with a pedophile.

Of course, such a conversation could never take place in Washington, DC. There he found the protection of gay teachers to be the topic of the moment. Gay lobbyist Steve Endean tells him of the Christian right's campaign against teachers across the country. He reveals that the ultimate goal is a federal gay rights bill. Interestingly that goal has never been met, even as marriage became the cutting edge issue. Endean estimated that one quarter of the staff on Capital Hill are gay, but closeted. Later, White meets plenty of educated professionals in the bars and social groups. But another special bonus to readers of this book is his meeting and talk with the great gay activist, Dr. Franklin Kameny.

The second edition, *States of Desire Revisited*, includes a new chapter on one of White's favorite topics, the Internet. He calls it "the 51st state" because it makes it easy for even the most far flung people to meet. When he first moved to Paris in the early 80s he learned to use the Minitel, a small 8" screen that the telephone company provided, on which you could dial up text information, shop, or cruise! There was a "pink line" where you could read sex classifieds, and exchange information with men. White recalls, "The Minitel gave me my first exciting experience of sitting in my underwear in my living room, unshaved and unbathed, erect and lying that I was twenty kilos lighter and twenty years younger than I actually was. I was all set for the Internet and its false advertising." By the time he returned to the States in the late 90s, he was sophisticated about Internet social sites, and continued to learn the latest possibilities for cruising and dating online. Since most readers are aware of all this too, he just gives a few examples of his experience, and warns of the dangers of online connections. As for health safety, he says practicing safer sex is safer than taking anyone's word for their status. At its best, White says, the Internet is a pathway to quality relationships. It also makes possible the benefits of a global community. Even those in the most dangerous homophobic countries can reach out to those in more fortunate places for information and hope.

The importance of *States of Desire* grows more obvious with time. It is the first major historical record of gay communities throughout the United States—not just on the two coasts. About a decade later, when everything was overshadowed by AIDS, two works followed White's lead. Neil Miller's *In Search of Gay America* (1989) focused on interviews in small town America. Political activist Darrell Yates Rist's *Heartland: A Gay Man's Odyssey Across America* (1992) tried to show there is one overriding gay community—and found this is not the case. Both are worthy books.

States of Desire remains not only the first but the most all-encompassing and engaging work of its kind. While the original edition had no introduction, it did have a brief epilogue which stated that its goal was to help gay people imagine other lives, other possibilities. That is still a wonderful goal for many today, and for everyone the book remains an essential part of our history, and a fresh and timeless reading adventure.

"That a life could be changed posited the still more thrilling notion that one had a thing called a life, a wonderful being that was growing silently inside like an infant."

—from *A Boy's Own Story*

A BOY'S OWN STORY

ROBERT GLÜCK

WHEN I RETRIEVED my copy of *A Boy's Own Story* for this essay, I was surprised by how short the book is—a little over 200 pages. By the time I finished it I had come to think of it again as a big novel. Why is that? The story is not grand; its events are poised between tableau and anecdote. Except for the narrator, characters don't emerge very far past the proscenium arch of the prose. Of course, it's the prose and the corresponding isolation of the narrator/hero that give the novel grandeur.

One is always guided back to the surface. For example, White abandons the conventional time-line of story about a boy's education. We don't travel with this boy into his future. He is fifteen when the book begins. He spends the summer with dad at a beach resort and has an affair with twelve-year-old Kevin. In the second section, during the previous summer, the boy is fourteen and working for his father. In an impressive display of *realpolitik* he negotiates his failed plan to run away into the purchase of a hustler.

He's seven in the third section; we learn about his parent's divorce, his life with mother. Then we go forward to his eleventh year, and the family drama extends to include eccentrics at home and at camp, where the boy has sex with a dysfunctional camper. In the fifth section, the boy, now thirteen-years old, rises to the call of popularity and falls in love with a girl. In the last section he's fourteen: he encounters more eccentrics at a pseudo-Anglo prep school, and he stages the betrayal of a teacher that heralds the onset of adulthood.

This manipulation of forward momentum sends us into the thematics of the story; it provides the leisure for these thematics to develop associatively and through figurative language. For example, the father's sexual life is described as follows. "This hint of mystery about a man so cold and methodical fascinated me—as though he, the rounded brown geode, if only cracked open, would nip at the sky with interlocking crystal teeth, the quartz teeth of passion." Two pages later the simile is revamped to include the son, a manipulation of imagery at once subtle and outlandish. "What if I could write about my life exactly as it was? What if I could show it in all its density and tedium and its concealed passion, never divined or expressed, the dull brown geode that eats at itself with quartz teeth?"

The problem set up at the start of *A Boy's Own Story* is, How can I put myself in relation to my dad, who is all-powerful? This problem is elaborated throughout the novel by means of a governing trope, the king or sovereign. The novel, you could say, magnifies the education of a boy through images of sovereignty. That a novel of sexual maturation addresses forms and relations of power is one reason *A Boy's Own Story* is so un-American, so French.

These images comprise a system or fundamental structure (like Hegel's Master-Slave relationship) because they are made to address such a broad spectrum of social relations. Sometimes they are mock-epic (home is a fake Norman Castle), but mostly they illustrate a continental wisdom: that desire and power are linked, that they are based on a kind of betrayal, a crime against love. These lofty images comprise a "theme and variations" that lend grandeur to the large movements and to the details. Images of sovereignty are brought to the isolation in the nuclear family, racism, male privilege, class privilege, issues that lift the book out of the box of psychology and the overheated nuclear closet. They remind me of Bataille, certainly Nietzsche, who might have written: "I even envied his sovereignty, though the price of freedom—total solitude—seemed more than I could possibly pay."

Many of these images center on the father, a Zeus, a deity, a king, and then they devolve onto the son as he matures. When he was alone he was "not a boy at all but a principle of power, of absolute power." In a nice twist, in the last of these images our young fag attains full royal stature—as a queen. "Or I felt like someone in history, a queen on her way to the scaffold determined to suppress her usual quips, to give the spectators the high deeds they wanted to see."

A Boy's Own Story appeared in 1982, and I encountered it, as I encountered everything in those years, as a gay man. Its publication was greeted by myself and others as both a literary and cultural event. We were grateful to find incontestable literature that applied to us—an expressive possibility had arrived. In the early eighties, few books offered a reading of our experience, and we approached them with the emphatic interest of looking into mirrors, testing new reflections against expectations. We were alert to every nuance of sexuality and always searching for possibilities of identification.

A Boy's Own Story was published by a trade press and we needed to see our new identities in the national forum. We wondered how this book, which treated our sex in such an offhand manner, got past the guards? It's not enough to say that its ticket was quality because other literary books—those of Genet, Irving Rosenthal's *Sheeper*, John Rechy's *City of Night*, for example—were published by wicked Grove rather than august E.P. Dutton. New Directions published Isherwood's *Berlin Stories*.

The answer, I think, is partly the times and partly the prose. Small presses had created a gay market, and suddenly editors working at large houses, like Bill Whitehead, could act on their interest in gay fiction. And in *A Boy's Own Story* every sentence tells a story—and that story is, "Look, this is literature." Sentences go to it like trumpets at Jericho: "I say all this by way of hoping that the lies I've made up to get from one poor truth to another may mean something—may even mean something most particular to you, my eccentric, patient, scrupulous reader, willing to make so much of so little, more patient and more respectful of life, of a life, than the author you're allowing for a moment to exist yet again." That is, this writing already comes to you from beyond the grave, a location more grandly French than English or American.

Perhaps this beauty "underwrote" the content, the recognizable (to us) push towards truth in sexuality. Two tykes are on an outing to buy Vaseline in order to ease the way. "He pulled it off without a trace of guilt, even asked to see the medium-size jar before settling for the small one. Outside, a film of oil opalesced on the water under a great axle of red light rolling across the sky from azimuth to zenith." So their sex is splayed out across sea and sky (before the days of water-solubility). You could say the prose safeguards the experience of being gay.

Still, the book was a bit confusing in 1982. Unapologetic homosexuality was not the only unusual matter it brought to the larger realm of American letters—its portrayal of aggressive child sexuality, its savaging of the nuclear family, its unapologetic love of surface and preoccupation with artifice. BOS didn't jibe completely with the smaller realm of gay community self-description—healthy, moral, natural—or nature that had been victimized. On the cover a boy in a tank top gazes outwards, to the sea, to the future—his promise of health and offer of physical beauty were certainly on the movement's agenda. But the boy between the covers is entirely corrupted by self-consciousness and the knowledge of gender roles.

A Boy's Own Story's claim to the largest forum was not only based on its lyrical prose, a feather in our cap, but on its negative vision, its grand homosexual theme of betrayal. Love is not something you give to others, but something you do to them. Sex and friendship are taken from people. It's a description of extreme isolation.

A Boy's Own Story is so amoral. The blurbs promised a cross between J.D. Salinger and Oscar Wilde. I'd keep Wilde for prose that generates at once feelings of precisian and incredulity, the great queen's aggression and assertion of surface that foreground the relation between writer and reader. But the moral anguish and problems of belief in Salinger are not even close. *A Boy's Own Story* may be a *bildungsroman* with a Dickensian enthusiasm for eccentric guides, but at heart it has more in common with *The Prince* than with *Catcher in the Rye.*

If *A Boy's Own Story* does resemble *Catcher in the Rye*, it's because both books ask, What constitutes maturity? Certainly every adult is an unacceptable model, and that is the joke of *A Boy's Own Story*. So, why not take revenge and betray one of these adults into revealing his false relation to life? That is, if your sex is viewed as a weakness, why not weaken an adult with it?

The hero has a lack of naivete that he loathes in himself; in fact, he is the manipulator that many of us felt ourselves to be. I am reminded of another wonderfully chilling child-portrait, that of baby Sartre in *The Words*. The hero of *A Boy's Own Story* is made unlovely because he is frozen on the grid of natural/not natural. He wonders, as we had, whether he is estranged by his sexuality, or whether his sexuality is just another symptom of deeper isolation. He can't take people for granted because his secret poisons every attempt to belong with them.

After reading *The Beautiful Room Is Empty*, I think I see an overall thematics in these memoirs. *The Beautiful Room is Empty* ends with the Stonewall Riots, the beginning of the present gay movement. White seems to be saying, you can't have love or moral life in a void—in a void you are just trying to survive. Moral life can't exist outside the context of a community.

A Boy's Own Story could be taken both as a model for the crossover novels of its period and as the novel that subverts the genre. Crossover novels tended to be family novels, tales of growing up and coming out, like Robert Ferro's *The Family of Max Desir*. The family remains the national forum, so it's no surprise that the family romance would fall to us just as we were claiming space on the national stage. Entrance into the mainstream would have to be a battle for public existence in the family.

But the family value White describes is lust for power: the indifference and brutality of those who have it, the craven self-loathing of those who don't, and the internecine battle to acquire some. And sex destroys families rather than binding them together. Hatred of the family and the assertion of child sexuality seem to go hand in hand. Dad is a philanderer; our hero mimes his father's sexual exploitation of Alice, the class evil made explicit: "I'd used and discarded him—just as my dad had mistreated Alice, the Addressograph operator."

As earlier forms are swallowed by later ones, I wonder if the theme of betrayal is domesticated here, its existential consequence replaced by a social one. The gay self (whatever it is) is extremely aware of itself as the product of historical and familial tensions.

In *A Boy's Own Story*, the existential terror remains, along with the sense of isolation—why should they be eliminated? But they are framed and "flattened" by an awareness of the self as a construct as they undergo a series of middle class remedies: prep school, camp, therapy, imported religion.

This awareness of the self as a construct is mirrored in *A Boy's Own Story* by attention to surface and by obsession with manners and mores, the nuances and ins and outs of communication. The message is always membership and status rather than specific content. Any society thus examined becomes every society. The outsider puts everything on a single plane, that of artifice. That is the wisdom of the closet: The anthropologist or imposter sees the extent to which everyone is playing a role with degrees of self-awareness based inversely on degrees of success.

Examining nuances that signal status and affiliation has been a practice of White's since *Forgetting Elena*. All gay people will immediately recognize that this examination is first the study and imitation of heterosexuality by a little fag. So here we have the poles of *A Boy's Own Story*. On the one hand, conversance is perfected. The outsider's imitations gain meaning through his struggle for self-preservation and his risk of being unmasked. Conversance—even when it's expressed as a highly ornamented surface—becomes a strategy for safety. "Somehow, but at what precise moment?—I had shown I was a sissy; I replayed a moment here, a moment there of the past days, in an attempt to locate the exact instant when I'd betrayed myself." On the other hand, this passage leads into an historical awareness, identification with (his idea of) Black people who were "exiled, dispersed into the alien population," and a wish for their community life. "I really believed I, too, was exuberant and merry by nature, had I the chance to show it."

But White does not conclude by giving the boy's suffering a pious moral value, because it is also linked to the will to dominate, to seize power. In the next paragraph White says, "I was desolate... I wanted power so badly that I had convinced myself I already had too much of it... I was appalled by my own majesty. I wanted someone to betray."

"No sooner would such a temptation present itself than I would smother it. The effect was of snuffing out a candle, two candles, a row of twenty, until the lens pulled back to reveal an entire votive stand exhaling a hundred thin lines of smoke as a terraced offering before the shrine. In this religion hidden lights had been declared superior to those that glared. Somewhere I was storing up merit, accumulating the credit I'd need to buy, one day, the salvation I longed for. Until then (and it was a reckoning that could be forestalled indefinitely, that I preferred putting off) I'd live in that happiest of all conditions: the long but seemingly prosperous courtship. It was a series of tests, ever more arduous, even perverse. For instance, I was required to deny my love in order to prove it."

—from *A Boy's Own Story*

A BOY'S OWN STORY

ALLAN GURGANUS

I

A BOY SOPRANO floats a tone like nothing else in nature. When that sound is hovering on pitch, it can come directly through you like sovereign daylight. But if ever a boy's note goes sharp, jump back: it's sheet ice guillotining off a slate roof. Suspense—can the kid stay up there?—is always part of the magic. So young a voice lives tilted—quavering—between boyhood's backyard pipings and the Niagara of puberty, roaring (basso profundo) dead ahead. The pathos, of course, is this timbre's brevity. The life span of a great boy singer's voice? I mean one strong enough to project through lungs nearly man-sized while still abrim with audible innocence. That, you must measure in months.

A Boy's Own Story is twenty years old. Can it be true? Oh dear, yes, I fear so. The Modern Library has chosen to provide a permanent choir stall for this youthful chorister whose curious range—now honeyed, now tannic, first sentimental, then intriguingly amoral—continues to command and enthrall us. Who is the child singing with such artful imbalance, now beguiling, now quite shocking? How has he fared in the stilled time of fiction? And, during his son's first few decades, to what uses has it been put? How can a boy and his epic solo survive such chores, such honors?

The subject of this book might be that brief eloquence between the fantasies of a dream-bound child and his implementing those through charm, sexuality, his wits. We trace the ascent of a playful yet sober young man who's made himself up out of wishes and books. We watch him become the erotically negotiable self-aware young "player" who ends this book with a chess-like coup of controlled plotting. It is a move that his wily executive father might've admired.

Nabokov, in a ventriloquized preface to *Lolita,* proposed subtitling his own masterwork "The Confession of a White Widowed Male." He attributes this medicinal foreword to one John Ray, Jr., Ph.D. (Widworth, Mass.). *Lolita,* published in 1955 during the golden age of analysis, approached the taboo subject of child sexuality by half-posting as a moralistic "case study." Nabokov's humorless, avuncular Dr. Ray advises, "Still more important to us than [the book's] scientific significance and literary worth, is [its] ethical impact; ... for in this poignant personal study there lurks a general lesson; the wayward child, the egotistic mother, the panting maniac—these... vivid characters... warn us of dangerous trends. 'Lolita' should make all of us—parents, social workers, educators—apply ourselves with still greater vigilance... to the task of bringing up a better generation in a safer world."

Edmund White's novel, appearing nearly thirty years later in 1982, needed no such apologia, however transparently comic. Atop the very crest of Sexual Liberation, this book arrived with the poise of a blond surfer. By then, into the most landlocked of our staid suburbs, wife-swapping had already reached its high-water mark, invigorating Friday and Saturday nights with license, killing Sundays with recrimination.

If *Lolita* trifled with the conventions of the scientific Case Study, this work might partake of newer traditions: self-actualized paperback memoirs concerning breakdowns en route to breakthroughs, soft-core works about trim, driven young men confined in groups at camps and schools, the confessional tell-all by some once put-upon boy who, now being "known," has transcended and must be worth reading. "Look, We Have Come Through," Forster titled one of his fictions.

As Twain does in *Huckleberry Finn,* Edmund White here subverts the revered American literature of self-improvement, the myth of sickly boys like Teddy Roosevelt, ambitious for a rough ride and an eventual Presidency. This novel's young hero quests are for meaning through acceptance, if not love—for phantom popularity. His chase lures him to at least one brothel, onto several couches, into more beds. His zeal to please might be influenced by other much-thumbed texts addressed to the adolescents of 1958; *'Twixt Twelve and Twenty*, by the singer Pat Boone, stressed teen kindness as the key to true teen popularity. It also urged much washing of the face (always pat dry).

The title *A Boy's Own Story* recalls those Victorian fictions designed for the moral instruction of colonial Britain's far-flung Youth. *The Boy's Own Paper* was a London-based periodical of the mid-to-late-19th century. Its many subscribers were impressionable, hungry for heroics, eager to implement weekly projects like "How to Stuff a Bird in Five Minutes." The bulletin featured serialized novels of youthful derring-do. Such fiction hinted that any pubescent boy's idleness, his over-many hours of reading by poor lantern-glow in stuffy upholstered rooms smelling of unclean hairbrushes, must lead said youngster onward/downward to more furtive and solitary vices. Parents were admonished to keep a boy out-of-doors where, from all sides, he might be watched. The suggested antidote for any male child's natural arrogance, erotic preoccupation, and lethal inwardness? Cold showers, brisk upland hikes, some nature-based nickname like "Rock-scaler." Seek out steady supervision by certain priestly males in no way softened by their spongy-making spiritual vocation. This seemed just the regimen for upgrading bookworms, velvet-robed Mama's-boy aesthetes, into the decent vigorous gentlemen required to rule so vast an Empire. My own boyhood public library once stocked countless illustrated versions of these inspirational boy-in-formation yarns. Their detailed wood engravings showed Amazonia waterfalls, many a shirtless rescue. I'm afraid I consumed such works indiscriminately as any fat lady will eat whatever chocolate is brought into her home at Christmas. Edmund White's novel posits the modern equivalent (psychic, sexual) of these bully-boy obstacle courses. Such novels abounded in mountaintop mishaps, brave St. Bernard dogs ripped with brandy casks while baying toward recent avalanches. The central heroic youth was soon buoyed—rowboat-like—along the locks and channels provided by a set of kind, worthy teachers. Each guise seemed skilled in a different practical art; each man proved versed in some code of earnest ethics. There was a best friend, another boy, as blond as our hero was brunet or vice versa. Strong bonds developed between these two ever-more athletic fellows, ties that—while always happily naturally physical—never got far below the belt of simple wrestling.

As in the present book, such foreground strengthening took place in relation to a remote and disapproving father. Usually titled, he was off in some locale more exotic and dangerous, he was exploring a mine or developing a product that would prove, to the Empire, invaluable. He had always viewed his pallid boy as unworthy of the family name. And it was only after some singular demonstration of this boy's physical courage—fishing a younger child out of a frozen lake was always good—only then did the father understand how his own son, by God, did after all possess the grit, the makings of a decent burly English gentleman.

I sketch this pattern to suggest the way White plays musical theme and variation with it and many others. His own mid-20th century boy's tale charts a new indoor Alpine course, one of habituating vices, class-based dangers, lubricous temptations, latent cures. Our representative youth falls in love with boys (the golden and admired if heedless Tommy); he falls in love with girls (the sophisticated yet voluptuous Helen). These beloveds are inevitably the favorites of everyone at school; that's the draw. And, even if our hero fails to make them love him, he—determined, almost cursed with the gift to please—at least contrives to *date* them both.

A room full of books and LP records (jazz and classical) at the end of the long corridor in some faux-Tudor mansion in Grosse Point might not seem the zone of conventional peril. But White renders—in prose of startling jack-in-the-box compression and dark-to-red Sargent-esque elegance—a treacherous route no less lethal than the 19th century's snowbound mountain passes. Of course, Grosse Pointe lacks the invigoration of physical danger endured in good male company. Here, a boy's story is merely his "own." This suggests someone made accountable at too young an age for the full burden of his personal narrative. White's novel alludes to works of self-actualization like Ben Franklin's witty autobiography. Then it comically tweaks our expectations of the typical young man's upward climb into solvent respectability, independence, possibly greatness:

> When I was fourteen, the summer before I went to prep school, a year before I met Kevin, I worked for my father. He wanted me to learn the value of a dollar. I did work, I did learn and I earned enough to buy a hustler.

We are far past the boy-victim implied by Dr. Ray's "wayward child." Here we greet an intellectual full-born in search of information one can learn only during the postcoital cigarettes, while lolling beside men or boys and girls either overqualified or unworthy.

This work charts the terror of being left too much alone with one's own intelligence. How soon all of that can turn on a young fellow! In the person of our narrator, we're up against a youth with the ability to register every nuance, aesthetic to erotic, but often while missing some essential hearty emotional reward. Progress here involves this child's relentless search or that one true fulfilling connection; when it fails, we find him quick to settle instead for a restless anatomizing, a cataloguing of types, the gathering of sensations for their own sake. White's achieved and textural prose is similarly questing, now referring to the natural world, now obsessed with high art, soon readily unbuttoning into the lowest reaches of fugitive erotic pursuit. But behind this moving-forward pressure toward the Great Love, one feels throughout the book an immense vacuum provided and maintained by our nameless boy's stunted, brilliant, shut-off father.

Among the work's gallery of vivid, contradictory, richly entertaining figures, this emotionally inert man comes to be the most powerful. Complacently fat, eager to seem athletically adept but actually a nonswimmer clumsy in a panicky way, this naked gent encourages his young son to serve as his live-in masseur. Kingly in reverse, as in photographic negative, the millionaire father offers no less potent an attraction for his own hiddenness, his nocturnal schedule. Loving best his Labrador retriever and Persian cat, the dad demonstrates a familiar fussiness, like that pet-loving terrorist villain from Ian Fleming. The young narrator's unmet affection and banked rage seem the fossil fuel driving his verbal acuity, his sometimes cringing wish to please, his dead-eye erotic aim. Here the boy traces such rage's lineage as his father beats him:

> He tugged my pants down and pushed me forward into the glossy spread. The belt fell again and again, much too long and much too harshly in my mind, which had suddenly turned strangely epicurean. The solace of the condemned is scorn, especially scorn of an aesthetic stripe. In that moment the viral energies retreated out of my body into a small, hard gland of bitter objectivity, a gland that would secrete its poison through me for the rest of my life. At last my mother, conveniently tardy, rushed in and asked for mercy...

Notice how the rhetorical phrase "to my mind" is dropped direct into the belt's line of fire: "The belt fell again and again... to my mind." Even "aesthetic stripe" seems to have absorbed a stinging lateral blow.

The scale of humiliation here is recorded in the depths of withdrawal from any serious connection to others—a lifelong habit, we are warned. What's left is a grazing, categorizing brilliance that has the avidity of love, the heat of erotic pursuit, but the camouflaging surface awareness of literary parody. This child's cerebral engine has a breathless, stalking, sexual energy. A skilled seducer must never admit to understanding the word "no." This vision has much in common with Proust's self-invented mission.

Edmund White shares with Proust an uncanny ability to let us guess what he was reading as he composed the book: now a work of marveling natural history, now a social novel; they all leave a tincture on the absorbent young mind guiding us here through an account of its twelfth to fifteenth years.

The novel's spurned young man can celebrate but one true sensory tie with his detached dad. Surrounded by Wall Street flow charts, the father might always seem shut behind a locked door after midnight; but the pair's beloved late-Romantic music reaches, includes, and ultimately moves them both. This provokes a telling passage about the missing person. That father stands, silent colossus, at the center of all those circuitous visitations with eroticized parental substitutes, the manic rounds that constitute the clockwise movement of this book:

I mention the constant music because, to my mind at least, it served as an invisible link between my father and me. He never discussed music beyond saying that the *German Requiem* was "damn nice" or that the violin and cello concerto was "one hell of a piece," and even these judgments he made with a trace of embarrassment; for him, music was emotion, and he did not believe in discussing feelings.

His real love was the late Brahms, the piano Intermezzi and especially the two clarinet sonatas. These pieces, as unpredictable as thought and as human as conversation, filled the house night after night.

Here, while marveling at a blocked father's grunted assessment of his favorite masterpiece as "nice," the author himself pushes on, calling that same composer's work, "unpredictable as thought and as human as conversation." What could better describe the ravishments, the surprise turns of late Brahms? Damn nice phrase, that. And yet, for the speaking child, the withheld human conversation can only be deduced via the music seeking to stimulate it. Art stands in here as a lonely substitute for some familial, personal eloquence that really should have preceded it, right? Left alone to itself, Art becomes an onanistic moral agent. Its lessons must be misapplied by however bright a child. He inevitably concocts a world self-serving and amoral, since it is a realm cut off from any deep emotive consequence to others.

And so, the father—who explains how men should only use the verb "like," not "love"—is assassinated by the author's phrase. It is a figure so apt, sad, opulent, Brahmsian. And yet this very summation seeks to show his "straight" emotionally retarded father how it might be done. This very book is a strange invitation to Dad for *A Dad's Own Story*. Which produces only silence. And this attempt to tell it all anyway—as an artful ventriloquist might—by the "thrown" voice of a boy soprano.

II

WHITE HAS WRITTEN fond dimensional biographies of those fellow gay rule-breakers: Proust and Genet. He shows us a Proust impervious to expected store-bought pleasures, susceptible only to surprises, shocks of joy and unforeseen betrayal that overtake him with the force of martyrdom. White also identifies with Genet, the congenital thief whose criminality begat a fictional formalism of such surpassing symmetry, such tuberose-scented beauty, it can elevate any jail cell to an altar.

Edmund White's own prose benefits from the examples of those willingly incarcerated French uncles: sealed in a cork-lined study or a cold stone cellblock, they must each make a great deal of seemingly little. How to find the heroic solace in one's own self-admitted self-administered condemnation?

White, born stolidly upper middle class, forever empathizes with the truant, the nervy, the dismissed, the oversexed and underrated. His life's work offers hundreds of love poems to such fellow recidivists. And in this novel, we watch as, one by one, such left-out figures step forward for their moment, attempting to either help or seduce the young leading man (or to help him by seducing him). To one and all, our boy usually proves a most apt pupil.

As it is with bright only sons from "good" families, this narrator always knows which brand names (in art and consumer culture) will or will not do. His father's boat is a Chris-Craft; his dad's ties are Countess Mara. Dad's favorite music is late Brahms, probably those recorded by Sviatoslav Richter. Here is a son who offers—as an incantation—all of Father's favorite products. It's one overliteral surefire way of describing a man so otherwise elusive. The boy recalls his dad with a strangely familiar combination of respect, contempt, unalloyed longing. This wish for a true connection comes to seem the book's greatest undertow, its deepest emotional riptide, its finally dubious goal. Though the story might appear that of a boy with two surviving parents, if divorced ones, White's novel really belongs in the literature of Orphanhood. A boy's "own" story. The possessive pronoun boasts self-reliance even as it admits to solitary confinement.

See *Huck Finn.*

This gifted child appears the perfect product of his private German lessons, prep school, haberdashery, and analysis. And yet, though any Ivy League college's admissions officer would see him as a likely candidate, as the son of evident privilege, he is really Oliver Twist's first cousin. Erotically and emotionally, his request usually runs "More, sir, please." And the very act of asking this aloud brings worse punishment down upon him. The boy is surrounded by so much space. Even in his crowded telling, amid his colorful toy-like succession of eccentrics and pals, he usually feels singularly alone. He always seems to be planning his next romantic "accidental" meeting, writing some outsized letter of admiration. Part of our sense of his isolation must derive from the amazing acuity of his adult-scaled observations. We note how these differ in scope from his boyish features, his outward insecurity, the lapses we picture as he bumbles and strives. White is never afraid to let his young hero's plaints veer toward the poignant; he knows that the very wit of their admission somewhat countermands their pathos:

> Unlike my idols I couldn't play tennis or baseball or swim freestyle. My sports were volleyball and Ping-Pong, my only stroke the sidestroke... My hands were always in the air. In eighth grade I had appeared in the class pageant. We all wore togas and marched solemnly in to a record of Schubert's "Unfinished." My sister couldn't wait to tell me I had been the only boy who'd not sat cross-legged on the gym floor but resting one hand on a hip like the White Rock girl... A man never gushes; men are either silent or loud. I didn't know how to swear: I always said the final "G" in "fucking."

III

SINCE EDMUND WHITE was born in 1940, he lived in round-number allegorical relation to the last six decades of our recent quick-change century. No intelligence stands readier to remember with perfect pitch a period whole-cloth: who else can tell us so exactly how its citizens then talked, dressed, contracepted, proceeded politically.

So, at age forty, just at the start of the sexually liberated eighties (in 1982, the year after HIV first sent its silent tentacles among the erotically adventurous in Manhattan and San Francisco), White offered the world a seemingly autobiographical novel. It appears to map a boy's coming to terms not simply with solitude, not just with his social destiny, but with a completely aestheticized vision only some scholastical and witty kid could so utterly perfect. The novel shows a child learning to face then exploit not just homo-sex, but sex in general. This work of principled sweep and great observational power also champions the centrality of Art as a governing quest. It offers this view with a faith that must recall Proust's life project, his attempt to hold all of time, its characters at synchronous ages, all its warring textures, in one head, one work. But crucially, White also places the Erotic on a level of expressive possibility alongside the pursuit of work itself.

"Love and Work." Freud promised us two choices, in that order. But here sex replaces romantic love, even while groping elsewhere for it. If Love, in modern life, is really Sex, then Sex, undertaken with concentration and ambition enough, can ascend to Work, can't it? The erotic is ranked, by the young man at the center of this fiction, as a great Darwinian organizing force for the good. We are told by White in 1982—using the voice of an erotically and cerebrally advanced fifteen-year-old facing his inaugural analyst—that life's great divide really seems between those who are sexual, are "getting it" on a regular basis, and the others, lonely and—because silent—powerless:

> My first sight of the analytic couch constituted the primal scene, for only its existence jarred me into recognizing that the world is governed by a minority, the sexually active, and that they hold sway over a huge majority of the nonsexual, those people too young or too old or too poor or homely or sick or crazy or powerless to be able to afford sexual partners (or the luxury of systematic, sustained and shared introspection, so sexual in its own way).

In 1982, this view of erotic power offered veriest catnip to the loud-because-too-long-silent cause of Gay Liberation. And *A Boy's Own Story*, with mixed results for the book itself, became one of that young Movement's essentials works. It was read not simply as the rich entertainment and provocation it is, but alas, as Theory.

Leading reasons for this novel's preeminence in gender politics remain clear: its impenitent candor about sexual activities, its fearless ability to say whatever can be seen or felt whenever two or three disrobe, its very picaresque structure reflecting a less than monogamous model for the way learning takes place, and, of course, the sheer forceful beauty of its coruscated rendering. And yet with the hindsight of twenty years, we must admit this book seems an odd one for Gay Liberationists to have made their very bible. While its cultural allusiveness and mordant humor might make its tone seem perfect for the Movement's usage, the work has one striking drawback: It does not, in fact, concern a youth's difficult if necessary and finally healthy "coming out."

Though *A Boy's Own Story* is still viewed as the classic late-20th century novel of homosexual emergency, we do have a little problem here. Read now, in light of the thousands of lesser works it inadvertently spawned (so much for the myth of gay sterility— see Proust, Wilde, Genet, Tennessee Williams, Warhol, et al.) we note that this book succeeds as fiction precisely in how it fails as a "Come On Out" brochure.

It never passed itself off as anything but a novel about a bright, agile, perverse imp. It is, in fact, the story of a child who would do most anything to "stay in."

Not yet fifteen, he seeks medical help, he begs to be sent to boarding school in hopes that male role models there might firm up his resolve to become a husband and father. He shudders at the thought of devolving into yet another aging "Gay," wearing Liberace ruffles, singing show tunes at the family piano for Mom's delighted bridge club. Instead he falls in love with a girl wonderfully named Helen Piper (making his conquest of her seem all the more theoretical). And when their romance founders on date #1, our hero suffers the tortures of Goethe's young Werther.

In the 21st century, we must read this work not as a tract for that painfully titled option "the Gay Life Style," but as an account of the one young man most eager to forswear his homosexuality. And, no, this is not just "a phase," his rabid denial. The book ends with definitive proof of his adult effectiveness, of his profound ambivalence concerning his unchosen sexuality. That foregone predisposition is visible to everyone else in the book; is visible alas in every line of its own exquisite expression. And here rests the source of much of this work's humor.

But movements, never known to get a joke, simply take what they need, extracting from whatever new work appears the vitality required for current propagandistic needs. This novel's importance for the Stonewall-era gay forces rested largely in its view that sexual exploration can be an absolute good. Set before the hideously corrective advent of AIDS, the book's youthful exploratory sexuality is here seen as a valid "occupation," almost an art form. It is not considered simply the naughty, harshly judged "preoccupation" that America's prevailing culture found so pathological in gay men's enviable (and therefore troubling) multiple partners.

But what the Movement seems to have missed, what makes reencountering this work such a tonic pleasure now that the fever heat of its political application has abated, is the far-ranging detachment of the sprightly invert-convert at its center. The analytic couch mentioned above is being approached by a boy most eager for the fastest possible "cure." The whole mentor of this refreshingly non-politically correct work is the heterosexual escape fantasy of a child who's terminally gay in his every molecule and synapse. The latent heterosexual. Very latent.

I do wish White had given his alluring-repellent narrator a proper name. I suspect his young narrator would, by now, have entered the national lexicon, an alternative roomie-companion to poor straight Holden Caulfield. The anonymous hero acts out his desire to be more than merely gay—carries it clear through to the book's strange yet somehow inevitable Gethsemane ending. The Liberationists, in their joy at the forthrightness of the book's sex—thrilling for its time and still startling in its full-frontal geometry and detail—overlooked how our boy protagonist's most fervent wish is always for Grosse Pointe normalcy. Such longed-for blandness, even if it's kinky as his father's brand, might seem a gross and pointless death wish. But that's precisely what the lad wants. He longs to remain in the country club's cozy dining room. He dreads being banished to a dishwashers' underworld that might constitute his sole means of support, his enforced self-disgusted subject matter. That could not be made plainer than in the following sustained analogy:

> I had a dream in which I was a waiter in an elegant restaurant where I served happy, elegant couples. That was upstairs. Downstairs the filthy kitchen was staffed by bald, grizzled men, convicts, really, mute, bestial with grief. They wore blood-stained aprons and gleamed with sweat. I was one of them and, although I could rise to circulate among the happy diners, I always had to descend back down to the hopeless workers, each suspicious of the others. And then the police van arrived and the help, all of us, were dragged out into the night street ablaze with revolving red lights. We were hauled off to prison, where we'd remain forever... Now [the diners] knew I wasn't one of them but one of the convicts.
>
> I woke with tears in my eyes . . .

IV

ON PUBLICATION OF this work, *The New York Times* announced—jingoistically perhaps, but with a certain aptness—"Edmund White has crossed J.D. Salinger with Oscar Wilde to create an extraordinary novel." What Holden Caulfield and Oscar Wilde might hold in common—at their varying levels of eloquence—is a strange hypervirtuous inability to defend themselves.

The same cannot be said of the hero of *A Boy's Own Story.* Unlike the aforementioned gents, our young narrator seems able to step from one conflagration, from one seduction and mentor to another, usually gaining more than he loses, all while destined, as Balzac put it, "to rise in the world." Here is a boy soprano gifted with a choric range. The soloist as an entire *Requiem* in white Brooks Brothers bucks.

As the book progresses, we feel more amazed by his philosophical and catlike sensuality, set alongside a more canine need for universal approval. And all refracted through his detachment, heightened by those unreasoning early punishments by his father. The narrator refers glancingly to his own rage. But it has gone, like the vision of gay men as "the hopeless workers" and straight ones as "happy elegant" diners, underground. He has engendered his own protective stance as a double agent in this rigged world: nothing escapes his astonishing perceptions. His eyesight seems laser able to, not simply register, but synopsize/diagnose every object and person in his purview. And yet this insecurity, his essential hiddenness in a world so ravishingly visible to him, makes for a strange parallax framing.

And yet, it is a split screen we soon adjust to. Using a term oculists employ, "we compensate for it," one eye giving the other rest then automatically trading off that function. Our young guide is utterly in love with the retinal world and capable of rendering it, now with the folkloric simplifying capacity of N. C. Wyeth, now with a detailed feather-by-feather Audubon notation. And yet, knowing he is banished by this very desire, he stands over to one side, commenting on the action, judging the dessert forks, remarking the relative allure of all those around him. He is unsparing of his own vanity, more generous with others'. We witness a fierce sustained emotional tussle, but one somewhat cushioned, offset, by an upholstered dictation of surpassing humor, knowing reference, compositional refinement.

We see this young man seek approval and admiration through clothes and savior faire; we watch him search for a loving community however small, for some scrap of his father's own vast distant power. And yet, this youth of the mid-20th century shows a potency quite different from that of those pinky-goldy youths in English pulp fiction. Selflessness does not rank high in his repertoire. His merit and clout stem from his cerebral allusiveness, his physical beauty and sexual precocity.

Like all prep school boys his age, he has been forced to read *Death in Venice*. But our young man's view of the work remains very much his own.

> I... luxuriated in the tale of a dignified grown-up who died for the love of an indifferent boy my age. That was the sort of power I wanted over an older man. And I awakened to the idea that a great world existed in which things happened and people changed, took risks—more, took notice: a world so sensitive, like a grand piano, that even a step or a word could awaken vibrations in its taut strings.

Music is still a distant father. And yet, who else in literature has ever identified, not with Thomas Mann's deranged older Venetian tourist, the poor man, his face streaming rivulets of orange hair dye, but instead with the roué's secret love, that Polish boy-aristocrat self-sated, ringlets tossing as he looks back over the shoulder of his form-fitting middy?

Our present narrator's merit depends upon his learnedness and his social wit; both these require and facilitate his endless mutability. Whereas the boy heroes of Victorian novels were praised most when they showed unbending ethical standards, when demonstrating their gift for withstanding cold showers and colder lakes, while evincing their willingness to forgo sexual pleasure till Marriage sanctified it.

A Boy's Own Story is hardly a traditional coming-of-age novel in which some innocent is tested then formed by a gallery of his elders. Instead, this preternaturally observant (and therefore dubious) narrator often seems the oldest person in any company, and yet his own gangliness, his dread of making mistakes, offer us the deadpan humor that makes this work so mortifyingly funny.

As in Buster Keaton's films, the hero is forever being thrust into professional and social stances for which he has no training. Picture Keaton trapped aboard a runaway locomotive headed downhill at terrifying speed, then retrofit this as Buster during his first bisexual three-way—a Buster flummoxed yet neutral-faced and, in the end, limber, ingenious, stoically accommodating. Both these protagonists somehow survive all such trials. Hilarity springs from their abrupt on-the-job training, their over-clever solutions to problems all too plain. We must pull for White's young hero as he places himself in ever more perilous positions, going after one idealized new friend then the next. What he fails to admit about himself is this: No one alive can resist his campaign to win them. Once he decides, they are his. The sole figure divinely outfitted to withstand such armor-piercing charm? His own father, of course.

Not exactly the perils of a stranded mountain expedition, but the consequences of exposure can prove as fatal. And this expedition seems more painful than any group trudge, since it is being endured so utterly alone. This book is crowded with a series of boy lovers, worthy if crazed teachers, shrinks who cannot listen, siblings incapable of anything beyond negative judgments and accusations of social sabotage. But any show of others' sympathy or sweetness can draw from this solitary observant child outlandish love letters written on vellum then slid under doors. The slightest warmth seems, to this boy with his stacked books and unlimited allowance, a declaration of love at last.

White's first novel, *Forgetting Elena,* was as cryptic and intentionally oblique as this work seems narratively straightforward, autobiographically inspired. At some point, the author appears to have applied his preternatural descriptive gifts to a pampered if desolate boyhood. Our narrator seems determined to find some way to transform, as in Proust's great organizing project, the ordinary pain and compromises of actual lived life into heightened and heightening prose. To himself in the present work, Edmund White proposes this very undertaking. The suggestion thrillingly reads like a top item on some artist's cosmic "To Do" list, one that will occupy the author for countless books to come:

> I thought that to write of my own experiences would require a translation out of the crude patois of actual slow suffering—mean, scattered

thoughts and transfusion-slow boredom—into the tidy couplets of brisk, beautiful sentiment, a way of at once elevating and lending momentum to what I felt. At the same time I was drawn to… What if I could write about my life exactly as it was? What if I could show it in all its density and tedium and its concealed passion, never divined or expressed, the dull brown geode that eats itself with quartz teeth?

How fascinating that the imagery of registration, that the picture of the self, should be merely mineral. Efficient, literally heartless, but exquisite in its clear chill geometry and, by implication, in its reason.

Twenty years later, looking back on this enduring and delighting book, the miracle seems that—as De Gaulle first described then embodied the French people, who loved what he showed them of themselves—Edmund White seems to have enjoyed and then outstripped his own utility to the social movement that tried making a mere flag from his exquisitely dyed silk scarf. It is a pleasure to see the work regain itself, and with the added footnote pedigree of its Liberationist utility. By being so comic, so informed, with a style so Nabokovian—when any good journalist's tiptoe-best prose might have done perfectly well—this novel was enlisted by a worthy cause that really would've settled for something far less good. And subsequently has.

Little else in the gay canon approaches the joyous control, the go-for-broke candor and high style of this work. If its young narrator kept breaking out of the closet he guessed to be his lifelong fate, gay lit has since set up housekeeping in that dark if capacious storage space. Journalistic romps through gay Savannah by gay journalists pretending—again for popularity's sake—not to be, that is what, a decade later, outsold but never supplanted this work. White's novel served its political purpose all too well. Happily, now we can simply read it.

James Agee once described the fiction of Theodore Dreiser as seeming the outpouring of some great Russian novelist but served up in a very poor English translation. White's oeuvre might have been first written in impeccable French, then translated by a party committee including Virgil Thomson, Gertrude Stein, Vladimir Nabokov. The ear for urgent casual speech exists alongside a topiaried control, a rigorous sentence-by-sentence reveling in the merit of "composition." The surface would surely gladden the heart of any Gallic schoolmaster, as its subject matter might disturb him. This novel's diction imitates the young character emerging at its center, the sort of boy who senses the history of everything he sees and touches, the kind of kid who could tell you in the middle of the night the name of the best chocolate on earth and where, on Michigan Avenue, you might acquire some at this hour. But under this knowing pearly overlay, the comedy remains as rude as it is suave. And the writing still feels so wet, generative, scarily honest:

> I hypothesized a lover who'd take me away. He'd climb the fir tree outside my window, step into my room and gather me into his arms. What he said or looked like remained indistinct, just a cherishing wraith enveloping me, whose face glowed more and more brightly. His delay in coming went on so long that soon I'd passed from anticipation to nostalgia.

What a splendid summation, both of this work's consolations and of its strange lingering suspense. Will our boy survive this boy's own harrowing story? Does Little Nell still live? We feel a worried breathless interest in this child, left too long to his own brilliant devices. We have enjoyed a kid's perspective, but one infused with an oracle's overview, with the aged Casanova's sensory knowingness. We hear the complaint of someone perpetually unloved, but he has sung all that in a Siren's magnetic tones, a voice literally irresistible to any passing human ear. The dare is invitational. We believe in his pain but are thrilled to the point of love, admiring how that pain explains itself. This schism helps account for the famously complicated ethics of the work's ending. At last our narrator seems to have found, only to discard, his very own admiring married man with children. "Daddy? Finally got your full attention. And now—you listening?—you're fired. No severance package, either, chump. So long, Pop."

All along, this boy's upper vocal register has been wonderfully complicated by the ventriloquism of his looking back and down on himself, by his having turned forty. He has found a safe place of his own. He has remained deeply engaged and bitterly amused by the comic sadness of his own first years. When we read Ben Franklin's autobiography we know that everything turned out all right for the suffering typesetting boy, because we bought the story of Ben Franklin; the kid did okay. In the way of these things, given the saving adoption agency run by Art itself, and generously supplanted by completest trust fund Memory, this book contains at least one kind father figure. That turns out to be none of the priests, counselors, professors, roommates, hoodlums who push forward wanting to lead or corrupt this child. No, the best dad present is the boy himself, matured into the wondrous teller of his own tale.

We have moved from the erection of hope—"anticipation"—to satiation's warming afterglow—"nostalgia." What, meanwhile, is absent? Isn't a real and active life missing in action after those formative years spent reading great writers, fantasizing superior lovers? What rests between pubescent underripe high notes and middle age's Brahmsian baritone refrains about regret, decay? What waits hammocked between elation at the prospect of a whole new life and its endlessly echoing Proustian ramifications? The core. Whatever is there, that is what's most thoroughly a boy's own. Hard-won. Is it often borrowed from books? Yes. It is a set of love letters written in exquisite diction and penmanship on parchment worthy of national constitutions. Are these petitions addressed to folks who will surely worry about the legal consequences of such a minor's love? Were poetic tributes sent to the very people who must find such pubescent admiration a form of stalking? Yep. And yet that *is* one's story. So often that's just what our quest for the Ideal leaves us holding. We enjoyed our beloved's favorite *Requiem* at the same time he did, but only from half a house away. And yet, who wise would wish away even one of love's indignities?

So now, prepare to be seduced by a song composed of hope. True, it goes all sweet and then all sour. But it always offers something glittering, permanent and yet while feeling as clearly transitory as that last, pure, held note of a gifted boy soprano. You hear the final quavering perfection before his whole mechanism, hormone-soaked, "breaks" at least. But here, for now, Nabokov's "wayward child" has not quite met—nor fully yet become—the "panting maniac."

As with the sound of all boy voices, the Celestial is closely underwritten by the Feral. Snakes, snails, springy pups' tails, umber-ocher gold late Brahms, plus the precious-metal purity of a boyhood forever on hold. He is someone just about to deepen and to change for the better. Someone close to darkening at last into becoming truly thoughtful of others. Our boy is someone finally confident as he deserves. He will soon be someone far less riven by those gravitational erotic drives that condemn us always downward—toward unworthy if fascinating others. He must soon become a grown man, tamed and calmed and civilized at least.

Not not yet,
not quite yet...

World without end. Amen.

"I who had so little power—whose triumphs had all been minor victories of children and women, that is, merely verbal victories of irony and attitude—I had at last drunk deep from the adult fountain of sex."

—from *A Boy's Own Story*

A BOY'S OWN STORY:

THE GRAPHIC NOVEL

BRIAN ALLESANDRO

AS A GAY man, writer, and someone who fancies himself well read, I'm embarrassed to admit that I arrived late to Edmund White. Most readers discover him when they are still in their teens or early twenties. For me, it was only three years a go, in 2016, and I was thirty-nine years old (of course, I had *known of* him since college). Though that introduction came through *Genet*, White's trenchant and tireless Jean Genet biography, the focus of this appreciation is on his coming-of-age trilogy, which includes *A Boy's Own Story, The Beautiful Room is Empty,* and *The Farewell Symphony*. I am adapting White's *A Boy's Own Story* into a graphic novel and screenplay with his husband, Michael Carroll, while also reimagining and incorporating thematic elements from the other two books in the collection.

A good deal has already been written about *A Boy's Own Story*, but my relationship with the material, as someone who is on some level making it his own while remaining true to the original vision of its author, has yielded perhaps an uncommon perspective. For me, someone with an advanced degree in clinical psychology and many years' experience teaching the subject, the work is about how passivity and accommodating personality types eventually give way to passive-aggressive spite. "I half wanted to be a man, a grown-up man, but a gallant one who could finally put an end to all this suffering. My other half wanted to have a man; I thought, I'd know better how to get one and keep him. Or else how to punish him for his neglect."

In fact, Carroll—whom I've become close friends with after meeting through the LGBTQ Writers Caucus, and who graciously permitted me to publish his memoir essay, *No Capote, or My 2016*, about his 22-year marriage to White in the inaugural print issue of my literary journal, *The New Engagement*—and I have had many long discussions about how we would give the unnamed protagonist—whom we've named affectionately and appropriately "Eddie"—more agency in our film and graphic novel versions. Visual medium enthusiasts are less tolerant of internal (that is, repressed) characters who are exploited without putting up a fight. Though, of course, at the end of White's book, he certainly, finally does just that. "He'd be powerless. I would have gotten what I wanted, gotten away with it and gotten rid of him: the trap-door beside the bed. At last I could betray an adult. This heterosexual hipster would be my momentary Verlaine."

The graphic novel format allows us to retell White's story in terms both literary and visual. Graphic novels have emerged as a conduit between literature and film or television. The medium has become so much more than "comic books for adults" (an old, but recently abandoned attitude held by many in publishing). It can earnestly be regarded as high art. I mean, Art Spiegelman's *Maus*, a metaphoric examination of the Holocaust depicting cats as Nazis and mice as Jews, won the Pulitzer Prize in 1992, Howard Cruse's *Stuck Rubber Baby* brought a frank and revelatory approach to scrutinizing issues surrounding homophobia and racism in 1995, Alison Bechdel's *Fun Home*, a piercing autobiography about growing up a lesbian with a closeted father who ultimately commits suicide, was turned into a Tony Award-winning musical in 2015, and John Lewis's *March*, about the Civil Rights Movement, won the National Book Award in 2016. Additionally, the graphic novel will come to complement the eventual film adaptation. With my background in writing novels (my debut, *The Unmentionable Mann*, was published by Cairn Press in 2015), drawing pictures (I've been exhibited in New York, Tucson, and Irvine, California), and making movies (my first feature, *Afghan Hound*, has been making the rounds these past few years), I intuit an organic relationship between written page, illustrated cell, and motion picture.

The vengeance that the unnamed protagonist enjoys at novel's end comes after many years of being taken advantage of. He must first endure everyone else's projections; they burden him with their own insecurities, their own resentments, their own desires. The unnamed hero serves as a blank canvas, a Rorschach onto which an unfair amount of pain is cast. The abuses of the boy's naivete and softness include Kevin's impatient sexual advances at his parents' lake house, the boy's mother and sister's manipulations and unfounded castigations, the boy's father's distance and domination, the hustler's seduction and deception, Marilyn and Fred's imposing mentorship, Ralph's degrading commands, Tommy's dazzlement and detachment, Helen's rejection, Mr. Pouchet's indifference, and the Scotts' marital and erotic theatre. The adult world disenchants him, but the world of his peers leaves him rootless, and thoroughly alienated. His betrayal of Mr. Beattie was necessary, as it served as a catharsis, a grandly obscene gesture aimed at the vulgar society who had harmed him. "I was able to punish [them] for not loving me. My German teacher had not loved me and Mr. Pouchet had not loved me. Tommy had not loved me. My dad had not loved me."

The *weltschmerz*—that awful process of becoming an adult, of letting go of the glorified version of the world held since childhood to make room for the disappointing and demoralizing understanding of what it really is—is found in the transition from put-upon martyr to active agent of aggression. The boy comes of age only at the end of his story, when he finally hits back. His time at the boarding school, Eton, both intimates the emergent rebel and provides the milieu. "Now at last, I, who had always been considered obedient, even docile, was rubbing shoulders with guys who were about to flunk out, who got drunk and totaled cars, who knocked up girls, who got into fist fights with their dads, who stole motorcycles and went off on joy rides, who had created such chaos at home they'd been banished to Eton."

If the protagonist is a blank slate for the other characters that inhabit White's wonderful and wonderfully complex world, then the book itself is a clean canvas onto which its reader can paint meaning. Of course, all good books do that. For me, *A Boy's Own Story* is about loneliness. That slow, agonized creep into isolation. The cool separation that timidity creates. The soul of the story works as a comforting guidebook to befriending the notion that we are alone, and will continue to be so, despite our best efforts to reach out and build bridges. Had I discovered the book "on time," as an adolescent, it would have saved me a few bruises, I'm sure. But looking back on it as an adult who was nearly the age White was when he wrote it, I'm proud to assert that I survived without a guide.

By integrating thematic elements from *The Beautiful Room is Empty* and *The Farewell Symphony* (and I stress "thematic elements," as we're not gleaning any characters or plot points or even language from those two books), Carroll and I delve into how the childhood experiences of the unnamed narrator colored his adult persona. Freudian and Proustian by design, our graphic novel and screenplay seek to explore how a receptive youth forges an assertive, yet reflective, adulthood.

The childhood spent in the capricious shadows of needy and fickle parents, teachers, and "role models" gives way to an adulthood rife with self-loathing, long and quiet reflection, an idealization of passing as straight, obsessions with station and power (the outmuscling of mortality, bigotry, and memories), and hysterical attachments. By considering the life of the narrator into his fifties, we cover a time span that ranges from the1950s to the1980s. Both nightmarish periods for homosexuals.

Being gay in White's universe is to be hedonistic, to be certain, but also to be alert and sensitive. Furtive, it being the 1950s. Perhaps, even a bit paranoid and contemptuous, by necessity. There's also a quiet and relaxed invincibility cloaked under a shroud of apathy. The persecution of the homosexual man had been so brutal, so callous, and so relentless for centuries that by the time he reached the hypocritical 1950s he was done with nearly everyone. The boy, despite his stabs at heterosexual validation, evolves into an emotional and social power broker in his own right. "Sometimes I think I seduced and betrayed Mr. Beattie because neither one action nor the other alone but the complete cycle allowed me to have sex with a man and then disown him and it; this sequence was the ideal formulation of my impossible desire to love a man but not be a homosexual."

Homosexuality is not the only mode of sexual want that White presents in his book. Incest, or the concealed tendency toward it, also finds its place. The vague incestuous longing at the core of the narrator's family presents an uneasy complexity. The boy desires his father. His father desires his sister. And his mother desires him. The only overt hunger is found between the narrator ("a boy") and his father. The boy's assessment of his father's body and breathing as he sleeps is at once tender and carnal. The infantilized adoration of the narrator by his mother plays out like a traditional Oedipal relationship between queer son and doting mother. What's powerful about White's writing is how he avoids making this psychoanalytic judgment. He simply allows his characters to be and become. They are imperfect—which is to say honestly written—people who fumble through a disingenuous and clandestine era.

There is much to appreciate about White's language. His style manages to be both sumptuous and concise, plain yet lyrical. He approximates moods and sensibilities and warring tones with an evenness and deftness that freights the book with an ineffable exuberance. Though there is nothing necessarily surreal about it, *A Boy's Own Story* finds its derealized moments. When the narrator studies sexually his sleeping father. When the narrator discovers the geographic location of his childhood home (behind a highway!). When the narrator encounters the hustler. When the narrator pictures his love affair with Helen Paper as a film beloved by audiences. When the narrator dabbles in Buddhism. "I tried to do everything beautifully, as in a movie of my life with Helen. In some way, I felt it was already being filmed—not that I looked for hidden cameras but I simplified and smoothed out my movements for the lens. When the dresser drawer stuck I winced—this sequence would have to be reshot." These dreamlike scenes are handled with a quick and quiet restraint. The novel's spare storytelling is matched well by its swift and minimalist pace. And, naturally, there is ever a clever, absurdist humor at play.

The challenge for me and Carroll in moving beyond appreciation of language and imagery and characterization and theme, is to distill all of it into a visual story that doesn't rely so heavily on White's words. A task we've decided was somewhat impossible. By culling some of what we've deemed the strongest passages and transposing them as voice over narration in the screenplay and captions for the graphic novel, we believe we've succeeded in adapting the book for these two vastly different mediums. Something that will pay homage to the source material and its author, while also becoming something altogether new.

Using Jean Cocteau's *Les Enfants Terribles* and Kubrick's *Barry Lyndon* as references on how to make voice over serve the adaptation rather than hinder it, Carroll and I made great efforts to match the visual sequences (sometimes montages, other times static master shots, and finally invented scenes) to complement the voice overs and captions, rather than allow it to do the heavy lifting. Lazy graphic novel and screenwriting is sometimes guilty of this.

The thematic elements that have informed the adaptation's development were drawn from the second and third books in the trilogy. Our adult Eddie's life in Paris works as a framing device, a la *The Farewell Symphony*. And the events of *A Boy's Own Story* and *The Beautiful Room is Empty* become flashbacks that correspond to encounters adult Eddie has with other men. Without giving too much away, the "thematic elements" center on GRID (Gay Related Immunodeficiency, or what became known as AIDS), conscious construction of a romanticized self, body image torments, promiscuous and anonymous sex (or as White fondly calls it, "toilet sex"), dubious relationships with women, a meteoritic career at *Vogue*, and the Stonewall riots.

In operating as a sharply observed exegesis on queer culture and the fleeting sweetness and bitterness of childhood, *A Boy's Own Story* did something important and groundbreaking. White melded genres—gay literature and the coming-of-age story—and the impact continues to reverberate throughout literary and LGBTQ communities. If the original thesis of his novel is about a person too pale in persona to have a palpable presence and all the intra-psychic turmoil it engenders, then this novel ultimately celebrates the unorthodox resilience and all too-human vindictiveness (vindication?) in even the meekest among us. Something that truly transcends sexual orientation and age.

"The Simplifying Grandeur of Destiny."

—from *Caracole*

CARACOLE

RICHARD CANNING

IN AN INTERVIEW with Edmund White which—the horror!
—took place over twenty years ago (on 25 April 1998), I mentioned in passing that the novel he was then working on—*The
Married Man*—was his first venture at novel length into third-per-
son narration since *Caracole*.

White, a little concerned, responded bluntly:

> EW: *Caracole* was a disaster… (Canning, *Gay Fiction Speaks: Conversations
> with Gay Novelists* (New York/London: Columbia University Press.).

And in many ways, this—White's fourth published novel and
always my favorite, as well as the one I go back to most often—
had been.

Caracole is an exercise that seemed to please almost nobody
(indeed, it almost seemed *designed* to please nobody).It alienated
White's new-found readerships in the UK, USA, Canada and beyond, which, having been won over by *A Boy's Own Story*, might
have expected a little more of the same, or something at least
somewhat similar; or something with a gay theme lurking in it
somewhere. (This "something," obviously, they would be granted
in 1988, with the publication of *The Beautiful Room is Empty*).

It also managed to offend many members of the artistic worlds in New York which White had frequented before he left for Paris in 1983. Some figures were more obviously targeted than others—most notoriously, Susan Sontag, many of whose quirks and eccentricities informed the characterization of the ridiculously cerebral Mathilda. Sontag used her various influences and networks to see to it that the novel was largely ignored, and it died commercially as a result. Other creative types, critics and commentators in America might have had cause to feel slighted too, however, for the novel ultimately ridicules not so much an individual as a whole generation, and a whole generational *ethos*: that those who wrote, or thought, or analyzed played a vital role in a country and culture's self-realization and *raison d'etre*. If Sontag could be identified as one of the targets, then, despite the deliberate indirections and imprecisions in White's imaginative canvas and fictive method in *Caracole,* the whole of opinion-forming Manhattan could suspect him of having them in his sights.

White's departure for France in 1983, year three of the AIDS crisis, moreover, was scarcely designed to win him allies stateside—much as the reputations of W. H. Auden and Christopher Isherwood never recovered in Britain, after they set sail for the New World in 1939. The comparison is woefully inexact and unfair, certainly, but to some minds, he had seemingly jumped ship just as a health crisis began that would decimate his gay peers, even when and as it would soon equally appear to threaten his own future. To a casual reader of *Caracole* it might also seem that White had lost interest in gay lives, subcultures and identities at the very moment that all three were under attack from all sides. (Of course, ultimately White's publishing career would show that he had done no such thing, and his co-authorship of *The Darker Proof: Stories from a Crisis* with Britain's Adam Mars-Jones in 1987 in particular was and remains one of the lodestars of early AIDS literature).

The apparent change of focus between *A Boy's Own Story* and *Caracole* could be taken to imply that White felt that gay themes had exhausted themselves in literary fiction—just seven years after the remarkable year in gay publishing, 1978, that had seen not just his second, crypto-gay novel *Nocturnes for the King of Naples* appear, but also his friend Andrew Holleran's epoch-defining *Dancer from the Dance*, the first of Armistead Maupin's *Tales of the City* novels, and Larry Kramer's splenetic but surprisingly regarded *Faggots*. In 1985, just a few inchoate and fragile beginnings suggested that gay literature might be beginning to be taken seriously. The phenomenon-that-was-to-be had gained few footholds, and the conceptualization of a niche gay readership that might be marketed to was still some way further off.

In short, American social and cultural politics and poetics in 1985 seemed to demand spokespeople, banner wavers, foot soldiers or slogan makers. Both White's self-exile and the publication of *Caracole* made it quite clear how different was the contribution to literature—gay and otherwise—that he then wanted to make.

Asked to reflect on the significance of *Caracole* to me for this volume, I've found myself forced to go back first to its author's own estimations quite extensively. This isn't because I want to defer to them. It's because I came to know Edmund very well from the early 1990s, and recovering the younger self who read it when he was "just" the implied author conjured up by this fictional text that you had bought, the one that you had clutched in your hand on the bus, has proven very difficult. If summing up White's literary career now strikes us as a baffling challenge – given its many achievements, its multi-facetedness, its restlessness, its winning changes of form, genre, appeal and focus—then so too the attempt at scrolling back to my earlier self—the nineteen-year-old reader of *Caracole*, at University and still shadow boxing against the closet—feels doomed. I'm not where I was.

So, it is worth quoting further from the 1998 conversation:

RC: You know it wasn't. How do you mean a disaster—in terms of ledger sheets?

EW: No—but that way it surely was. It was the worst-selling of all my books. But I think it was also a book that profoundly confused people. It has six major characters and shifts in a very pell-mell way from one point of view to the other... *Caracole* was my homage to one of the great failed books of all time: Nabokov's *Ada*, which has Terra and Anti-Terra. Nabokov was trying to imagine what it'd be like if there had never been the Russian Revolution, and if America and Russia had been the same country, Amerussia, and you blend their cultures together. It was a hybridization, too, and a kind of alternative version to history as we know it. I was trying to do something similar. I have said of *Caracole* that, if you were taking a course in world literature, went to sleep the night before the exam and had eaten too much Stilton and had a bad dream, then this is what would come out. It seemed to me at one and the same time this sort of compendium of European literature, with a heavy emphasis on figures like Stendhal and Proust, plus a hybridization of straight and gay America and Europe. (Canning)

The link to *Ada* here was compelling—not least because White had long claimed that his ideal reader would be someone like Vera Nabokov—a brilliant novelist's equally brilliant wife, that is, and someone, moreover, capable of being engaged by any topic, told in any way, if told well enough. But had White's ideal reader, in the case of *Caracole*, implicitly allowed an excess of Nabokovian virtues to creep aboard, a surfeit of word-play, tricksy allusion and literary techtonics, at the expense of... well, truth-telling, directness, or control over a story? I didn't articulate these concerns then—and I certainly didn't have in mind what now strikes me as the most Nabokovian moment in the novel: the absurd dispatching of her love rival Edwige by Mathilda at the ball in the book's closing pages, and the still more absurd self-justifications which the narrator relays as she prepares to commit the murder. The following passage from *Caracole* is surely spun out from the self-regard in, as well as the aestheticising regard of, Nabokov's most fully realized and most deeply comically un-self-aware protagonist, *Lolita*'s Humbert Humbert:

> Her ironic self snickered at the preposterous melodrama she was instigating, but her tragic self moved with gravity toward her goal. Primitives did things—attacked, killed, struck back—and sobered up later to regret their impetuosity. Civilized people did nothing and prided themselves on the self-consciousness that had tranquilized them. They didn't understand that their inaction, far from proving how highly evolved they were, actually demonstrated that they were suited only to belong to the chorus. They could comment on the deeds of the principles but not step out to become one. Of course every educated person found anything bold ridiculous; and of course any action of any sort creaked with the awkwardness of the discernibly real. Yes, how wonderful that we should exist; how hilarious that we should do or make. But someone worthy of being a protagonist finally steps forward and, no matter how stylelessly or inopportunely, plants the axe in the stomach.

Mathilda decides that to murder is right, since she will do so with the foresight and self-awareness of the "artist," just as Humbert Humbert's own unreliable retelling in *Lolita* renders its own storyline throughout by way of aesthetic embellishment, self-repression as well as self-regard and misrepresentation, willful and otherwise—including regarding Humbert's planned murder of Charlotte Haze, Lolita's mother, and his actual murder of Clare Quilty, the abductor (who all too conveniently makes Humbert's ethical culpability appear a little less culpable).

White's savage, hilarious exposé of Mathilda has all the mordant, ironic weight found in Nabokov's 1955 masterpiece, as this supposed genius casually distinguishes between two crude formulations of human, the "primitive" and the "civilized," flat-footedly insisting upon an absurd "either/or" contrast between surface and depth among human motivations. It is Mathilda's own binary reductionism too which informs her self-division into "ironic" and "tragic" selves, not White's or his narrator's. Above all, Mathilda's reflections return us to the intrinsic moral simplifications and certainties of the stageplay world, especially that found in opera or ballet, as she invokes "melodrama," "chorus," "principles" (for principal performers) and focuses on herself as a "protagonist." Mathilda makes a further cardinal mistake, in presuming that people in life will act and should act like those in the plots of our preferred works of art.

Yet she speaks a sort of unwitting truth, in the sense that the world of eternal reflectiveness with which she, as an intellectual, has happily been associated, is about to be up-ended by the reunion of Gabriel and Angelica, and by the former's leading role in the incipient revolution—and indeed also ended by her own violent action, since the murder of Edwige is precisely what is needed to bring these two climactic plot developments about. Her running commentary, meanwhile—as White's narrator renders it—reads more like the program notes for an Italian *verismo* opera than a plan of action, or the arrival at genuine inner resolve. For Mathilda the murder is justified by the claim that she will "do something in full knowledge of its meaning," but the fundamental lesson conveyed by the intricacies which unfold in *Caracole* is that *full* knowledge of the meaning of anything—immediate or permanent—is never possible, including even in the acts of sex or murder, each shared by two partners but then subject to interpretation by many others.

What strikes me most about White's comments, though, is the radical intent and the peerless pursuit of his interests in writing *Caracole*, even as they came to fail to align themselves so comprehensively with the incoming era of identity politics, niche marketing and a widespread and incremental Western drift towards nationalism, inward-lookingness and cultural conservatism (which latter was found as stridently in American subcultures, often, as it was in mainstream culture). A compendium of European literature? At this moment, readers wanted books which summarized a circumstance (being gay, being young, being Midwestern, being effeminate), rather than complicating it, or—still worse, and for me one of the enduring pleasures of *Caracole*—seeking wryly to change the terms (context, genre, allusion) by which it might be judged. Eighties readers—like their counterparts in 2018 in so many ways—were drawn to simple if invented statements and storylines, by which both characters and readerships could converge, with the implied author, in a closed-in world of certainties (and usually commonplaces). Each of White's novels is a rebuke to such formulaic and predictable plotting and literary stylistics, certainly—but *Caracole* is the novel which most openly trumpets its defiance, in celebrating a renewed, and also partly reinvented high modernist aesthetics which sought only to destabilize or complexify.

Still more challenging were White's ambitions towards a "hybridization of straight and gay America and Europe." Gay characters, it was felt at the time, had only just gained any sort of permission to speak and act in their *own* fictional stories, and to live their own equally fictional lives: E M Forster's *Maurice*—published in 1971, only after his death, and one of the first entirely gay-themed novels to be published in English at all—was, in 1985, still a *current* title; the Merchant-Ivory film version which followed the publication of *Caracole* by less than two years in a sense confirmed the "market friendliness" of such "new" (if already deeply historic) gay titles in the still more conservative context of film. (Coincidentally, White has told comically of his dissuading Louis Malle from turning *Caracole* into a film—see

Canning, p.88). If gay men and women were earning their own spurs in 1970s and 1980s fiction, including in White's own novels, why was the author suddenly seeking to bring together or "hybridize" anything else?

The 1980s saw things falling apart, with the purported or traditional social and cultural centers failing to hold. *Caracole* seemed to take inspiration from a hectic, sometimes cacophonic arena of literary voices inside its author's head: it argued for a reader either steeped in such reading and attuned to such voices (very much, then, a minority reader), or else for a reader who could be seduced by the scale of the challenge (ditto). In terms of bringing gay and heterosexual cultural and literary traditions together, let alone gay and heterosexual storylines, White was decades ahead of the pack, and indeed it really has only been in the very recent past that we have seen novels of literary caliber written by heterosexual writers on gay or sexually marginal themes; books which might count, that is, as the response to the call which *Caracole* then made: John Irving's *In One Person* (2012); Sebastian Barry's *Days Without End* or Rose Tremain's *The Gustav Sonata* (both 2016).

I argued to White in 1998 somewhat along these lines—that it was simply a "book for which the time isn't right." I also suggested that *Caracole* might be a sort of vengeance that the Nabokovian side of White's split literary persona was wreaking on its counterpart—the gay, auto-fictionalist, Isherwood-like demi-persona; the one who—through the *A Boy's Own Story, The Beautiful Room is Empty* and *The Farewell Symphony* trilogy in particular—became the White novelist most readers know, and, where they do know of his more avant-garde strain, remains the one which they invariably admire. The idea of one side of White's authorial persona sabotaging the other was, unsurprisingly, not too appealing to the author, and in our conversation White parried, admitting at least that he had been satisfied with *Caracole* on its completion:

EW: I thought: "This is a book I've labored on long and lovingly. Every detail seems to me burnished or high-finished. Maybe there'll be people who dislike the whole conception – and there were plenty—but I think that, within its terms, it is one that is realized." Its terms are very peculiar, and mostly invented by me. It's not like they were preestablished. I remember in Germany, people hated it. They thought it was like Thomas Mann; "Weltkulturliteratur" or something. There was something repellent for them about that. They wanted something like David Leavitt: short, minimalist, modern, and contemporary. (Canning)

German critics and readers were not alone in feeling alienated. Far from it—*Caracole* has continued to be a minority pursuit, even if there have been keen advocates amongst White's admirers, including the English novelist and playwright Neil Bartlett, who reviewed it for Toronto's *Body Politic* magazine. The British magazine *Time Out* considered *Caracole* "something to revel in: elegant, fabulous, almost sublime." Almost? But even positive reviews inadvertently pointed to its challenges: Phyllis Rose in *The Nation* found it a "devastating panorama of life in a high-powered city," but also nominated it as "the finest French novel written in English"—an award, obviously, for something which cannot literally exist. In *The Unpunished Vice*, coincidentally, White is droll on the historical accident, whereby the French novel whose formal traits *Caracole* most immediately resembles, Julien Gracq's breathtaking *Le Rivage des Syrtes* (1951)—or *Caracole*'s "glorious, superior antecedent" (White, *Vice*)—was unknown to him until after *Caracole* had been published. Intriguingly, Gracq's novel was only published in English as *The Opposing Shore*—translated by White's long-term friend Richard Howard—in 1986, almost as if it had no right to appear until *Caracole* had itself been published.

Nicholas Radel reminds us in his excellent monograph *Understanding Edmund White* (Columbia, SC: University of South Carolina Press, 2013) that *Caracole* both preceded and postdated *A Boy's Own Story*, White's breakthrough work—and also the one which seemed to lay to rest the experimental style that I have characterized as Nabokovian. White set it aside to write *A Boy's Own Story*, but returned to it immediately thereafter. For Radel, this justifies it being bracketed together with the first two novels, not only in formal terms, however, but thematically too. For Radel, *Caracole*'s "highly intellectualized" society evokes those found in *Forgetting Elena* and *Nocturnes for the King of Naples*. *Caracole* also affords its protagonist, Gabriel, a world "rich with possibility for someone open to novelty" and a set of "pleasures and possibilities" which involve a welcome opportunity to throw off inherited moral codes, but also contain elements of risk and hazard, initially not easily identified or avoided (Radel). Each of these things had, equally, been promised in White's earlier novels

The biggest development, however, lies in the erotics of these initations, for Gabriel—who, we deduce, is seventeen when the novel opens—is to be tempted by a younger, native girl, Angelina (who must have been fourteen when she seduces him—though we have to wait most of the novel to learn this). White's first novels may have used sleight of hand and decorousness and ambiguity to prevent the reader from identifying too obviously the homoerotics within and beneath the stories told. Here, however, White went further—in reimagining all the potential and all the shortcomings with which gay male relations are associated (or might be),including those involving differences in age, status or experience, and projecting them instead onto a series of non-gay relationships which in turn themselves prove unorthodox, exceptional and deeply disruptive, destabilizing to the social fabric, and therefore queer.

Caracole opens by presenting Gabriel's father—"a silent, stubborn man," evocative, from White's other writings, of the author's own in broad temperament, but equally exaggerated, metamorphosed and rendered entirely fantastical (*Caracole*). This sort of universal, almost Baroque embellishment of character, with dark and perverse exaggerations and emphases sets the tone for the entire novel, and it likewise makes sense of White's mention of both Dickens and Balzac, two authors commonly constrained within simplifying critical conventions concerning 19th-century literature, stressing mimesis and naturalism, when they both were capable of creating entirely unrealistic plots and characterizations, and then, still more disturbingly, incorporating these alongside the more instantly credible.

The "larger-than-lifeness" also bears comparison to *A Boy's Own Story*, where pathology is never far from the surface whenever adults appear, however matter-of-factly the novel's narrator might seem to render it – he, after all, normalizes all manner of things, not knowing any different. In *A Boy's Own Story*, a similarly unorthodox seduction takes place as the one in *Caracole*—though it is of one boy, by another who is younger still. The heterosexuality of Gabriel originated largely from the novel's heavily fictionalized source material, in the early years spent in New York by White's own nephew Keith Fleming, who had turned up on his doorstep and been taken in by his gay uncle, following a very troubled upbringing.

But White, in utilizing essentially a Brechtian theatrical "alienation effect"—*Verfremdungseffekt*—to recount the fictional. coming-into-maturation of Gabriel as something hard to fathom not just for himself, but hard to render at all in a novel, radically applied a gay sensibility or aesthetics to a heterosexual storyline. In this sense, *Caracole* can be seen not as the obverse of *A Boy's Own Story*, but as the autofictional novel's counterpart, each one confirming a universal truth: that the arrival of youth into the palace of adult sexuality is an alienating, destabilizing and universally queer moment. Those critics who praised *A Boy's Own Story* for its universal qualities were, I think, making the same point in reverse.

In *Caracole*, Gabriel's imprisonment by his father after his first sexual initiation (and a sort of marriage initiation) by the native (racially other) Angelica marks an all-too-obvious attempt to contain the growth of his son, his independent-mindedness and implicit threat to his father's own power and potency. It is only with the arrival of the very differently tempered Uncle Mateo from the capital that Gabriel is released—and has an opportunity, returning to the capital with Mateo, to become his own person (and for his threat to move on to pertain to his Uncle).

There is much that is operatic or pantomime-like in White's plotting from the outset—with the opening scene or prelude set in the jungle necessarily giving rise to Gabriel's need to escape to make his fortune, like any pantomime hero. The meaning of the word *Caracole* itself suggests a further debt. In French it means "prancing" and in English, a "caper": White's novel included these definitions on its book jacket for many years, in case this might help. Is *Caracole* a sort of simple dance between characters of different classes, races and ages, a sort of "dance to the music of time," to co-opt the title of Anthony Powell's novel sequence? Not only this. In English, by association, "caracole" is not just any sort of dance, or prance, or capering step: it is a half-turn made by horse and rider, a step which is therefore a sort of half turning away, or a first step of resistance. But the French verb "caracoler" (to prance, and ultimately from the Spanish *caracol* or snail) put me in mind of one of White's favorite authors, the Edwardian novelist Ronald Firbank (1886-1926). Firbank's only successful novel in the USA was entitled *Prancing Nigger* (1925), a title nowadays considered objectionable: in fact, however, this was a vulgarising retitling by Carl van Vechten, Firbank's chief American advocate, of the novel Firbank himself had called *Sorrow in Sunlight*.

In any event, here is an English precedent for the word "prancing," in a novel written by an author—Firbank—whose other novels included *Caprice* (1917), a title which equally identifies the work as a series of narrative "capers." *Prancing Nigger*—set in a highly fictionalized Cuba (with Jamaican elements)—does not open in the jungle exactly, unlike *Caracole*, but it does announce the moving to the capital, Cuna-Cuna, of the entire, deeply provincial Mouth family in an attempt at social betterment. White's novel does not imitate Firbank in all stylistic particulars, but its title—intentionally or not—calls to mind Firbank's formally innovative, modernist Baroque precedent. Moreover, *Caracole* is replete with examples of non-naturalistic dialogue, theatrical embellishments and fairytale-like plotting, all quintessentially Firbankian traits.

Where Firbank deployed unattributed contributions to conversations to create a highly wrought interpretative challenge to the reader, this arch degree of non-naturalism in dialogue was, in fact, far more redolent of what we actually hear in day-to-day speech than the cleaned-up dialogues found in literary naturalism. White did not use such rapid shifts between speakers to confuse and destabilize his readers, but he did use shifts in perspective and subjectivities (who is thinking, speaking) in comparable ways, drawing not only on Firbank but on any number of high modernist fictions.

The succession of complex emotional triangles in *Caracole* owes little to Firbank—or to White's nephew's real-life experiences. But it fully makes sense as an imaginary, projected queering of the heterosexual relations in *Caracole*, undertaken by an author in the epicenter of gay liberation's radical testing of sexual and relationship *mores*. White gives us, in the maturation of Gabriel and Angelica (who will follow him to the capital, forming a dependent relationship with Mateo), and the enablement of it by Gabriel's uncle, a sort of first fictional queering of heterosexualities. This might make *Caracole* feel like a book very much ahead of its time, which in many ways it is, but it is also one whose alienation and estrangement (*Verfremdung*) of such relations has antecedents in writing for theatre—by Brecht and others. White had begun his literary career aiming at becoming a playwright, of course, and stageplay conventions and devices recur in many of his novels, nowhere more prominently than in this one.

Might not *Caracole* be indebted to that sensational contribution to avant-garde theatre *La Ronde* (German title—*reigen*),written by the Austrian playwright Arthur Schnitzler in 1897, published privately in 1900, but not performed until 1920? That play—set in *fin de siècle* Vienna—progresses by way of ten sexual encounters, each scene featuring two protagonists, one of whom progresses to the next scene in a way which finally confers both a circularity as well as a linearity upon the play's structure:

The Whore and the Soldier
The Soldier and the Parlor Maid
The Parlor Maid and the Young Gentleman
The Young Gentleman and the Young Wife
The Young Wife and The Husband
The Husband and the Little Miss
The Little Miss and the Poet
The Poet and the Actress
The Actress and the Count
The Count and the Whore.

Where Schnitzler's plot requires its ten scenes to combine two characters in a new way, White's characteristically more ludic plot development depends on the complex circling and recircling of three three-way relationships:

Gabriel—Mathilda (his sexual educator)—Mateo (her former lover and father of her son);

Gabriel—Edwige (an affair of Gabriel's, and Mateo's unresponsive beloved)—Mateo;

Mateo—Angelica (his dependent lover, but also Gabriel's wife)—Gabriel.

Yet this very loose, initial comparison between *La Ronde* and *Caracole* offers more: Schnitzler's title refers to a round dance; White's to a dancing half-turn, partly in on itself (and thus snail shell-like and also somewhat resistant). Schnitzler's play develops by passing the story along and around, finally returning it to a character from its opening, the whore, now presented in very different circumstances. White's novel progresses likewise, with the girl Gabriel loses his virginity to at the outset becoming once again his (prospective) lover at the novel's close (with Edwige dead and Mathilda already rejected), but in a sense to an entirely reconstructed Gabriel. Schnitzler's whore progresses from Soldier to Count (scene one to ten), though this supposed development in fact equally underlines her highly non-dramatic social stasis. Gabriel in *Caracole* is transformed—not into a Count, but from a boy into a budding Soldier, and advocate for the Revolution to come.

In her anticipation of her crime, Mathilda contrasts two *personae*, the "soldier" and the "thinker." For Nicholas Radel, the promise of Gabriel reuniting with Angelica lies in their shared and learned potential to bring closer, if not to unite, the poles or axes of intellect (mind) and desire (body), between which all characters fluctuate. The novel may involve sexual advancement and education, but (self-)instruction and -tutelage equally take many non-erotic forms, and a disciplining of the mind proves as advantageous an achievement as physical release for the body. Equally, as befits an author who befriended Michel Foucault and who came to know and draw on all his ideas, power relations in *Caracole*—both in terms of libidinal and intellectual exchange—prove paradoxical and capable of sudden inversions. Gabriel, having been tutored by Mathilda, comes to recognize not only how he might take advantage of the situation, but in doing so, reverse its power dynamic entirely. When she seeks to downplay the "originality of [his] situation," Gabriel immediately understands the danger of being or becoming familiar or routine to someone like her, but perhaps to anyone: that it will next inspire indifference, contempt and finally rejection. This truth is equally implicit in the circle-like structure of *La Ronde*: people (who can) *move on*.

In Gabriel's world, this means that to remain important (not just to Mathilda, but to the novel itself), he must remain aloof:

> Gabriel was ready to do anything to make Mathilda like him. But on the other hand he recognized that only a measure of independence was likely to attract her; he must insist she please him. For an unrelated reason (fear of devils) he'd moved his chair away from her. This little act, which she'd seen as a slight, had given him an advantage. He suspected

she'd do anything to tame him but that if she succeeded she would lose interest.

Though Mathilda and Angelica are entirely unalike, as desiring women they can still, to a certain extent (an erotic extent), be read in the same way—and Gabriel, a very quick learner, soon finds in Mathilda's eyes the "same sequence of desire that would twitch jerkily through Angelica's." Gabriel now immediately knows how to take advantage of the signals he reads, and moves physically back towards Mathilda to do so:

> She was still seated, of course, when he came over to her and stood beside her. They both watched the blue silk pleat of his pants stretch and fill. They exchanged a funny little glance, incapable of questioning this development but still nonplussed by it.

The sequence of desire in Mathilda's eyes both catalytically creates the opportunity for Gabriel to assert himself, and renders the outcome inevitable. Such sequencing of desire equally informs the plotting of Schnitzler's play: sexual need alone moves it forward (on stage at least), but sexual release marks the end of each scene. This in turn suggests Peter Brooks's brilliant, Barthes-inspired formulation in *Reading for the Plot: Design and Intention in Narrative* (1992) concerning Balzac's characters: that they constitute "desiring machines", without which his plots cannot make headway and whose autonomy in the round is severely constrained by this narrative function.

In coming to understand Mathilda's physical neediness (through his uncle's guidance), Gabriel realizes that, though he has nothing to contribute to her soirees, he can simply speak an entirely other language—through his body:

> No one was as smart as Mathilda, that was obvious. Luckily, he had no points to make. By touching her, by putting their two bodies into contact, he'd shifted their exchange onto a more shadowy plain where she was less sure of herself. Most young people… apparently wanted to win the attentions of older people in conversation but were unwilling to make love to them, or so Mateo had explained.

His "speaking" will be beyond *lexis* entirely—hence the silence with which they both receive the visual evidence of Gabriel's arousal earlier—an arousal which is figured metonymically, his part very much however becoming detached from his whole: it stands (up) for itself. This returns us to Ronald Firbank, whose frequent "non-lexical" expressions invariably denote a sexual act, allusion or inference might be contained elliptically and symbolistically within an absence of words, but a presence of punctuation: "…"

Paradoxically, whereas Mathilda holds all the aces in *knowingness*, she lacks not only bodily self-regard but a corresponding self-awareness, for in dismissing her own guests in front of Gabriel— to flatter or put him at ease—she also, fatally, dismisses her own distinctiveness: "Is there anything more loathsome than an intellectual?" she asks. In seeking here to keep at bay the rivals for his affection, including his next lover, the beautiful Edwige, Mathilda diminishes herself in a literal sense (although Mateo informs Gabriel that the boy is supposed to protest in reply that intellectuals are a fine species, and that she herself is first among them). Likewise, when Mathilda kills Edwige, she will be acting not so much in a self-liberating vein as in a self-enslaving one. A testimony to Jean-Paul Sartre's thesis in *Being and Nothingness* (*L'Étre et le néant*, 1943), she shows herself as "condemned to be free" and also as willing to enslave herself by murdering the other woman, by which act she will perpetuate forever—as Sartre argued all murderers do—the very relationship between them that her action seeks to end.

It is a fatal—or fateful—mistake for Mathilda, but it is also the means by which the novel, its own Balzacian desiring, devouring machine, can move on—just as in Arthur Schnitzler's play. Equally, White's characters suggest comparison not even so much with those in Schnitzler, but those trapped within the powerplay of desire and intellect in the French Enlightenment playwright Pierre de Marivaux's (1688-1763) comedies. Particularly pertinent is his *The Triumph of Love* (*Le Triomphe de l'amour*, 1732), in which the young Spartan princess Léonide (partly in disguise through the play as a man, Phocion) comes to be juggling three contradictory and incompatible relationships, as does Gabriel in *Caracole*. There are many Marivaux-type moments in *Caracole*, inevitably perhaps, since the dramatist's interests lay in staging through paradox, wit and plot inversion a highly disruptive, destabilizing and even nihilistic view of sexual relations, at odds with the values of, and inimical to the interests of, hegemonic cultures.

*

In his most recent discussion of *Caracole*, White neatly refers to it as a "traitorous" book, as opposed to *A Boy's Own Story*, a novel *about* treachery (White, *Vice*). The author continues:

> The book was divided into three parts inspired by Roland Barthes and Michel Foucault: uncoded, coded and decoded, as if I could represent an Edenic state before society imposed its rules on the individual, followed by the years of education in which someone (Gabriel) acquired a knowledge of the world, finally leading to a period when that person shed all of his acquired manners, beliefs, and attitudes. It was based on my nephew, Keith, who deeply resented it because I mentioned his bad skin. I had made him a Stendhalian hero—a Fabrizio, I thought—and all he could focus on was the acne I described.

Of the queerness of White's attentions towards heterosexual sex, glanced at in these comments, a fine, if very disturbing example, lies in Gabriel's reaction to his first sexual encounter with Angelica. He enters her, only to become confused at the sensation that "it seemed the gift, the gift-giving, was all hers." The "pleasures of being taken in, of being *housed*" develop in his imagination, since her rootedness, her acceptance, her *accommodation* of him offers the first time and most importantly place in which he can experience a sense of belonging. This feeling, and the desire to continue to belong, informs an imminent, quite extraordinary account of macrophiliac obsession—one which only someone as sexually open-minded and well-schooled as White could have written:

> No, he'd rather shrink down to the size of an elf (or a penis) and climb in, wiggling past coils of wet muscle into a sloping corridor leading all the way to the pungent source of that clove scent she harbored, two sacs that filled—veined, whistling—and then deflated, flooding the world with rich but invisible roe. His dream of wandering through her body— past the heart as stately as a frog at night, through entrails more passionate than his own hands stroking her face, restlessly feeling for a new fault through which he might enter her—this dream made him hard again. He dug into her with his sore penis. He pressed his skull against hers; he wanted in there, too. He kissed her; he knew her mouth was another way in.

Their lovemaking is juvenile, even, virtually, prelapsarian: they are "bewildered by what their bodies had done to them" and neither can own it or take possession of it fully. Hence their marriage is a sham—they lack the self-knowledge to know what love is, and to make the gesture have enduring resonance. But each will receive erotic tutelage—Angelica from Mateo, Gabriel from Edwige—which in turn will enable their more knowledgeable, more sexually aware reconciliation—promised at the end of the novel, if not shown. In Gabriel's sexual tutelage under Edwige, White again was able and prepared to articulate this in terms of extremes of desire rarely expressed in literature (outside of D.H. Lawrence, perhaps):

> Gabriel was nothing but a flat chest sluiced in sweat and he restrained a leashed animal whining to be let go, to shoot off in the pursuit of the one prey it was born to hunt. And Edwige was no longer the arrogant dispenser of favors but this gleaming white rump (the deckling had faded) and its smell. He loved the smell of her shit because it smelled of the most shameful act of the day, the one no one dared to share.

Ultimately however the novel's most important and pivotal relationship is not sexual or romantic at all. I think this is the aspect of *Caracole* which caused me so much excitement, as well as concern, on my first, deeply-teenage reading. The most realized, enduring and important love proves not to be erotic but simultaneously legitimated by and also threatened by all of the novel's erotic games. It is that between uncle and nephew; the one which Gabriel already realizes a third of the way through the novel is "as genuine—that is, as compromised—as any other sustained feeling must be"—and here, once again, there is the qualifying adjective to unsettle ("compromised").

The transfer both of potency and thus implicit political power and will from Mateo to Gabriel is absolute, even if it is hard for Gabriel to achieve, and still harder for Mateo to accept. In a bravura few pages, Mateo reflects on the tensions as well as the rivalry within their developing relationship: he reflects on how, had Gabriel been a girl, she might have made play with him in a sensual way that would be considered "an entirely respectable violation, one that garnered the smiles of every witness." As it is, Mateo is stuck with a boy (just as White may have reflected on inheriting a heterosexual male nephew, not a female one, and not a gay male one either): "Far from being a consolation, a boy could only be competition."

Perhaps only White could have dared to write not only of the faux-repulsion Mateo feels at his new rival's "ugly and vigorous" appearance, but then to risk eroticizing the very charge of repulsion which (chiefly) drives the heterosexual Mateo's thoughts on, as he smells the boy's seed amid the "cast-off clothes, the cast-back sheets, the downcast gloom of such intense sexual loneliness": "If two men are not lovers, they can only acknowledge each other's yearning with embarrassment and yearning," continues *Caracole*'s narrator, then settling on the ignominious self-regard which pursues Mateo as he overhears his nephew going to the toilet: a scenario which is as enveloped in jealousy as it would be, in a gay context, with naked desire:

> At times when Mateo heard the boy urinating he envied him the force of his piss. To the boy, pissing was surely nothing, just one more dull mystery, but to Mateo, listening, it was the sound of animal vitality.

Mateo must succumb painfully to the phenomenon of ageing—"Young men he was introduced to started calling him 'Sir'"—watching the chance of its satiation recede even as desire itself—increasingly toward the young—increases. The passing on of sexual opportunity to the next generation symbolizes, in a generational transition, the passing on not only of other strengths or capabilities, but of responsibilities and authority and opportunity too.

In light of these examples, Nicholas Radel's comments on the relevance of *Caracole* to gay politics in the 1980s are helpful: "Readers who were initially inclined to dismiss the novel as something of a retreat from White's concern with homosexuality miss the ways in which it is about the power of sexuality in general as a social phenomenon and force" (Radel). *Caracole* daringly took the preoccupations, experiences and prejudices of White's own generation of gay men, and projected them among a range of non-gay characters, to see how they might be seen in a different light, if played by a different type of actor or actress, on a different kind of stage; to test, perhaps, whether they were universal.

The author—who would soon embark upon his biography of Jean Genet, a writer against whom he would invariably cast himself as in opposition—might be seen to be attempting in prose fictional form something akin to Genet's achievements in his greatest play *The Balcony* (*Le Balcon*, 1956), also a work set in an unnamed city which is undergoing a revolutionary uprising in the streets. Much of the action in Genet's play takes place within a brothel that functions as a microcosm of the regime under threat, so, similarly, most of *Caracole*'s developments in terms of its macropolitical storyline take place with and through sexual courtship, role playing and intrigue.

I remember now. When I first read *Caracole*, it didn't seem to be about heterosexuality at all, but about all the vital, inescapable associations between power—symbolic and actual, social and political—and sexual desire and desirability. That's pretty much everything my younger self was likely to think about anyway in daylight hours anyway. Its penetration of these matters was so original, so poignant and in some cases so hard to take (even, occasionally, hard to understand), that of course this novel stayed with me, and has continued to stay with me. How could it not? The older, implied author invited his much younger reader to a sort of unequal dance or caper. In so doing, he required me to think for myself, learn for myself, act for myself and, whenever necessary, to resist.

"Come with me, then, up the concrete steps to the toilet door, place a dime in the box, turn the chrome handle, open the door a crack, and slip in.

You'll be surprised by how many silent men are standing around. This businessman has rested his expensive leather briefcase on the filthy sink and is leaning against a tile wall. On the floor a bum, reeking of sweet red wine, is sleeping it off, snoring loudly, a sound that draws a red line under the conspicuous silence. Both stalls, one doorless, the other with its door half open, house men sitting right on the porcelain (the seats have long since been stolen). Both occupants have dropped their pants to the damp floor but are leaning forward to conceal their erections. The mood of the room is a cheap alloy of tension and boredom. A train clatters in, you can hear the doors open and shut, then shoes ringing on the pavement in the cavernous station.

And then you lean against the wall and, enduring seconds that pulse in your ear, stretch out your hand toward the crotch of the man beside you. Your action triggers vitality all around you. In a second this raw country boy at the urinal with the rosy forearms and red knuckles, the sickle of a vein superimposed on the hammer of his hand, has turned toward the room, brandishing a big red penis. An instant later everyone has converged on him, the men in the stalls emerge, one is kissing him, the second licking his testicles, a third man the penis, and another is standing beside him, arm around his waist, as though to lend him courage and companionship. The businessman with the expensive briefcase has planted his face between the farmboy's buttocks in total disregard of his expensive trousers, which are getting damp and dirty on the floor, wet with backed-up sewage. He's lapping and lapping; I can see his eyes drifting peacefully from side to side, dreamily independent of the suckling action.

Then the man sucking the cock comes up for air and you take his place, fitting yourself around a tumescence still warm and tasting of the other guy's spit. You look up as someone else unbuttons the country boy's shirt, revealing a hairless chest marbled by blue veins and decorated like a piece of wedding cake with two candle sockets in pink frosting—the erect nipples.

Now everyone is at work on him at once, breath in his ear, lips on his lips, mouths on his balls, cock, and ass, that arm around his waist, as though he really is a bride and this the last-minute flurry of seamstresses fitting him into his gown.

When he comes, he lets out a cry. His body stiffens and he leans back. You swallow gratefully the surprisingly meager but sweet semen, and the boy's ecstasy sets off his bridal attendants, who shoot and shout in a chorus around him. The drunk is still snoring.

In two seconds you've buttoned up, wrapped your raincoat around you, and rushed out into the flood of passengers flowing up the stairs and rivuleting into the night. Your hair is rumpled, your face flushed, and your hand still smells of the country boy. At the subway entrance you catch sight of the businessman just behind you. Without thinking, you glance at his trousers, not too bad, he looks at your wet knees the same moment, and you and he exchange the tiniest smile of wintry complicity."

—from *The Beautiful Room is Empty*

THE BEAUTIFUL ROOM IS EMPTY

IAN RAFAEL TITUS

HOW DO I describe those times? The early to late 90's as a college student in New York City. How do I describe what it was like to go on the hunt and to be the hunted—the *haunted*. Hunting for men to validate me, to desire me. Wanting to be pursued, wanted, grabbed, fondled, stroked, caressed, kissed. Did I believe the touch of all the strangers I desired in those places, those *rooms* (the adult theaters, the booth stores, the hook-ups in unknown railroad apartments and outer-borough homes) would make me beautiful, turn me from ugly duckling to swan? Did I believe my self-esteem would rise with each kiss, with each cock that found its way inside me? Did I seek salvation from the baptism of cum on my face?

There was something deeply spiritual in many of my encounters. Kneeling before a man, looking up at him, adoring his flesh as if a god seethed within that body. Seeking his approval at my carnal skills, seeking his adoration, his desire, yes, even his love if I was inflamed enough, enthralled enough, bewitched enough. And haunting those places for what seemed a never-ending quest to repeat those seemingly few and precious embraces that had felt like I had wrestled and fucked with gods and demons. That unquenchable thirst for more.

That's what Edmund White's *The Beautiful Room is Empty* captured so unnervingly well for me. There, in those pages I returned to again and again, spoke a fellow traveler about desire so fierce, so inexhaustible, that reason, self-care, and dignity could be forsaken despite one's best intentions. A fellow traveler who knew the weight of countless hours awaiting gods but making do with mere mortals. But also someone who sought love, companionship, understanding, intimacy. Someone who wanted to be loved, adored, cared for. Valued. Validated. Be seen as beautiful in a beloved's eyes. I wasn't alone in feeling such conflicting desires—throwing myself at countless men but yearning for The One who might put an end to the days and nights of constant searching, constant craving, constant self-loathing. What a revelation!

No wonder I dog-eared the pages which contained such wisdom, such familiar scenes of debauchery and tenderness, loss and self-acceptance, fear and defiance. Some of the passages seemed lifted from my own journals, yet written with such poetry, such visceral self-examination, it was more as if they had been pulled from my own thoughts, and most not as fully-formed or as aware as White's narrator.

What was it like? Often stepping from the sunlit crowded sidewalks into the dimness of the Westside highway and East Village theaters and booths lit by screens both large and small. Hearing the moans and groans and dirty words, not always knowing which came from the videos and which from the patrons in the seats, aisles, restrooms or booths. Sometimes the rooms would be as boisterous as the streets outside, at other times the rooms were sparsely occupied or empty, but they were never beautiful. And the smell—that stale aroma of desire, lust, made up of sweat, spit, cum, cologne, alcohol, piss, that heady and unmistakable aroma that always assured that you were in a home away from home, that you belonged there.

Does that paint a full picture? What about the men? Suits seeking lunch-time relief, laborers looking to get off, old men wandering like phantoms, men of all races and creeds and social classes, united inside these kingdoms of lust, where their differences did not matter much, where desire ruled supreme.

I first read about *The Beautiful Room is Empty* in a New York magazine book review and I bought it in paperback a few years after its 1988 publication. I was attending art school in New York City, exploring my sexuality and stepping out of my sheltered family life with the help of my new college friends and the gay men who came into my life. In Edmund White's book I found a protagonist with an interest in the arts, a young man who lusted after other men and who, like me, found himself seeking love and sex with strangers in the most unlikely of places. And like me, when he lost the man he loved, Sean, the narrator grieved with an intensity that was soul-shattering, grief so overwhelming nothing but the possibility of that lover's return seemed of any significance.

Beginning in the 1950s Midwest and ending with the Stonewall Uprising in New York City, *The Beautiful Room is Empty* continues the story begun in White's autobiographical novel *A Boy's Own Story*. It starts with the narrator in his junior year in prep school, his world about to expand beyond his wildest expectations. Taken in by a group of artists at the college across from his school, the narrator experiences the thrill of living like an artistic outsider, befriending charismatic individuals like the painter Paul, Ivan the sculptor, and Maria, who will become his best friend. Yet he fears what would happen if they were to know about his attraction to other men.

During one of his visits to Paul, "the best painter at the school" and the narrator's "first genius," he has these thoughts about him:

"I tried to imagine kissing those dry lips, wrapping my arms around that tall skinny body, but I couldn't thread that particular loop of film through the projector. As half-consciously I inched toward my desires for men, I clung to my official goal of stifling those desires."

Passages like this resonated because I used to imagine myself in the arms of some of my fellow male art students and struggled with wanting to stifle those longings. The narrator has been seeing the psychiatrist Dr. O'Reilly, with the consent of his parents, to rid himself of his homosexual tendencies, a battle he fights throughout most of the novel with much anguish and self-loathing. To be a homosexual was to be considered an aberration not only by society but by the medical field. The narrator wants desperately to rid himself of his sexual desires for men, trusting that seeing Dr. O'Reilly will help him, yet it becomes increasingly clear to him as he grows into adulthood that his feelings for men are more powerful than his need to be "normal."

During his last year in boarding school, the narrator meets Tex, the owner of a bookstore, and his assistant Morris, two gay men who teach him the life and language of the urban gay world. Tex is at first discreet about his homosexuality, snapping at the more flamboyant Morris for things like pulling up one trousers leg, caressing his calf and saying, in front of the narrator, "I'm feeling so gay tonight." Yet later it is Tex who opens up to him about his current lover, a straight cop he's given money to pay for his wife's abortion. "Aren't we mad," he later tells the narrator, "we gay boys, starving ourselves to sylphlike fragility, all so we can attract a straight cop with a beer belly?" The narrator goes to a gay coffee shop with Morris and some of his friends and becomes exposed to their sharp and often vicious wit, and their loud, explicit exchanges catch the attention of the heterosexuals at the next table. Noticing that they are staring back at him with disgust, the narrator declares:

> For the first time I'd crossed the line. I was no longer a visitor to the zoo, but one of the animals." He is acutely aware of the strength of his desire, even wondering if others could perceive it, if it was steaming off him like a bad smell (something I used to wonder myself). It is with mixed feelings that he approaches and finally arrives at this world he has been longing to know.
>
> Ticking steadily inside me was the thought, half-thrill half-fear, that within my grasp, or almost, lay this other world. This "gay world," you might say, with its mood swings turning slowly, then slamming you to one side like a roller coaster on a sharp turn. This world with its child-like enthusiasms and vicious attacks.

At the University of Michigan, to please his father, the narrator joins his father's fraternity, Alpha Tau. Though his father knows of his homosexuality, they never discuss it, and he later finds out from his stepmother that one summer his father put him through "a strict regime of yard work" as a way to drive the gayness out of him. But when the narrator discovers the toilets in the student union, there is no turning back.

Gay men, forbidden from being open about themselves, unable to date openly, were forced to seek love and sex in places like the labyrinth of public restrooms, parks, and bars. The narrator wanders into such a restroom and it changes his life. White vividly describes these places: the men silently lined at urinals, the clinking of belt buckles on tiled floors, the men in stalls groping each other under partitions, the smell of cigarettes and disinfectant, the sighs and exclamations of pleasure, the sound of approaching footsteps and the men scurrying to compose themselves until it's safe to resume their carnal transactions.

Obsessed, the narrator spends every free moment between classes cruising the toilets, sitting in a stall for hours "studying a book on Chinese social structure or Buddhist art, awaiting an interesting customer, like one of those gypsy fortune-tellers who prospect clients in storefronts where they also live."

When I read some of the sexual passages in *The Beautiful Room is Empty* I experienced a secret thrill that a literary novel was exploring not only what it was like to be a young man coming to grips with his sexuality but that the activities I'd previously only seen depicted in dirty stories and pornographic films were being described in language that was often poetic, haunting and spellbinding.

One of the passages that still resonates with me occurs toward the end of the book, where the narrator invites the reader to put himself in his shoes as he walks into a subway toilet and participates in an orgy. How bold of White, to have the reader imagine himself a participant in actions considered shameful and inexplicable by many, including the narrator himself, who is powerless against his need for sex with strangers, powerless against the loneliness he continues to feel despite all of the men he has been with. The reader, at least for one moment, is turned from spectator to complicit player in the erotic drama that is the narrator's life. In his description the narrator likens the blond country boy being adored to a bride, and the men worshiping him to bridal attendants. When the country boy reaches his climax it triggers the others to "shoot and shout in a chorus around him," and I could visualize the incongruous image of the farmboy swooning in a wedding dress and the men, dressed as bridesmaids, crying in ecstasy, overcome with emotion at being allowed to feast on this object of fantasy made flesh.

For me, this scene is crucial in how it mirrored my own experiences in New York City's adult theaters and booth stores. And how it captured the spiritual fervor I felt in some of my carnal encounters there. White had been in places like these before me, had felt anticipation and shame mingle with lust just as I had. Like me, he had craved and experienced the touch, the taste, of countless men, lost himself in a world of seemingly endless sexual gratification. I cannot emphasize enough how extraordinary it was for my younger self to find a work that gave me a sense of belonging, of feeling that I wasn't alone in my hunger for connections with men.

On his journey towards self-realization our narrator assumes and sheds various guises as he seeks to survive in a world where he must live a secret life: fraternity brother, Chinese scholar, writer, loading dock worker, gay bar denizen, overweight man, weight-lifter, and ultimately rioter at the Stonewall uprising. On my own journey as a young adult, I went from closeted art student to published writer in a community of queer artists. The assuming and shedding of guises has been (and continues to be, despite our medical, political, and social victories over the past several decades) an essential survival skill for many gay men. Being found out could mean being ostracized by society, family, and peers, being arrested and labeled a sexual deviant by the law. It could mean facing physical assault. It could mean death.

White creates a marvelous cast of characters who jump in and out of the narrative, some staying for the long run while others appear only briefly yet still manage to leave their mark on the narrator. Some of those who play larger roles in the narrator's life, besides the aforementioned Maria and Dr. O'Reilly, include the charismatic and manipulative law student William Everett Hunton; suicidal Annie Schroeder, a fellow patient of Dr. O'Reilly's; and Lou, an older advertising man who becomes the narrator's lover and closest male friend.

As the narrator makes his way through college, he continues cruising for sex with strangers even though he still believes that he will someday be able to stop being a homosexual. Yet he is perfectly aware that his feelings for other men are nowhere close to disappearing. Those feelings deepen as he interacts more with gay men outside of the public restrooms. He develops a close bond with Lou that goes beyond the physical. And it becomes increasingly clear to him that Dr. O'Reilly, who is supposed to help cure him of his gayness, is a drug addict whose life is coming undone. How could he have put his trust in a man whose own life is in such disarray?

White's nameless character, and how fitting, that the color white itself designates blankness, that which we can project ourselves onto, starts to date Sean. He obsesses over Sean, someone he meets outside the cruising grounds, the kind of obsession that, when reciprocated, can be considered love. They share an intimacy I craved (I was once infatuated with someone named Sean), getting to know one another's bodies, the little details that you can't discover in the piss-drenched corner of a porno theater. Sean struggles with his homosexuality and flees, which triggers a mental breakdown for White's character. As someone who experienced depression and anxiety I often feared I'd end up in a mental institution, so reading about the narrator's breakdown over lost love resonated. Our narrator rallies and leaves his college town to permanently relocate to the playground that is New York City. There, at the end of *The Beautiful Room is Empty*, he's hanging out at Stonewall when the riot starts, and the story ends with this movement from the personal to the political.

We know *The Beautiful Room is Empty* to be an autobiographical work; White is our nameless narrator and he uses the novel as a platform to meditate upon his life in a way that frees him from the formalities of a straightforward autobiography. The intimacy in the narration, the raw vulnerability expressed throughout this novel, shine a light not only on particularly gay experiences but it lets us turn our own experiences outward, and into a universal tableau.

"We looked down at ourselves in the mirror, not as one might watch pornography starring oneself but to confirm the happy fiction that we were in each other's arms."

The third book in White's trilogy, *The Farewell Symphony*, was to come nearly ten years later. Nothing in the previous two novels could possibly foreshadow what was to come, but did these preceding tribulations somehow make the unendurable endurable? We all survived to read these words, after all. As that college student, I'd impatiently skimmed *A Boy's Own Story*. I coveted my copy of *The Beautiful Room is Empty*. I wasn't white, I wasn't part of the upper middle class, but I wanted to join the same world of art our narrator craved. I now work for a museum and make art. Like the narrator I longed to be a writer; not only have I had some of my work published but I found a small community of like-minded queer writers in the process. This searching roadmap of lust showed me that I wasn't alone in my quest, and more importantly, I wasn't alone in enjoying sex but wanting love.

I'm still looking.

"Gay writers are not just reporting the past but also shaping the future, forging an identity as much as revealing it."

—from *The Faber Book of Short Gay Fiction*

THE FABER BOOK OF

GAY SHORT FICTION

LEO RACICOT

LIKE THE VERY best jewels from the family vault, Edmund White, in 1991, gathered together these 32 stories about and by gay men. Spurred on in his idea by a very enthusiastic Robert McCrum, renowned editor of the equally renowned Faber and Faber, White set about to unearth as many gay treasures as he could: those he remembered liking the first time he read them, those he had heard positive words about, along with a few outings from (at the time) new writers, lending the collection a contemporary as well as an historical feel.

The Faber Book of Gay Short Fiction is a valuable and valued anthology. More than twenty years after its publication, its stories crackle with vitality and talent. Here is a gala gathering under the roof of one book of every legend of gay culture and the gay literary world, men now gilt in myth, gay history and the magic of words. So many versatile writers cover these pages, it is difficult to know where to begin…

Henry James's "The Pupil," quite the most amusing of the lot, delights with its tale of a near-unresolvable bond between a teacher and his young student. Gore Vidal's bitter vetch piece,

"Pages from an Abandoned Journal," appears here and the old contrarian's voice rings out eager and strong. Here also to be found is the tenderness of Denton Welch's alarming encounter at a Swiss ski chalet, as well as the always salty, backwater perversities of James Purdy. Readers must rejoice in Alfred Chester for his surprising paean to toilet sex, *In Praise of Vespasian*, a piece so brave and needed, and the revered Tennessee Williams' naughty camp horror fest, "Two on a Party," and revel in the universality of Christopher Isherwood's "Mr. Lancaster," a salute to gays as a group, a global community rather than as a particular person. Here, too, for a reader's excitement are E.M. Forster, William S. Burroughs, Adam Mars-Jones and Paul Bowles, Andrew Holleran, Alan Hollinghurst, James Baldwin and Bernard Cooper. White's own "Skinned Alive" is included, hands-down the shining star in this heavenly sky of writers. The story of a middle-aged expatriate author in Paris, it climbs ivy-like upon White's precise, lyrical prose, a fine, keen-eyed meditation on the never-before-explored emotional and romantic repercussions of POZ men in the 80s.

White's radar in choosing these works was right on target. If there is a common theme, it is "Displacement." The gay man knows a permanent sense of alienation from the tribe, but also the unwillingness of parents and relatives to forgive or understand, the often unwanted company of women (viewed as intrusive or unnecessary), hearty boyhood affairs, randy, never-to-be-forgotten liaisons, courtships and lovely bodies and Style, lusts, longings and sorrows—a gay Panorama egg of a subculture's customs, costumes and secret languages, multiple forms of gay expression and male beauty. The ardor and variety of these stories is a brilliant mix, truly. Not only was the *Faber* a milestone in its time because it was unequalled in both scope and the level of talent represented but also because surprisingly very few anthologies of its caliber have been published since. It made history and it also has kept its cache, a high watershed place in gay literature that has not, I think, been toppled.

Criticisms against the book when it first appeared were mild. A Eurocentric bias permeates selections but this served to draw readers to discover (or re-discover) lesser-known and/or foreign writers. The stories, of course, also summon you to read more works by the authors and also led admirers to further explore White's work. One man in 1993 wrote, "If Edmund White selected these stories as his personal favorites, it made me want to read and know more about him."

As to the criticism that the collection omits black authors (other than the always divine James Baldwin), White said, "I read dozens of stories by dozens of black writers and I didn't find anything too suitable. And I thought it was wrong to include them just because they were black."

Robert McCrum reports, "My memory is that the book was well-received. There were some quibbles about the title—and why we had not made it *Gay and Lesbian Short Fiction*—but nothing serious. Having Ed White do it more or less guaranteed a smooth ride. No specific reviews stick in my mind but it was a success and I'm proud of it."

I want to be bold and say I believe *The Faber Book of Short Gay Fiction* initiated a queer renaissance. The collection resurrected the reputations of forgotten authors or made readers aware that certain beloved authors like E.M. Forster, James Baldwin and Langston Hughes were homosexuals. White has rescued from obscurity men like Glenway Wescott, Denton Welch and, more recently, the too-long-neglected John Horne Burns and Jean Giono. He gave the work of Adam Mars-Jones a needed, important chance to be seen. The *Faber* acquainted readers with The Violet Quill, a group of seven gay creators (White, Felice Picano, Andrew Holleran, Robert Ferro, George Whitmore, Michael Grumley, Christopher Cox) formed to read and critique one another's writing. Picano recalls the group was established because straight editors and literary agents were not being helpful with gay-themed work. As of this writing, only three members of The Violet Quill: Holleran, Picano and White remain.

The *Faber*'s wise inclusion of foreign authors generated a starburst of exploration into gay writing outside the United States. Readers discovered Machado de Assis whose anti-Realist hybrid prose lent credence to the hypothesis that he was gay. During these years, the great Cuban scribe, Reinaldo Arenas, came to prominence (in 2000 his autobiography, *Before Night Falls*, was turned into a film of the same name). The journals and diaries of Antonin Artaud were re-discovered. And certainly, Armistead Maupin's story in the *Faber* helped bring widespread success to his *Tales of the City* series.

White's elimination from the collection of one of the most celebrated gay authors of his time, Truman Capote, was due to the amazing fact that Capote never published a gay short fiction. (Interesting aside: rumor had it that a casting couch element similar to the one that existed in Hollywood for actors existed in the publishing world and that Capote's earliest gay-themed submissions were snubbed by publisher Bennett Cerf after Capote refused to give Cerf a blow job. To Cerf's request, as the rumor goes, Capote, incensed, fired back, "You can blow me!" and stormed out the door.)

Before I tell you about the first time I met up with Edmund White's work and with Ed, I think it is good to tell you about Miss Stanley, my kindergarten teacher who taught the class a little dance, nothing too elaborate, because we were kindergarteners. At the end of our baby ballet, she instructed, "The boys will bow (here, she demonstrated how to bow) and the girls will curtsy." (She showed us how to curtsy.) We did our tiny turns to the music and at the end, you can guess, of course, what sissy little me did. I *curtsied*. I was rather self-pleased until a wall of laughter and derision knocked me over like a bowling ball. If I could have crawled under the floorboards or jumped out a window, I would have.

It is small wonder I chose, then, to hide what I felt for other boys and men. It was the 1950s and 60s. There was no name for what we were other than the names we were being called by haters—Fish, Faggot, Fruit, Nancyboy, Nelly. Plus I was fat, homely and shy, and in the gay world—three strikes and you're out! I related to and with no one of my kind—I did not know my kind was out there. I wallpapered my room with magazine photos of Julie Andrews and spent long, lonely hours on my bed listening to Verdi and Puccini. I dreamed I would turn into Maria Callas.

A chance encounter (though is there really such an animal as co-incidence?) directed my eye to *Forgetting Elena*, high upon a library shelf. I was drawn to its exotic cover, to the handsomeness of the author's book jacket photo but more so, to its rich, lush, almost tropical prose. I devoured it in a day, a Holy Grail found when I wasn't looking for one. This was not a book I held in front of me but a mirror. Not a gay book, strictly speaking, *Forgetting Elena* nevertheless offered an open invitation to a gay sensibility. Ed's sentences lay across me luxuriantly, like reclining magnolia. Ed's writing is always deeply moving without being manipulative. In natural, unsentimental, unaffected ways, Ed manages to strike just the right pulse of a story. I find myself, again and again in his books, touched in unexpected ways. Less gifted scribes will utilize cornball, maudlin grooves to woo and unspool you. Not Ed; he knows that the root of nostalgia lies in words, not feelings. "If you get the word order right, feelings emerge—naturally." To write good fiction, a writer needs empathy and Ed possesses it in spades. He defies the writer's dictum to "show, not tell" and in welcome and satisfying prose he chooses to *tell*, and tell he surely does, lest a reader miss out on every scrumptious drop of exposition and wit. I make a beeline to the bookshop or library whenever a new title by Ed appears!

I was thrilled when Ed sanctioned me as his official bibliographer. Bibliography is a discipline of discovery, a detective hunt. Librarians are, by nature, archaeologists. My excavations on behalf of Ed's work have led me on many a delightful journey—to Yale's wedding cake-shaped, windowless Beinecke Library where dozens upon dozens of boxes holding his work await the Edmund White enthusiast. Also, to colleagues and friends of Ed: J.D. McClatchy and Timothy Young at Yale, Nancy Roche at Vanderbilt, Christopher Bram, Wilfrid Spiegelman, Steven Dansky, Tiziano Sossi in Italy, Ed's brilliant, devoted Michael Carroll; their help was invaluable. Google is, of course, an indispensable research tool. Yet pre-Internet materials are not always easy to find. Truth be told, one wild goose after another led to featherless dead ends, empty nests. A major assist from Patrick Merla, editor of three now-legendary gay publications: *Christopher Street, New York Native* and *James White Review,* helped me track down a fascinating packrat in Florida who'd hung on to every, single issue of Patrick Pacheco's divine milestone of 60s, 70s, 80s entertainment, *After Dark,* many of which contain Ed's early essays and interviews.

There is no exaggerating the value of Ed's own assistance; he has opened his home, his vast personal collection, his memory palace to me, a grateful visitor. Whenever I find myself neck-deep in the quicksand of what became over 3000 citations, his is the rescue rope that keeps me from sinking.

A fervor for the bibliography led directly to the idea for a needed, new biography. And my own personal and private passion for the history of the Gay Liberation Movement in North America sees me embarking on a new project: *A Pictorial and Oral History of Gay Lib.*

Diligence. Discovery. Delight. This, for me, is some of the most important work I will ever do—to catalogue a great man's work in literature, in history.

As a friend, I find Ed divine. Whether you like to walk or not (and I do), Ed will pedestrianize you—Ed loves to walk and look and talk and to have you "see." Not even four consecutive strokes and heart bypass surgery can stop this locomotive of a man. And what a delight it is walking the wide and winding avenues of his marvelous mind. He is, quite simply, brilliant. I admire Ed profoundly, the man and the myth, the wordsmith and the punster, the raconteur and the fashionista, his endless generosity of spirit...

His work stands the test of time and will last and have permanent value. Ed wrote not to have the world's prejudices against homosexuals eradicated, rather, to show others what it is like to walk in our shoes. He never peddles a false creed. He says: This is us. Take us or leave us but if you don't like us, let us live our lives as we choose. He does not and will not accommodate convention. His honesty washes over the reader like refreshing fountain water. This truth-telling energy and output landed him in the catbird seat, paralyzed his contemporaries and gave a voice to generations of gay men. With clarity and vision of purpose, he gathered us safely under the umbrella of his bravery, revealed to us an auspicious sexual and cultural Eden that knows no bounds.

Edmund White—a true social, sexual and cultural pioneer—led us out of the dark when The Closet was very dark indeed. He marched us out into the light of Liberation to a place of not only self-acceptance but of real and a lasting pride in who and what we are.

"Genet was a deeply contradictory man who resolved in his work the warring elements that tore his life apart. He was a loyal friend who believed in treachery. He was possessed of a courtly sweetness that often gave way to fits of rage and pettiness. He alternated between staying in palaces or hovels and consorting with thieves or princes. Several of his writings express a direct political concern, but even these works are far from 'committed.' Beauty—as judged by the dandified author, the arbiter elegantiae—remains Genet's ultimate measuring rod."

—from *Genet: A Biography*

GENET: A BIOGRAPHY

ANGELO NIKOLOPOULOS

2018: IT'S SUMMER in New York, and I am packing for Greece.
I've just accepted an invitation to write a short essay on Edmund
White's *Genet: A Biography*. As a procrastinating, confessional
poet, I can't think of anything less pleasurable than writing about
someone else's life. Buoyed by the thought of a Mediterranean
vista (Aperol spritzes by the sea, etc.), I put the assignment out of
my mind.

*

Which is to say, I prefer to think about pleasure instead.
There's the pleasure of experience, of course, but what about the
pleasure of description? Is this the nature of biography, the joy of
sifting through the debris of one's life to create order? It is, in the
end, a kind of tidying up. But where does one begin?

*

White's biography begins, more or less, with place and physicality:

> At 14, two weeks after his arrival at an educational centre run by Public Welfare […], Genet ran away. An official report was immediately filed, his body subjected to a 'scientific' description:
>
> > Height: 5 foot 1 inch
> > Nose: Average
> > Mouth: Average
> > Chin: Long and round
> > Eyes: Black
> > Pale complexion
> > Effeminate look
>
> The document was dated 3 November 1924.

*

"Genet always ended his letters with a witty remark," White mentions. "He was never cruel but he liked to tease." I am not certain of my cruelty, but I will begin by teasing: J. and Ed, I'll call them. And why not? Who's to say we're not intimate strangers?

*

Athens, Greece: I have made a leap in time, seven hours to be precise. At sunrise, my jetlag has me on the balcony overlooking the ancient Agora, north of the Acropolis. I am smoking a cigarette; I am reading. "The art of biography," Ed writes in his introduction, "is often supposed to trace the small steps an individual takes in a clear direction, but no one could logically account for the extraordinary leaps Genet made from the beginning to the end of his life." I think I am conflating the term leap, but all the same, here we are on the balcony at twilight: three gay men regarding the ruins.

*

1998, Charter Oak High School: in the north, the San Gabriel Mountains poke through the smog like an earnest monument, but in the flatlands there is Carl's Jr and Vons. There is, at the intersection of Glendora and Grand Avenue, a Younger Self who has ditched fourth period—played hooky, is truant—for no other reason than because he is in love:

Height: 5 foot 7 inch
Nose: Grecian
Mouth: Average/petite
Chin: Short and round
Eyes: Brown
Pale complexion

*

Do books find you when you need them the most? I am not sure of this, though poets often surrender to mystical thinking. I've faith, instead, in chronology: at 16 I met a boy I loved. G. was not particularly bright. He was blond and boyish, which mattered to me. In gym glass, I'd focus my entire being on the thin crest of skin, between his underwear band and shirt, as he lifted weights. In a biography, one might describe this as a shift in the trajectory of my young life.

*

1998: With me is Ed's tome *Genet: A Biography*. Its hardbound 728 pages weigh heavily in my vinyl silver backpack. In the park, I sit with my back pressed against a large walnut tree. The empty green field before is cinematic. Armed with black velvet, and my teenage misanthropy, I rest J.'s fractured portrait on my crossed legs like an icon. I am, as mother says, a sensitive deliberate child. In truth, the compendium of historical data in Ed's text bored me. Mother had driven me to a library a town over for research. The assignment was to present a book I'd read independently that summer. Mine, *Our Lady of the Flowers*. I planned to intersperse passages of J.'s *Divine* with images of Divine, the drag queen made infamous by John Waters' cult films. Ed's text, I came to learn, was what we call a secondary source.

*

In 1998, Bill Clinton is president, and there's conflict in Kosovo. Don't Ask, Don't Tell carries over, for many, into the life of a suburban high school, where I do not have the luxury of passing. Later, in college, a roommate names it: *effeminate look.*

*

1972, Pink Flamingos: Divine, as notorious criminal Babs Johnson, delivers her manifesto:

> Kill everyone now! Condone first-degree murder!
> Advocate cannibalism! Eat shit!
> Filth is my politics! Filth is my life!

*

"Genet's work pushed far beyond the tenents of dandyism," Ed says, "but it was his starting point. The dandy topples traditional hierarchies of value and order and replaces morality with an aesthetic rule of his own devising. The Beautiful replaces the Good." This is what we call transvaluation. This was also, for me, the appeal of the flamboyant, triumphant fag.

*

In 1949, J. says: "As for me, I've chosen; I will be on the side of crime. And I'll help children not to gain entrance into your houses, your factories, your schools, your laws and holy sacraments, but to violate them."

*

In the end, my presentation earned me a two-day suspension, for profanity and insubordination. At home, unmonitored: I jerked off endlessly to Bobby G. videos of seduced straight marines. I read Ed's *A Boy's Own Story.* I was, more or less, happy. *Advocate cannibalism! Eat shit!* My body sang: *Filth is my politics! Filth is my life!*

*

While I admired Ed's attention to detail, I cared less for the inventory of J.'s life—the minutiae of soldier life or touring Spain. Instead, I scoured the text for homosexual coordinates—a kind of intergenerational triangulation of lust. And I found, as if presented by Ed on a predella of joy, the young Villeroy at Mettray Colony, and the silver medallion of the Sacred Heart around his neck:

> After I'd swallowed his sperm and kissed the tangled hairs of his body, my mouth would rise back up to his. When I moved past his throat he dropped the silver medal back into my mouth.

I felt deep admiration for a stranger who presented these images to me, folded as they were within the authoritative voice of scholarly work. It was like the sudden pang of delight I experienced when G. parted the branches behind his parents' house for me to pass through in the night. It was the pleasure of being shown the way.

*

J. was, undeniably, a sissy. And if "he grew up as a darling in a world of women," Ed spoke the language of this world, thereby introducing my Younger Self to an unfamiliar lexicon of gayness. Before I had any terms for it, Ed articulated a butch/femme sensibility I'd previously only attempted through clothing (see black velvet, silver backpack):

Genet's lovers had been older and tougher; now he was drawn to smaller, younger men with pretty-boy faces and tough-guy ways, boys who had served time for petty crimes, boys with milky skin, slicked-back hair, fine features, tattoos, bad grammar and teeth and moods that alternated between snarling and pouting. (See ROUGH TRADE.)

Genet had been the 'femme' in butch-femme gay relationships, a role that at his age (he was thirty-four) and his incipient baldness no longer made flattering. (See READING.)

Genet's new ambition to be the 'butch,' the tough guy, the 'man,' [...] would be more imaginary than real, as Genet's failure in real life to make the transition would make him bitter about homosexuality. (See SHADE.)

*

ROUGH TRADE (cont.): At the boy's colony, "after his first lover, Villeroy, joined the navy, Genet was married to another tough guy [...]. Genet, as the bride, is married to Divers at midnight in the chapel while twelve other couples of Family B look on (*the most beautiful day of my life was this night*)."

*

I am writing this on a ferry from Athens to Mykonos, and I am struggling to imagine the church of Panagia Paraportiani as I'd left it the summer I was 16, where I was fucked for the first time against the white wall. Or, as J. would put it, where I was made into "a high born lady."

*

"If you walk beyond Babylon you'll find the church of Paraportiani, literally *Our Lady of the Side Gate*," a Gay Travel Europe site reads, "as its entrance is a side gate from the Kastro area." Later that day, beyond the side gate, I let another man enter me, bent over at sunset. "It is an important religious monument in Greece, dating from the 1400s but now the old doorway that used to house monks is a gay cruising site. The narrow rocky beach behind Paraportiani is also full with guys looking for a partner for the night."

*

If reading J. compelled me to be a poet, Ed's work inspired me to get laid. And both equally galvanized my desire to be in love. If there is a subtext in *Genet: A Biography*, it is the subtle portraiture of a man chronically cruising for love. Peppered throughout the text, a litany of first encounters:

1940: Genet met Jean Decarnin that August. Decarnin was a teenage Trotskyite. He was handsome and heterosexual; but he was willing to have some sort of affectional and even sexual contact with Genet.

1943: In prison he met a young man, Lucien-Guy Noppé (known as 'Guy'), who occupied the cell next to his.

1944: Genet met Nico Papatakis [...], a handsome man with dark skin and blue eyes.

1945: Genet met the eighteen-year-old Lucien Sénémaud.

*

What is biography, then, but an inventory of flirtation?

*

FLIRTATION INVENTORY (cont.):

1947: During a visit to Cannes, Genet met a twenty-two-year-old half-French, half-Russian man named Java.

1952: Genet writes: "In April, at X..., I met a twenty-two-year-old hoodlum." Apparently he was a handsome Roman prostitute (some people said effeminate).

1974: Genet met the last important companion of his life, Mohammed El Katrani. Genet was in Tangier and saw a young man sleeping on the pavement...

*

2011: Freshly equipped with an MFA in Poetry from NYU, I am hired to be an administrative assistant at Princeton University's Creative Writing Program, where Ed is teaching. My responsibilities include managing the reading series, handling student issues, and making coffee. It appears I am also here to help restore Ed's forgotten email password, as he's invited me into his office on the heels of a tedious faculty meeting, at which we've met for the first time. Once inside Hotmail, Ed's face turns to me brightly, as if presenting a reward: *And now don't you want to see my Italian boyfriend's dick?*

*

The problem with biography, if there is one, is that the subject subordinates the author's personality. In telling another's story, you take a backseat. You have to pipe down. Those who know Ed know him to be a conversationalist. His impulse is to entertain, to gossip and exchange indiscretions. It's no surprise then that throughout the heavy text of the biography there are moments of Ed's effervescence and camp, slyly inserted. Even in writing this passage, I can't help but insert myself: the last I heard of G., my high school boyfriend, was in 2006. He was doing porn and living with a director in West Hollywood, strung out on meth (a bad cliché). I can't say with any certainty if he's alive today. In his film *California Gold 1*, which I sometimes watch, he's alive and well, riding his motorcycle through the Hollywood canyons. During the opening credits, he pulls to the side of the road and pisses along the thistle. He emits a grunt of pleasure and straddles the bike; the narrative begins.

*

J. died alone in a one-star hotel in Paris. It was 1986, five years after my birth, and four years after the publication of Ed's seminal novel *A Boy's Own Story*. That year in the US, 24,599 AIDS-related deaths were reported. I do not mean to suggest that these observations point to a grand, cosmic plan. But I do have an untested faith in the value of collage and assemblage—that the scant, arbitrary details of a life can, in the end, produce a meaningful tapestry, when viewed in hindsight with lucidity and grace. I believe the relics we collect along the way can, in some small way, ignite a spark in the abyss.

*

1952, J. in a letter to Sartre:

Instinct turns me to my own sex. My pleasure will be endless. I will not embody the principle of continuity. It is a silky attitude.

Marginalia, circa 1998—beneath the above passage, in a dazzling display of youthful arrogance, in my own handwriting:

I think Genet would have liked me.

*

2013, Princeton: In the evenings, after everyone's left, I'd often sneak P., a graduate student, into Ed's office for quick, unvarnished sex. *I need to unload,* he'd message. Tonight, after he's bent me over Ed's desk, he pins my face flat against the cold surface, his forearm firmly against my neck. *This is what you want,* he asks, again and again. *Is this what you want? Is this what you wanted?* When he's done, I think to myself I will never see him again. This is, in my mind, a romantic gesture. On the tabletop, as if festooned, I see a garland of his ropy cum. I think for a moment to clean it up, and then I do not.

"Whereas most writers who emerge from obscure origins are quick to disown them, Genet became the apostle of the wretched of the earth."

—from *Genet: A Biography*

GENET: A BIOGRAPHY

SARAH SCHULMAN

IF WRITING IS a committed utopian action, then the Jean Genet of Edmund White's engaging, impressive, transformative biography (Knopf, 1993) was the epitome of manic depression. Genet wrote his five novels in five years, from 1942-47. After seven years of sadness and silence, he wrote his three best known plays in two years. The subsequent 1960's were filled with death as his lover, Abdallah (a high wire performer) committed suicide, his agent and English translator Bernard Fruchtman committed suicide, and Genet himself tried to commit suicide. Then he entered into the other utopian endeavor: activism. From 1970 until his death in 1986, Genet was aligned with oppressed people and supported them in energetic ways, on their terms and on his own terms. Ed calls him "an apostle of the wretched of the earth."

Ed's use of the word "Apostle" is, of course, an open invitation to question. Apostles believe that the mortals they adore are not mortal. And in that way they err. Sartre, who White points out was an atheist, called his homage "Saint Genet," so there was an ironic anti-religiosity. But Genet was a man for whom adoration was deification and he literally described lovers as Gods. Genet's love was possible, encompassing, invigorating and annihilating. And since many people can only love in one way, one could assume that he might emotionally connect with oppressed people in the same manner that he loved his Nazi soldier lover/apparition turned underdog when left behind in liberated Paris in the novel *Pompes Funebres*.

Edmund White has loved far more rationally than Genet if his life's works are an indication. He has been torn open, sure, and impulsive and destructive, i.e. human, but he has also been sensible, reasonable and accepting. His books are often a process of coming to terms. I would not use the world "Apostle" to describe Edmund White as a lover, but the concept of "wretched of the earth" more readily unites the two. When Ed co-founded Gay Men's Health Crisis, in 1982, he got up from the typewriter on behalf of a despised group of people, with no rights, abandoned by their families and societies, living in illegality and facing a terminal disease for which there was no epidemiological information, no treatment and no cure. However, Ed—openly HIV positive for decades—was exactly one of them. Genet, on the other hand, died at the beginning of the epicenter of the AIDS crisis. And, although he had been poor, outcast and incarcerated, was never, for example, Palestinian. There are universes of difference between the conditions of people with AIDS and Palestinians, though when I began to become a conscious active worker for Palestine, I did notice some resonances. In both cases these were categories of people who were profoundly oppressed, who were treated with brutal abandonment and indifference, who were falsely cast as dangerous when they were in fact endangered, and who were treated like predators when they were the ones being attacked. So both people with AIDS and Palestinians have been lied about, pathologized and literally inhumanely discarded. If a despised gay man who had spent his life unjustly blamed when he hadn't done anything wrong, truly understood his own condition, he could—perhaps *should*—relate to Palestinians. That would be a rational response to oppression. Unfortunately history shows that oppressed people often identity more strongly with the element of their demographic that still connects to domination. Many white gay people aspire to the unjustified powers of whiteness. Many male homosexuals rue any obstacle to male supremacy. When we are debased by ruthless ambition, we look up longingly towards the corruption of domination as we wish better for ourselves.

Born in 1910, Genet had already been arrested eight times by the age of 17 for running away, taking trains for free, embezzling money to go to a carnival and for stealing pens and notebooks. He was sentenced to two years at an agricultural prison for juveniles. White tells us that in order to get out of Mettray (a place that looms large in his work) Genet joined the army, was promoted to corporal and "volunteers" specifically for duty in the Levant. In other words, at age 19 he chose to be in an Arab place, in this case Syria. So the Arab world offered escape from the pain of France that never let him run away, ride trains or watch freaks unpunished. The Arab world is to French Genet what France becomes to that little Ed from Ohio, a place of permission. And permission is a kind of romance. It's a rhapsody of relief, indulgence, light-headed elevation. Of course arriving as a French soldier gave Genet a different source to his permission than Edmund White, who not only loves men but also graceful stylish beautiful things, sophisticated ways, and elevated traditions. Genet also found male beauty, ancient cultures and intoxicating aesthetics, but his permission came with the power of the French state. He had a uniform, a gun, a rank, an historically imposed social role. The marginalized, despised, punished and alienated Genet came to his place of peace as a colonial. White had only the willingness to be reconstructed as a Francophile, and of course the U.S. dollar.

Ed describes Genet's commitments to Palestine and to the Black Panthers as support for the "homeless," and of course both American blacks and Palestinians are living in exile, diasporic displacement and elaborate fantasies of resolution and repair. Even Edward Said understood Genet's pro-Palestinian position as the identification of one oppressed person with another. "Genet made the step, crossed the legal borders, that very few white men or women even attempted. He traversed the space from the metropolitan center to the colony; his unquestioned solidarity was with the very same oppressed identified and so passionately analyzed by Frantz Fanon." And while it is easy and truthful to say that Genet also was homeless, in the most intimate sense of the word, unlike Palestinians he did have a nation state, a passport and *la langue natale* which allowed him to be a writer with readers who also have passports, nation states and their own indigenous language. White reports Genet's perspective of himself as an exception in the eyes of the various Arab communities he was sent to occupy. Of course, we don't know what the Syrians actually thought of him, but we do learn that he felt they saw his difference in a positive light. Like Genet, I also see myself as a "friend of Palestine" and yet I do understand that that has nothing to do with whether or not individual Palestinians like me. Political relationships of solidarity are rife with the problem of supremacy, no matter how alienated or excluded the dominant party feels from their own society. And it is easy to project one's own enthusiasm of connection onto the less powerful partner. And White wisely acknowledges this by pointing out that one of Genet's favorite fantasy tropes is that of the benevolent/enamored cop, or complicit soldier, transgressing the rules of punishment because he is so moved by a vulnerable fictionalized Genet.

At 21 Genet re-enlisted, this time volunteering to go to Morocco. In 1934, at 23 and out of the army for only six months, he signed up for a third round, this time volunteering for Algeria. In 1936 he did not show up for roll call and deserted. He falsified his passport with the name Gejietti, was arrested in Albania, then arrested in Yugoslavia, then arrested in Vienna, then arrested in Czechoslovakia where he asked for political asylum. Despite some kind of shelter, he left, was arrested in Poland, crossed Nazi Germany, (Nazis were never a problem for Genet) got to Paris and was arrested in a department store for stealing 12 handkerchiefs. Over the next two years he was arrested and incarcerated for desertion, expelled from the army, arrested for more free train riding, for stealing bottles of aperitifs, carrying a gun, stealing a shirt, vagrancy, stealing a piece of silk. At age 30 he spent ten months in prison for stealing a suitcase and wallet, then four months for stealing history and philosophy books. He worked as a bookseller on the Seine, where he met readers, writers and intellectuals. Then he was arrested in front of Notre Dame and sentenced to three months for stealing a volume of Proust. In prison, at age 31, he started writing his first novel, *Notre Dames des Fleurs*. Two former customers, one of whom was a right-wing editor, introduced him to Jean Cocteau, who helped him immeasurably. Arrested again for stealing a rare edition of Verlaine, he was then eligible for life imprisonment, but Cocteau argued in court that Genet was "the greatest writer of the modern era" and he was instead sentenced to three months, during which he wrote *Miracle de la Rose*. Three weeks after being freed he stole more books and was jailed for four more months.

It's a manic cycle, and most obviously filled with repetition and pervasive disregard for the obvious consequences of actions that might have alternatives. In this place and this time, Genet was a man who could not solve problems, unless his goal was to remain in prison. Certainly the meeting with Cocteau was lucky, but even luckier was the fact that Cocteau helped him at all, and to that extent. I have to disclaim here that Edmund White, himself, helped me by reviewing my lesbian erotic, formally complex, AIDS revolutionary 1994 novel, *Rat Bohemia*, in the *New York Times* and thereby elevating me with his accomplishments in the tradition of Cocteau. But I assure readers that most people with real power in literature do not help people who cannot help them back. That Cocteau, himself the homosexual author of *Les Enfants Terribles* (about a love affair between a brother and sister), "got it" and bothered to make the effort is just a fluke of history. Lucky, lucky Saint Genet.

It was now 1943, in the midst of the Nazi occupation of France. French people, Jews among them, are being deported to concentration camps in Poland and exterminated. And Genet found himself dangerously held in Camp des Tourelles, a deportation site. He was visited by Marc Barbezat, the powerful publisher of the magazine *L'Arbalete* who, with other powerful people, got Genet released. I have no idea what role this publisher or Cocteau or any of Genet's other powerful supporters played in interfering with the deportation of Jews. Cocteau did flirt with the German power elite, and other artists like Max Jacob and Robert Desnos were deported and exterminated for being anti-Nazi or Jewish. Genet's friends were not deported, and continued to publish. So, despite his homosexuality, his desertion, his endless incarcerations for crimes petty and pathetic, this homeless man's life was saved in a period in which thousands of citizens of far greater social standing were sent off to be murdered because they were Jews, Communists and Resistants. I would like to know more about this and to understand more about Genet's feelings about Jews, French anti-semitism and the European holocaust. Sartre claimed Genet as an anti-semite, but understood it as a revulsion of other oppressed people. White quotes Sartre: "Since Genet wants his lovers to be executioners he should never be sodomized by a victim. What repels Genet about Israelites is that he finds himself in their situations." But actually, no, he was excused from their situation. So, given that he had more power than Jews, just as he had more power than Arabs, there is a contradiction in the theory of Genet as pro-Palestinian *because* he identified with the oppressed.

In 1944, still under Nazi occupation, Genet's first novel, *Notre Dame des Fleurs* appeared in excerpt in *L'Arbalete*. He met Sartre, also still in France, at Café Flore, which was still open despite the Nazi seizure of resources and severe rationing. And Genet's lover, Jean Decarnin, died on the Communist barricades fighting to liberate Paris. Strange juxtaposition of events, I would say. One dies, the other drinks coffee. From then on most of Genet's important love relationships were to be with Arab men. The Nazis were defeated in 1945, three years later Sartre and Cocteau petition for amnesty for Genet. In 1951 Gallimard published the complete Genet while all his books were banned in America until Grove Press broke the ban in 1963. This was another good reason for Edmund White, future author of explicitly gay literature, to be enamored with France. It offers him a legacy of freedom. There is such a strange imbalance of values in all of this. A France brutally colonizing the Arab and African world, and deeply complicit with the deportation of Jews, listens to its own intellectuals and frees, publishes and awards its own homosexual experimental writer ex-convict. Then again, perhaps the things that made white homosexual men intolerable to American culture: principally the refusal to build families and reproduce, didn't really matter that much to the French. Overt empires reproduce in their own brutal ways, and histories like Adam Hochschild's *King Leopold's Ghost* about the colonization of the Congo by Belgium, depict colonial culture as a homoerotic, homosocial and in many cases homosexual refuge. Similar perhaps to our own genocidal westward expansion and cowboy culture.

In 1970, Genet was arrested with Marguerite Duras at a demonstration protesting the death of four African immigrant workers. As a Frenchman, he had often traveled in Africa, especially in French colonized countries. Yet he had little contact with African Americans outside of those individuals like James Baldwin, in sexual and racial exile in France. But once he surfaced as an activist, Genet was contacted by Black Panthers Connie

Mathews and Michael Persitz to speak out on the jailing and government murders of much of their leadership. How the Panthers
made the decision to ask him for help is unclear to me. A lot has
been written about the macho nature of the Panther party, and
much of that has also been softened retrospectively. Huey P.
Newton, party chairman, famously said "The homosexual may be
the most revolutionary" which is certainly very far from the white
left, busy yelling "Pull her off the stage and fuck her" when Marilyn Webb of Women's Liberation tried to talk feminism at an
anti-war rally that same year. Certainly the handsome Panther
Chairman Huey P. Newton and stylish rank and file were a lot
sexier than white Leftists whose torn, baggy jeans and flannel
shirts de-sexualized working class clothing, which would soon be
tightened and re-masculinized by gay clone culture.

Wanting to help the Panthers, Genet was denied a visa by the
U.S. because of his homosexuality, and so crossed the border il-
legally from Canada. For two months he traveled the country.
Genet gave many public talks at universities and to the press on
behalf of the Panthers. His many American adventures include a
cocktail party at Stanford's French department where he compared the Panthers to the Marquis de Sade due to their shared
authenticity. He had a crush on Panther leader David Hilliard,
Jane Fonda proposed doing a film with Genet, and one night he
danced for some Panthers in a pink negligee. He may have been
a Marxist, but he was still camp. The Panthers gave him a black
leather jacket. He met 26-year-old UCLA Philosophy professor
Angela Davis who was a fluent French speaker from a family of
learned French speakers. On May 1, he spoke to 25,000 people in
New Haven; his speech was published by the Black Panther Party.
He then hastily departed America when contacted by the office
of Immigration. Back in Europe he published a defense of Angela
Davis, who was now on wanted posters named "Public Enemy
Number One." When she was arrested, he agreed for the first
time to go on television where he delivered a talk, "Angela Davis
is at Your Mercy." In *Prisoner of Love* Genet reflected that "The
Panthers symbolism was too easily deciphered to last. It was accepted quickly, but rejected because it was too easily understood."

As the Panthers fractured, back in France Genet became
friends with Mahmoud El Hamchari, the Paris representative of
the Palestine Liberation Organization. His wife told White that

Genet would come to the house unannounced and have long talks with El Hamchari about the divisions and corruption within the Panthers. So, as one political partner crumbled, another was born. White writes, "After following events in Jordan that proved disastrous for Palestinians, known as 'Black September,'" Genet "accepted an invitation" to visit Palestinian refugee camps for one week. He stayed for six months and returned four times over the next two years. In November 1970 he met Arafat for less than 30 minutes. He gave Genet a pass permitting free travel in any PLA territory and asked him to write a book about Palestinians, which he completed 15 years later. White writes that Genet:

> preferred to think that the Arab world should be Palestinized rather than the Palestinian revolution should be Arabized. To Genet the only positive vision of the future should be socialist, not theological: his analysis of the failure of Zionism was that it had begun as a socialist experiment but had degenerated quickly into a theological state.

Just as in Syria, we don't have much information about how the Palestinians experienced Genet; most of the information comes from his version of the relationship. As in Syria, he described himself as well liked. Genet says that he shocked Palestinians by telling them he was homosexual and an atheist, "an avowal that made them burst out laughing." But, who knows what really happened? I am fascinated by Genet's "invitations." As an openly lesbian woman who is a "friend of Palestine" I wonder if Genet is the first out queer in political solidarity, as opposed to colonials whose only investments were a sexual interest in Arab men.

This visit took place after the 1967 war, and much of the world was troubled by the Israeli occupation of more territory, the creation of yet more refugees on top of the people still in exile from their expulsion by the founding of the Israeli state in 1948. Although Palestine is and was a "place," the specific geographical boundaries of this "home" were different in people's minds than in legal realities. In fact "Palestine" was now The West Bank, Gaza, The Golan Heights, Refugee camps in Jordan, Lebanon and Syria, and a global diaspora of refugees from Kuwait to London to Detroit. "Palestine" was also the memories, the still-standing houses now lived in by Israelis, and the land, sea and hills that many Palestinians would never see again. His visits stimulated a series of articles and photo captions, petitions and participations with Foucault on anti-prison work and with Deleuze in support of Arab workers in France as well as the rights of North African immigrants. At 64 he met his last lover, Mohammed El Katrani in Tangiers. They lived together in a small apartment in the Saint Denis suburb of Paris. At age 72, with throat cancer, Genet moved to Morocco. From this base he traveled to Lebanon with Leila Shahid, a young Palestinian activist. In September 1982, Genet was in Beirut when Israelis invaded. This assault enabled Christian Militias to massacre Palestinians in The Sabra and Shatila refugee camps where Palestinians are still living to this day. Jim Hubbard and I visited Sabra with Lebanese queer activist Lynne Darwich in 2013. Genet was one of the first outsiders to enter Shatila on September 19 and found the place strewn with corpses. He wrote "Four Hours at Shatila" which was published in *The Journal of Palestinian Studies*. I don't know if he chose this venue to support the journal, or if the piece was rejected by more widely read and mainstream publications. Returning to Morocco, he started to write *Prisoner of Love*, based on fifteen years of notes about the Black Panther and Palestinian experiences. On April 15, 1986 he died of cancer at age 76 and was buried in Larache, Morocco. *Prisoner of Love* was published one month later.

If Genet ever had a "home," it was in the Arab world, a world he first entered as a colonial soldier. It was as a colonial soldier that Genet had his first experience of authority, group belonging, sway. It was in the Arab world that he found lovers, often younger, poorer, with less social currency. It was Palestine that "invited" him, while America refused his request for a visa. American homosexuals now have, what Rutgers Professor Jasbir Puar has named, "Homonationalism." That is to say that those of us who are white and male, who marry and reproduce, who are documented, who are not incarcerated, who have homes and who support the military and U.S. imperial wars, we are now invited to identify with the American, Canadian, British, German, French, Dutch, and Israeli state apparatus of punishment and enforcement. Despite being a homosexual convict, Genet experienced this elevation by being a French soldier. But the status of Palestinians has not changed since Genet walked into Shatila and witnessed murdered civilians lying on its grounds in 1982.

Palestinians are still mass murdered, denied a "home." It's a difficult question and one that is implicating for all of us who, like Genet, work in solidarity. The question for us to grapple with is to understand to what extent Genet's support for Palestine—which was unusual, energetic, sincere, effortful and significant—was rooted in the identification of one homeless person with another, one marginalized unjustly punished person with another. Or, was it simultaneously a relationship of a French person, whose only place of supremacy in his own cultural framework was in relationship to Arabs, Arabs who he could love, who he could afford, to whom he could make a difference, Palestinians and Black Panthers who needed Jean Genet.

While Sartre's *Saint Genet, comédien et martyr* established this unique, tragic, sexually and politically alienated writer in the public imagination, in 1952, it was more of a personal philosophical musing than historical document. Today, the work is almost forgotten for English speakers. Clearly, for the American reader, Edmund White's *Genet: A Biography*, a rigorous historical telling of the facts of one singular man's eclectic life, is the go-to reference work for thinking about the context of his novels, plays, speeches, loves, transgressions and dreams. It is this rare and generous homage that remains one of Edmund White's many gifts to the world, one that stands triumphantly beside his own heart, his own novels, his own life.

"The famous mordant gay humor, which always attempts to cancel the sting of any jibe by making it funny, has sought, I think unsuccessfully, to camp on the 'sickness' metaphor; you can often overhear one queen telling another, rather affectionately, 'You're sick, honey,' or 'My dear, I love you, you're a madwoman.' But this approach, no matter how charming, brings little relief."

—from *The Burning Library: Writings on Art, Politics and Sexuality: 1969-1993*

THE BURNING LIBRARY:

WRITINGS ON ART, POLITICS

AND SEXUALITY: 1969-1993

CHARLIE VÁZQUEZ

I WANDERED THE aisles of Powell's City of Books in 1995, on an afternoon of seeking titles I'd memorized in a running list while allowing random treasures to tempt me. Powell's boasted an extensive "Gay and Lesbian" section even back then, those frightening and ecstatic times of personal and artistic exploration. Gay literature and culture were still new to me as a young musician who had only been out since 1992—a fresh universe to navigate.

So different from my roots, the Bronx, New York City's black sheep county that spit me out; where residents fled burning buildings imploding in the night in the 70s and 80s. I chilled with dread each time a neighbor, another African American, male IV drug user, shrank toward death during the first wave of AIDS. The crack crisis followed and tore families apart, finishing what heroin started, which my father succumbed to. A high school friend murdered point blank mere weeks after I left for a life out West: those were tough times indeed.

And I had it good for the hood… I went to live with my mother's family in über Anglo Oregon in 1988, a much-needed break from the urban decay and drama that shaped me—what I knew best in the world. Time away from the noise and aggravation that drove me to pack my book-bag and lose myself in the world of the New York Public Library on 42nd Street and Fifth Avenue, where I studied for Regents exams in the 1980s. The tragedies and inhumanities that forced me to sneak into the New York Botanical Garden to climb trees and meditate on existence—I left all of it behind.

My dreamier aspects emerged while in Portland, where forests swept into neighborhoods minutes from the city center; a town with just enough cultural attractions to keep my New York City-refined curiosity entertained. Powell's City of Books became my sanctuary for learning and reflection. The thrill of pulling books at random felt the same as it did when I was a boy at my local library. That same curiosity urged me to investigate a certain book spine one cloudy afternoon—*The Burning Library: Essays* by Edmund White. The title brought the Roman sacking of Alexandria's Great Library to mind, an account that perplexed me as a young reader.

The cover featured a black-and-white photograph (a Mapplethorpe I would learn); a handsome face with wise and penetrating eyes that beckoned further scrutiny. I traced my finger down the table of contents to find familiar names such as Burroughs, Williams and Capote, as well as others I'd yet to hear of such as Pasolini, Schuyler and Barthes. I sat on the floor and read the first essay, "The Gay Philosopher," mesmerized by the authority and urgency of White's voice, his surgical examination of art and society. I bought the book and finished it three days later.

Something I sought in those fatherless years was a mentor, my own gay philosopher. My ex-band mate's dad Michael Cervenak would fill that role in my early 20s. The wisdom he shared as the only survivor among his peer group, all taken by AIDS, would serve as an amulet for my deeper exploration of the complex, and often hostile, gay underground. This would transform into queer life once I moved beyond gay male circles to forge friendships and alliances with lesbians, bisexuals and trans-identified folks.

My father could've never provided me with the guidance required to embark on the journey of becoming a queer writer.

The Burning Library showed me that William S. Burroughs, whose novels I learned of through junkies I knew in Portland, was as crazy as his stories were. Burroughs gave me the confidence to write graphically about sex. So it wasn't a coincidence that my first published stories appeared in erotica anthologies. The piece on Truman Capote touched me most at the time, an awkward encounter with Robert Mapplethorpe in tow. White presents the reader with a semi-coherent interviewee who fans himself obsessively during a New York heat wave, closing with his ominous warning about the torments of the writing life.

The essay on Nabokov prioritized my reading of *Lolita* in the weeks that followed. I also bought a used copy of Yukio Mishima's *Confessions of a Mask* after reading "Movies and Poems: Pier Paolo Pasolini," eager to understand the foreign points of view. White people accounted for over 90% of Portland's population at the time. *The Burning Library* launched me back into a universe whose subjects originated from all corners of the world, however; a cast of artists and thinkers of international renown. It also showed me a side of New York City I never could've known about as someone from a different generation and socioeconomic class.

I returned to the Bronx in 2006, in search of a community where being queer and Puerto Rican made sense. The need to network arose after a reading organized by Emanuel Xavier for an anthology he edited (which I was included in): *Best Gay Erotica 2008* (Cleis, 2007). The collection also included stories by wonderful writers and peers such as Lee Houck, Sam J. Miller and the dearly-departed Taylor Siluwé. The reading at the now-defunct Rapture Bookstore in the East Village attracted an amazing crowd. I didn't want the fun to end and launched the PANIC! (and then HISPANIC PANIC!) queer reading series soon after, hosting dozens of writers over a three-year run at Nowhere bar on East 14th Street.

*

The Bronx Council on the Arts hired me to direct the Bronx Writers Center in 2014. I ditched the downtown bar scene, which I came to resent as the city hyper-gentrified and the underground was dissolved; a bittersweet return to the neighborhood I fled in the 1980s. What I didn't know at the time was that my work for the Bronx Writers Center would double as one of the most transformative periods of artistic growth for me. The opportunity to serve some of the nation's most underserved and emerging writers put me in the role of mentor at times, something I hadn't anticipated—the gift of sharing everything I learned on my own writing journey.

The revisiting of *The Burning Library* over twenty years later brought surprises as might be expected. "The Gay Philosopher" and "Writer on a Hot Tin Roof: Tennessee Williams" endured as timeless cultural examinations that withstood the storms and upheavals of difficult decades for our community. Others essays and articles resonated with the vibe of the times they were written in and didn't have the same punch they had in the 90s. The entries on Foucault and Isherwood will retain currency for a long time as definitive markers of 20th century gay culture.

"Genet's Prisoner of Love" made much more sense after reading most of his work since. Genet, like Burroughs, inspired countless writers to publish transgressive work. So much so that I tracked down almost all of his books and plays upon finishing *Our Lady of the Flowers* in the late 90s. White's reporting of Genet's radical alliances, his solidarity with those in revolt against colonialism worldwide, appealed to me as someone who survived the ravages of misogynistic Caribbean machismo, its mandates on suffocating gender roles and homophobia.

Other Edmund White books wound up in my hands over the years. I enjoyed *A Boy's Own Story* and *Nocturnes for the King of Naples*, though *Arts and Letters* and *City Boy* taught me so much more. I've referenced the meaty Genet biography dozens of times as well. The first time I saw Edmund White read was at the aforementioned Rapture Bookstore, where he launched into an essay from *Arts and Letters*, about a role-playing encounter. White's thoughts drift off to exotic European vacation locales while he's tied to a chair and ruled over by a rather serious and incompetent dominant in the account, which inspired fiendish laughter from the audience.

The Burning Library reconnected me to a world beyond the seductive, although provincial, Pacific Northwest of the 1990s. It taught me to live life on my terms, to write about it. I started composing my first book while visiting the Bronx soon after, scribbling the first drafts of short stories in the tenement hallway where I studied as a boy, amidst cigarette butts and the sting of ammonia. Those accounts would later merge into a novel I self-published (however foolishly) in 2005, called *Buzz and Israel.* The completion of it was proof that I could do it, however shitty my first attempt at it was—I could start at the beginning and reach the end somehow.

While my worldview as a working-class Latino was forged by my Puerto Rican and Cuban heritage, my art history and cultural education, the studies and intellectual guidance I sought and found upon leaving New York as an American, was largely informed by queer men, their lives and their work. *The Burning Library* deepened my understanding of art and culture as a New Yorker in exile. The innocent act of learning about The Stonewall Resistance and Cormac McCarthy's Southern Gothic sensibility prepared me for more than I could've imagined at the time.

SKINNED ALIVE: STORIES

MICHAEL CARROLL

MY LETTER WAS the only useful thing I've written in years. It doesn't get me to Paris but it will get me into his apartment. Earlier I got off an overnight bus; I'm checking in at Le Mije, a youth hostel which as it turns out is only blocks from where he lives. I'm trying to lose my self-consciousness about being thirty and staying in a youth hostel, but when I see my bunkmates (all clearing out for the afternoon as instructed), who are all hairy and straggly-maned and from their ripe garlicky adult-male smells haven't used the showers and are of ambiguous age, international youngish travelers—the kind I never really was (raised work-ethic-proud)—I ignore them and set my backpack on my lower bunk, the only bunk left in the room I'm assigned. Crouched over my wafer mattress, careful not to be overseen and clocked as an unbohemian, thus suspicious type, I remove my camera and head out. No one's talking to me. I'm actually that kid again, the flimsy nerd no one wanted to talk to in school because the smell of my sissy peculiarity is detectable—a scent that from having read and closely reread him I've smelled in Edmund White's pages.

I wander around the Right Bank. I discover that in order to make a coin call you find a bar tabac that has this kind of heavy phone sitting on the bar near the workers drinking wine and smoking cigarettes at ten a.m. Before picking up the receiver, you ask the owner or bartender if you can use it, using standard polite French, and so I call him after putting it off and he says to come for coffee, and on my way I buy white tulips. He has a boyish, sometimes reedy voice I contemplate after hanging up. I'm disarmed, charmed—of course not knowing what to expect.

I find the address on rue St.-Martin and punch in the code he's given me over the phone.

I speak a tiny amount of French and I hope no one speaks to me but when they do they're very nice. I make a note to tell him this. Sweating, I climb the four winding flights of stairs. After the cold early morning in the ugly suburban bus station, and having taken the RER (can't pronounce it), I had climbed into sunlight at the Hôtel de Ville Métro station, and the day's been getting warmer, this Thursday before Easter, 1995. I'm over-layered for March, with a thick cotton tennis sweater weighing me down, and I'm most worried about my thin hair slicking against my head, and when I ring his doorbell, which sings in high, thin-metal chimes, I hear feet rumble on carpeted floor.

He opens and is barefooted and sturdy-calved in khaki shorts. The sleeves of his oxford-cloth shirt are rolled up and his smile is broad. His voice cracks: "Oh, what pretty white roses!"

> We arranged an evening and he arrived dressed in clothes by one of the designers he knew from the club. Not even my reactionary father, however, would have considered him a popinjay. He did nothing that would risk his considerable dignity. He had white tulips in his surprisingly small, elegant hand.

Well, my hands are small at least, and in one I'm carrying white tulips as an allusion.

I say, "Parisians are so nice! Americans say they're such snobs, but they're all so nice!"

He gives me a kiss on the cheek and invites me in. I've been further studying him during my year in the Czech Republic. I've been finding him more and more in the library of the British Council, his essays, reviews, articles, those books I've yet to read still, stories in anthologies and literary magazines I've heard of but never gotten my hands on. Apparently the English like him much more than folks in America. But then, I've been an unsuccessful missionary of his sacred word back home, where I've evangelized but not gotten many takers. My ex-boyfriend and I are among the few who've decided his work has saved, transformed and dignified us. He was a grad school passion of ours, then Patrick and I broke up and each of us found ourselves alone with his books—the way a reader ideally finds himself alone with any book that ends up mattering to him more than almost any other. More than Fitzgerald, Salinger. He tells the truth about us—that we don't have to be perfect, we can exult in our own individual forms, thrive and be whole in our personal shapes. If we can no longer be together Patrick and I can still spark off our love and our enthusiasm and gratitude for Edmund White, whose work even now pursues me. We loved each other even more when we talked about the books, then went off separately to try it with others. A foolish not yet disabused part of me still believes eventually I will go back to Patrick.

> Even so, I thought there was something all wrong, fundamentally wrong, with me: I set up a lover as a god, then burned with rage when he proved mortal. I lay awake, next to one lover after another, in a rage, dreaming of someone who'd appreciate me, give me the simple affection I imagined I wanted.

And:

> He warned me from the first he was in full flight. What I didn't grasp was that he was running toward someone even he couldn't name yet.

The sentences. How to write a sentence. His short stories, which I've been catching up on because they haven't been collected yet, are novels crammed into short story bites, and these condensed novels are comprised of sentences that capture in-breaths of entire experience-gulps.

> Paul had a photographic memory, and, during the hours spent together in the car in Morocco, he recited page after page of Racine or Ronsard or Sir Philip Sidney. He also continued the story of his life. I wanted to know every detail—the bloody scene on the steps of the disco, the recourse to dangerous drugs, so despised by the clenched-jaw cocaine set. I wanted to hear that he credited his lover with saving him from being a junkie, a drunk and a thug. "He was the one who got me back into school."

I feel that I haven't had so many dark and dramatic experiences, as someone who fears an HIV conversion but only for the stupidest reasons. After Patrick (we broke up when I was in my mid-twenties), I've had a very minor love life. I'm gun-shy. My small-town psychology having made me an old maid long before I was thirty. My next thing with a Cuban undergraduate while I was still a grad student has only reduced my confidence. As the object of my affection and the light of his female relatives' eyes (in Havana they'd fed him grilled-cheese sandwiches when he was a boy in the bathtub), Luis had this habit of going silent. In Ohio, when it seemed that our break-up was inevitable, I said, "I want you to leave me if that'll make you happier. These guys you're seeing, okay. You come home more cheerful but quieter. Hey, no need to keep secrets."

(I was lying.)

He'd never been faithful to anyone before. In fact, he'd preached against fidelity, which he'd considered as barbaric as female circumcision.

The apartment in Bowling Green, Ohio was minute. The bed took up most of the narrow slot the landlord called the bedroom. It was separated by this stiff, accordion-fold curtain from the room, even smaller, where I finished my thesis. If we cooked, it was me doing the cooking. I supplemented my income on weekend evenings delivering Chinese food. And in the summer I went back to work for the county board of mental retardation, supervising adult males in a group home, making sure they got their Tegretol and antipsychotic medications. Luis lived on student loans and Pell grants, never working. He was going to be a high school teacher and figured that he could work later. If I cooked his mother's Cuban recipes (chicken and yellow rice a favorite), he wanted his black beans blended. He had a childhood horror of beans in their solid form, and so using my mother's cast-off Oster blender I poured in the black beans I'd cooked from scratch and cooled and I hit Frappé. They came out as a runny purple-gray paste, and he liked this. But only just. He was sullen and spoiled and immature, the way I'd never imagined myself to be.

He still had a thing for a guy in Dayton, where he'd started college, and I knew I couldn't have what I'd had with Patrick, a marriage-model monogamy, with another guy, guys having too much on their egotistical minds all the time, guys with themselves in their brain-centers always.

> Like other brilliant young men and women he dissolved every solid in a solvent of irony, but even he had certain articles of faith, and the first was Paris. He liked French manners... He had a lively, but somewhat vain, sense of what made him interesting, which struck me only because he seemed so worthy of respect that any attempt he made to serve himself up appeared irrelevant.

Luis, a Marielito obsessed with hygiene and neatness of appearance, showered first thing in the morning, often skipped class, and when I came home would be watching Seinfeld on the portable TV set I'd brought to the union but never watched because books were my thing. Only gradually, after the sex quickly died, did it occur to me that my love bored him to silence, and he once said to me, "I don't know how you do it. Like, if I wanted to be a writer, I'd give myself a year and if it didn't work out I'd move on and find something else." When he was horny, he let me know after the lights were off and we were under the covers—his right hand locating me, his lips finding the courage to urge his face toward mine. In time, he stopped conveying even that.

> After this brief, irresponsible flaring up of lust, which had followed the sexless year of George's dying, Ray had gone back to celibacy. He thought it very likely that he was carrying death inside him, that it was ticking inside him like a time bomb but one he couldn't find because it had been secreted by an unknown terrorist. Even if it was located it couldn't be defused.

We lasted, the good parts and the bad, for two years, beginning and ending in summer.

The summer Luis and I weren't talking, I chewed a bag of peanuts roasted in their shells whole, chewed and swallowed them the way we often did in the South, salted shell and all.

I woke up with purple-black blisters on the insides of my cheeks, which I imagined to be KS lesions, dark shiny-wet beans exposing my shame where it belonged: in my mouth, where I hadn't done much sexual work but had only longed to after a while, next time apart from Luis. I wouldn't get tested. A positive test only meant you were certainly going to die at the time.

They both expected to die. "I just hope I graduate first," Ned said. "I'd love to finish one thing before buying the farm." Mark had an attack of shingles. Before his doctor diagnosed it, Mark looked at the spots across his solar plexus and panicked and said out loud to his reflection in the mirror, "Dear God, I'm not ready to die." The same week, after learning what was wrong with him, he read that shingles in someone under fifty was an accurate "tracer disease," a sure sign of dangerously lowered immunities.

My writing was pale and watery—I hadn't lived much except as a student and a mostly monogamous gay man hiding from most of the straight world, even my parents until recently—but the masterpiece I was composing in my head (where it would stay) was a bombastically epic tragedy about a gay kid who suffers because the younger guy doesn't love him because he loves himself too jealously. He meets undergrad classmates he talks about. He and I talk about them in bed when we grope and mutually masturbate under the covers. This is a real gay life and get used to it! Before AIDS and dying, there's nothing to look forward to out here in the sticks...

He recovered. In May when he saw Hajo in Berlin they went to the hospital for a blood test. Hajo had insisted on it, although Mark had warned him, "You know how it'll turn out, you'll be negative and I'll be positive and then we'll break up. It's just that simple."

Before the purple-black lesions went away, in two or three days, and before I could ever get myself to see a doctor (I didn't have health insurance), the climax of this unrequited passion deal running through my head was this: I would take my MasterCard and fly to Greece. I would choose a high, chalky cliff and fling myself off it into a wave-crashed cove of the blue Aegean.

He begged Ned to take more precautions. Ned said that Luc had swollen glands in his neck and under his arms and night sweats. He also had athlete's foot and bad skin. They hugged their bear and Ned said, "Peters, I guess it's curtains for us." They agreed that if they became ill they'd travel to India and commit suicide beside the Ganges. It was Ned's idea: "We've never been there. It would be an adventure. We should do something absolutely new. Anyway, they know all about death and cremation there—it's their specialty."

Luis and I decided we were going to leave Ohio. I was going back to Florida to take my chances in a low-paid service-industry economy sucking up to corporations who would relocate and take advantage of desperate unskilled laborers who would work for a dollar or two above the minimum wage without benefits, and he was going to take a good high school teaching job with union-supported benefits in Houston, and the inevitable was happening. We were breaking up.

The week before we packed up and moved, we drove to a club in Toledo and staked out separate beachheads on opposite sides of the dance floor. I met Jim, a poet who was unhappy in his native Glass City, and we talked and kissed and I think danced. He was tall, better-built than me, with luxuriant and skillfully trimmed straw-color hair. We were both writers, and I had been living with someone planning to teach history and geography who couldn't be bothered to read a textbook (he could memorize maps), who dropped the history component when he found out that he could still get a decent teaching job as a geography teacher in Texas since he spoke Spanish. I got Jim's number. I was going to call him but I was still going to move. I'd already planned it (Luis and I had planned it together) and let the apartment go and rented the U-Haul, and like Jim I didn't want to stay in Ohio. Again, my life was over—it was over for me every couple of years.

> He gave me a story he had written. It was Hellenistic in tone, precious and edgy, flirting with the diffuse lushness of a Pre-Raphaelite prose, rich but bleached, like a tapestry left out in the sun. I suppose he must have had in mind Mallarmé's "Afternoon of a Faun," but Paul's story was more touching, less cold, more comprehensible. That such a story could never be published in the minimalist, plain-speaking 1980s seemed never to have occurred to him. Could it be that housed in such a massive body he had no need for indirect proofs of power and accomplishment? Or was he so sure of his taste that recognition scarcely interested him at all?

In all my time in the MFA workshops at Bowling Green State University, I wrote only one story I thought was at all good. It was my one sure bet for literary greatness but not for love. I flattered myself that because the story was unabashedly gay (and yes of course about coming out, a theme soon to be discarded in New York publishing), it was sufficiently pioneering for the journal that had accepted it for their issue the fall I returned to Florida, said good-bye to Luis, and put in my application for the Peace Corps—a year-long process involving FBI fingerprinting, background checks, the fetching of nine letters of recommendation, and a round of doctor and dentist visits.

Publishing my first story did not change my life, but being alone a while probably did. I got hungrier and desperate during my interim year back in my hometown of Jacksonville. I was a college English instructor and on the weekends I was a janitor at a gay bathhouse across from a Southern Baptist church, picking up spare cash (I had no health insurance, only debts) and things to write about. I experimented with tone more than content, creating nothing new in that addled year I'd want to bring with me overseas to Yemen, when my number in Washington finally came up. Whenever I felt discouraged and lonely, I opened the journal and reread my published story, thrilling at its professional layout, and sighing and smiling damply at the prose's many not-well-disguised borrowings. I've brought a copy as a "gift" to Edmund White, one of several copies I have lugged halfway around the world without knowing for whom any of them is intended. It's my single pride, this professionally typeset and immaculately proofed story text. It's all I have.

I tell him (I've poured this all out to him more or less in the letter I typed in my little sky-high Czech apartment, a studio called a garzonka, derived from garçon; a letter I sent him via his New York agent, and which he responded to by postcard): "You don't understand, I've only ever lived in small places, the one where I grew up, the one where I went to college and the one where I went to grad school, and the ones in the two countries where I've served in the Peace Corps."

"That's probably why you're still alive and why you're negative."

The days in Crete were big, cloudless hot days, heroic days, noisy with the rasp of insects. They were heroic days as though the sun were a lionhearted hero... Oh, but hadn't he just read in his beach book, The Odyssey, the words of the dead, lionhearted Achilles: "Do not speak to me soothingly about death, glorious Odysseus; I should prefer, as a slave, to serve another man, even if he had no property and little to live on, than to rule over all these dead who have done with life." He'd cried on the white-sand beach beside the lapis-lazuli water and looked through his tears, amazed, at a herd of sheep trotting toward him. He stood and waded and waved, smiling, at the old shepherd in black pants with a curved stick in his hand, which itself looked carved; Ray, expensively muscular in his Valentino swim trunks, thought he was probably not much younger than this ancient peasant and suddenly his grief struck him as a costly gewgaw, beyond the means of the grievously hungry and hardworking world. Or maybe it was precisely his grief that joined him to this peasant. Every night he was dreaming about George, and in that book about the Greek death rituals he'd read the words of an old woman: "At death the soul emerges in its entirety, like a man. It has the shape of a man, only it's invisible. It has a mouth and hands and eats real food just like we do. When you see someone in your dreams, it's the soul you see. People in your dreams eat, don't they? The souls of the dead eat too." Ray couldn't remember if George ate in his dreams.

The clean phrasing, the being-alive in the middle of his prose. No one can outdo him.

He says, "I want to read your story."

We go into the bedroom and he sits on the floor Indian-style under the light of a lamp and I lie on the bed on my side facing him and he reads my short story's piss-elegant phrasing (which only comes to me now as pretentious), without faltering delivery. I wince. I love him so much!

Done, he nods and says, "Well it's very Jamesian, but good. No, it's very good! Bravo!"

And though he doesn't mean to make me feel this way, my sensation is one of smallness. I've come from a very long distance to hear my master pronounce my story "good"—and, in this pat, clean, warm pronouncement, I realize how far I have yet to go. I used to think my story was hot shit, but now I understand it's okay, and though I'm scared I don't feel like a complete loser.

Aloud, Edmund White has just read my story and he rushes in, "You're a real writer."

I've told myself that the only thing I've lacked is a mentor, and now in his gentle nodding I have my judgment. None of my writing professors were so involved in my work unless they'd decided I was trying to be the next Carson McCullers (whom I'd never read). So I love Ed—yes, Ed—for his tender honesty. He says, "I just finished another story, but it's not as good as yours."

I laugh and say, "Oh, sure," knowing I've tried poaching his style to not such great effect.

He says, "Do you want to hear it?"

"Are you insane?"

He reads from the notebook he wrote it in, and tells me he always writes his fiction in one of these thick-paged hardbound deals from an expensive papeterie. I am the first to hear it—or if not, that's the way I'll present it to friends when I leave the Peace Corps for the States in August. He begins:

"When I was a kid, I was a Buddhist and an atheist, but I kept making bargains with God: if he'd fulfill a particular wish, I'd agree to believe in him. He always came through, but I still withheld my faith, which shows, perhaps, how unreasonable rationality can be."

A two-sentence paragraph. Nothing out of place. Since I realized that my contemporary, Michael Chabon, is the only writer of my generation I've read who can pull off the epigrammatic style convincingly, seamlessly infusing a quick, witty epiphany into the swelling narrative whole, I've vowed to stay away from trying to go 19th century. It either comes out as a bad Oscar Wilde imitation, or I get lost trolling a Flaubertian estuary of shallows and tangles in search of an outlet to the bracing open sea. My story (dully, abstractly titled "Afternoons"), I see in an instant listening to Ed read his "Cinnamon Skin," is trying too hard in its quest to reach *The New Yorker.* The first sentence of his second paragraph—"One of God's miracles occurred when I was thirteen." —keeps the rapidly undocked vessel humming and chugging and making for the waves and then the perilous storm-lashed depths beyond the coast. (Since then, too, I've also all but given up on mastering figurative language, and especially those extended metaphors my English teachers had worked so hard to show us the authors we were studying had rigged out seemingly effortlessly.)

He reads out breathlessly, sitting in front of me Indian-style, facing me and hunched over the creamy pages of a notebook he will sell to the Beinecke Archives at Yale, laughing at his own jokes and once farting without comment, reading, and when he's done I just say, "Wow. Wow."

"Really?"

"Really."

"What do you like about it?"

And now in memory words fail me because I don't remember what I said, just some crap about what a good storyteller Ed is, always was—with what over the next twenty years I'll learn, along with charm (if you can muster it), is the most important quality of writing. Some suspense, a flair (learnable, as I now believe) for seducing a reader, disarming, charming the reader—who's holier to you the writer than book smarts, gorgeously complicated sentencing, and piss-elegance.

Easter weekend is long and involved, and I only return to Le Mije to recover my backpack with my not-elegant clothes. His gay cousin Austin and Austin's lover Stephen are in Paris for the first time, too (Ed has never met them but Austin becomes Ed's web designer). It turns out that Austin and I overlapped in Sweetwater, Texas. So we are something of a family.

I return to the Czech Republic and Ed gives me an AT&T number to call him. My little garzonka doesn't have a phone, and I have to dial him from a pretty wooden phone booth in the lobby of a coffeehouse next to my university department, the Beseda, predating the Communist era. I am, after all, in Europe. As I'd always imagined, I was in Europe. I belonged in Europe.

"Listen," he says, while I'm away from my friends and colleagues ordering cheap nectar-grade espresso in the beautifully decorated dining room, "I'm in love with you. Move to Paris!"

And so with a lot to learn, I do. I become friends with his friends. We stay in Paris three years and when it's time to leave together and go back to the States, I realize more than anything I am a story writer. So much of my short story writing began when I read *Skinned Alive*.

I meet the people who inform his fiction, and I learn that the best fiction, which is part of his secret, comes from real life. I remember this line from the title story of *Skinned Alive*:

My French friend Hèléne nudged me and whispered, "There's one for you."

In 1990 when we were living in the United States, [Hubert] started to acquire his characteristic line, his *patte*, through hundreds of hours of drawing cartoon figures. They were seldom elaborate—in the beginning they were just a dash and a knot, a stick and a ball, a ponytail and glasses: a rapid jet of lovely calligraphy.

And from the first these little people, *ces bonhommes et bonnes femmes*, were integers in a storytelling calculus of his own devising. He saw stories and, as with the ancient Egyptian scribes, his columns and columns of figures and animals were intrinsically narrative. He'd satirize himself as the acid-tongued Frenchman among well-meaning American hicks. Or he'd imagine the Chinese couple who cleaned for us once a week as spies sending back to their government a confused, hilarious report on our peculiar activities. The amorous adventures of our friends were also subjects for his sharp if affectionate eye. Of course his great theme was cultural differences.

I'm writing this page with his beautiful Art Pen, which he always forbade me to touch; today I couldn't find anything else to write with, and I wanted to—needed to—give a form to my grief that he would have approved of.

—from *Our Paris: Sketches from Memory*

OUR PARIS: SKETCHES FROM MEMORY

PHILIP F. CLARK

GRIEF NEEDS ITS palate cleanser. *Our Paris: Sketches from Memory* was Edmund White's. This memoir is the concise, raucous, irreverent, at times painful and ultimately loving celebration of The City of Lights, and of the artist White met there and fell in love with, Hubert Sorin. Written while Sorin and White lived in Paris it is a document of the many people—the very *bonhommes et bonnes femmes*—who surrounded their lives, and the adventures—there is no other word for it—they encountered in such company. It is also a testament to and document of the life of Hubert Sorin, who was dying of AIDS during their time together. He succumbed to the disease in March of 1994. Sketches both verbal and visual are the heart of this book, in its delectable evocation of their crowded life together among the city's antic panoply of famous, infamous and everyone-you-can-imagine-in-between. It is a love story as well of the city, and a catharsis; it would be the book whose memories were later hauntingly recreated in depth in White's novel of 2000, *The Married Man*—which has its own connection to the trilogy *A Boy's Own Story*, *The Beautiful Room Is Empty* and *The Farewell Symphony*.

Though its voice is that of White throughout the book, the visual *chansonnettes* of Sorin's artwork is a perfect accompaniment and cicerone for the reader as White takes us through neighborhoods—Île St. Louis, the Marais, Isle de la Cite, Les Halles—in which they encounter the city at its best, its most vulnerable, or most beguiling. Appearances are made by such personalities as Azzedine Alaia, Naomi Campbell, Billy Boy, Julian Schnabel, Jean Genet, Madame Pompidou, President and Nancy Reagan, Rachel Stella, Ernest Hemingway (in drag), even Garbo. But the treasured caricatures of the inhabitants of White's and Sorin's neighborhood and travels are the real face of Paris: the garrulous prostitutes, the over-zealous concierges, the restaurant staffs, the market vendors, the chars and the "snowy-haired matrons." All of whom, celebrity or not, are captured with perfect pitch in Sorin's delicate drawings.

Sorin's acrobatic and captivating pen and ink drawings fill the book's sixteen chapters with his incisive eye: with Aubrey Beardsley lines and sardonic—though not black—humor, the citizen-characters of their Arrondissement come to life and lead us on from chapter to chapter. As White regales us with the antic and yet charming idiosyncrasies of such personages as their concierge Madame Denise, who after a day's long work, will confab with the local prostitutes, all of whom she knows by name; or the local "handsome" butcher, who would prepare for White and Sorin *moutard* rabbit dishes of incomparable flavor and simplicity.

The City of Paris is pure energy here—risible and tactile; its inhabitants a continual catalyst and inspiration for innumerable adventures in leisure as well as professional work. White wrote for such publications as *Vogue* at the time, articles and short portraits on innumerable celebrities and their lives, homes, and escapades.

White is a deft archeologist of Paris's history and culture. Throughout the book we are served specific descriptions of its past, present and future. He has an acrid observation of the *milieu*, in such statements as, "Everyone in Paris seems to be the son or daughter or nephew of someone famous. The famous people themselves belong to the city's glorious past; their relatives, like Parisians in general, are living off their patrimony." He understands the milieu, and the connotations not only of correct use of language, but of the perfectly upturned gaze. One can be succinctly dismissed with as little as a raised eyebrow or a pall of silence. The book is a catalog of the language itself, and one comes away with a whole vocabulary of French terms in the colloquial and the formal. White's deep love and knowledge of Paris, coupled with Sorin's, make for an inimitable introduction to the city on so many levels. Much as he did in *The Flaneur*, White entrances us with small, deft vignettes that are more apt to the *contes* style of the poet Francois Coppée than the travelogue. As he notes: "Paris is of course, in constant flux. Before 1850 it was a smelly, cramped, chaotic, medieval collection of villages; after 1870 and the changes wrought by Napolean III and his master builder, the Baron Haussmann, it was a modern city. Everything in Paris—from the twelve avenues radiating out from the Arc de Triomphe to the graceful layout of the new Bois de Boulogne with its two artificial lakes, from the innovative design of the glass and metal stalls of the food markets at Les Halles to the botched transformation of the Ile de la Citie´ from a dangerous but picturesque medieval slum to an arid administrative center— everything was thought out and calculated down to the tiniest detail by the tall Alsatian workaholic, Haussmann, the Prefect of the Seine." And it is from this sense of transformation and history that White is able to make palpable the many people and places that are remembered here. Behind each of them is Hubert Sorin—the book's shadow and light.

Though AIDS does make its appearance in the book, it is more a side glance than a deep look in the mirror. White's Introduction and Afterward make clear that the memoir was written during Sorin's illness, and that the passage of time was elementally symbolic—as Sorin completed the illustrations, White would write more of the sketches, both knowing there was an inevitable end in sight, and an inevitable desire to prolong time. The center of the book is his and Sorin's life together; vibrant and stimulating, mundane and surprising and filled with a deep celebration of *living*, not dying. White was HIV positive as well; yet he was healthy and thriving with it, as Sorin was slowly wasting. White strode two sides of the fence:

> I kept thinking he'd live on and on. I'd been diagnosed as HIV positive in 1985 and my health had in no way deteriorated. Hubert was receiving two different experimental treatments, one of which seemed promising. I suppose I let myself be seduced by the current cant about AIDS

becoming a manageable chronic disease like diabetes. It's no such thing, but I was encouraged to hold on to this fantasy by my love for him and my fear of losing him. He knew the truth, though, and in his last three months longed to die in order to be freed of an existence that had become almost entirely one of suffering.

That very aspect of being healthy or sick while infected reflects what was happening at the time in the mid-to-late 90s: new therapies and medications were making many men well even as many still sickened and died. And why? Chemical genetics? The luck of the draw? I got those genes and you got these? It doesn't matter here. White is concerned with the fact that his and Sorin's story—their life and love together—was about acceptance and drive. The inevitable is held off for a while here; there is a concentration on other things, though each knew what was to come. AIDS and HIV were still taboo. People were kind at best, and silent at worst. Amongst the dark, the book has its humors. Edmund White's wit is as sharp as his vision, and as rapier. In describing taking their dear Dachshund Fred out for a walk: "At the corner is the always busy fountain designed by Niki de Saint-Phalle and her husband, Jean Tinguely, with a pair of red lips, water squirting from the tits of one of Niki's famous ladies, or *nanas*, a top hat that spins, and treble clef in black metal, and so on, all bubbling and twirling—and soaking passersby on windy days. Fred likes to walk by here because I encourage him to defecate on the grill above the underground center for experimental music, directed by Pierre Boulez, who once refused to give me an interview." Sorin's brilliant and detailed depiction of the fantastic fountain—and Fred's delight in relieving himself—is a source of complete *sourire* for the reader. White regales us with an anecdote of Father Riches, a priest and friend. "Allen Ginsberg's latest twenty-two-year-old came through Paris on his way to Italy not long ago. He phoned and promised to contact me on his way back through town. When he came by a month later he said he'd stayed with Father Riches in his charming parsonage on Lake Garda. The young man shook his head and said, 'It was terrible!'

"Really? Did he try to seduce you?" I asked, concerned. "No. He tried to convert me."

As the memoir comes to a close, the language of loss grows ineluctable. In the guise of a travelogue and memoir, *Our Paris* pays tribute to the life force that Sorin and White both embraced and lived. Even at the end, dying in Morocco, Sorin sought and filled his eyes with beauty, constantly wanting to recognize art and creation:

> On the last full day of his life we traveled by automobile from Erfoud, in the Sahara, to Ouarzazate, passing through one oasis after another. It was the end of Ramadan, and the men were dressed in festive white, the women in black and sequins, woven red belts around their waists. He saw a camel grazing at liberty. We went through the entire towns of shaped and incised earth mixed with straw and cement or chalk. Hubert kept murmuring, 'Superbe, c'est superbe.'

How could one write of such a life, of such a loved one, without looking through a lens of constant and fractal devotion in the face of what poet Edward Hirsch so beautifully says, *"Poor Sisyphus grief / I am not ready for your heaviness / Cemented to my body."*

That so much was lived in so short a period of time, and so much deeply enjoyed is the real core of this memoir. *Our Paris* is a constant reminder for us to truly *see and feel* each and every day. The final Afterword is a eulogy of the remarkable clarity and intent that was Sorin's gift. White remembers him with complete love, and Sorin is captured with resonant memory. Yes, of course it brought me to tears. It brings you that deep. You realize this is no small offering. It is a love letter as much as a book.

"Leonard saw me reluctantly and when I stood hesitantly in the sickroom doorway he mumbled while saying his black rosary and he kissed the silver crucifix that dangled from it. He didn't look up at me. I was broken-hearted and angry to see my big, brave boy reduced to this cranky, creaking prayer wheel. I was sorry that he had lost his confidence, his belief in everything he'd so beautifully achieved."

—from *The Farewell Symphony*

THE FAREWELL SYMPHONY

LYNNE TILLMAN

I

IN THE EARLY hours of June 28, 1969, the Stonewall Inn's gay clientele had had it, and took to the streets to fight the police and their relentless harassment. On June 23, 2015, the Stonewall Inn was designated a historic New York monument.

On June 27, 2015, the Supreme Court of the United States ruled 5/4 that gay marriage was legal in all 50 states—no more state referendums or Federal Courts overturning legislatures one way or the other. Two unprecedented events occurred, while I was rereading Edmund White's novel *The Farewell Symphony*.

The first time I read it, in Xania, Crete, it was 2000, four years after protease inhibitors had been discovered. The cocktail, a flighty term for a life saver, turned AIDS into a treatable condition, like diabetes. But the terror of AIDS between the years 1981 and 1996 in NYC, where I live, was vivid, and not a memory. So many friends, young and older gay men, and some who shot heroin, had become sick and died. Everyone died very fast, and four words were numbingly repeated: "He's gone." "Already? No."

Post-war Americans, "baby-boomers," thought "uncurable" was impossible. Polio had been cured; Neil Armstrong had walked on the moon. AIDS revamped that version of reality, when everything changed, and some illusions were shredded. Since there weren't always cures, inviolability had left the room. Some people became inured to the inevitable, and could not feel anything, a dead kind of mourning, devastated by memorial after memorial. Artist and writer David Wojnarowicz told everyone he didn't want a memorial, so the day after he died, friends marched on Second Avenue from the base of his apartment building to Astor Place, and there someone lit a militant bonfire, a red fury of protest, not a sad mourning, which Wojnarowicz had wanted—rage. These were traumatic years.

The Farewell Symphony chronicles several decades before the AIDS epidemic, into the advent of Gay Liberation—the protagonist participates in an early gay-consciousness raising group. Before AIDS, gay men partied as if the future were curable: White writes about a gay internist who shot everyone up with antibiotics for syphilis, gonorrhea, and other sexually transmitted diseases, without worry.

In the beginning, no one had a clue, no one knew why gay men were getting sick. The novel recounts this and continues through to AIDS' being named, then as it furiously claims life after life, into the time when there was no time left, no future. In a way, *The Farewell Symphony* is the consummate, embodied witness, stunned like a survivor of Hiroshima or the Holocaust.

The novel also tells the tale of a young man and his beginnings, and that of its writer's life and career from its beginnings to a book's first publication. "I had found an exhilarating if suicidal liberation in my rejection slips… " It covers a family history and a history of books read and loved, of knowledge gained, naivete lost. It is a formidable social commentary, astute, informative, witty, and sometimes caustic, with an exacting class consciousness and analysis that most American novelists abjure. Each character whom the unnamed protagonist meets—presumably "Edmund" but his namelessness is part of the fiction—has a place in the American social system, its culture, class, politics, and all play their roles faithfully.

White's alter ego worries about his worthiness and "sincerity." "What I failed to accept (until a few years later when I read Rilke's *Letters to a Young Poet*) was that a *distance* necessarily separates any two people. Separation is the most human aspect of existence and to rail against it is puerile…" Throughout the novel, sometimes like a bildungsroman, the reader learns as the protagonist learns. And because this is an American novel, it is very concerned with doing the right thing, even the so-called "wrong" things the right way. "I was living with Maria, but I felt out of place. She was fastidious, calm, unambitious, whereas I was sloppy and driven by my twin appetites for sex and success, both of which struck me in her presence as hairy and unwashed."

When the narrator takes his sister Anne's son into his home and parents him, he does the right thing, without complaint. He finds him a school, making sure he does his homework and eats well, and reveals another side of his own many-sided character. While he despairs of family, especially the heterosexual model, also for love and sex, he creates it. "I craved love, sex, fame, money, food, and drugs, and yet I never suspected I was addicted to these things because my specialty was hopeless love." His list might also include a craving for family: his close friends are his family, but he also shows loyalty and devotion, with ambivalence, to his sister and mother.

Unlike many contemporary novels that focus on a single, dramatic event and its consequences, or upon the author's inexperience—I call these "novels of inexperience"—*The Farewell Symphony* insists upon broad and complex experiences, the writer/protagonist's, and the reader's responses to these. White's novel has a unique affect: somehow it involves readers intimately in these various experiences of another. The dizzying number of experiences, hundreds and hundreds, in *The Farewell Symphony* drew me in, and I was living it, feeling and thinking about this man's life, and as I read on, forgot it wasn't mine.

> We do not know today whether we are busy or idle. In times when we thought ourselves indolent, we have afterwards discovered that much was accomplished, and much was begun in us... All our days are so unprofitable while they pass, that 'tis wonderful where or when we ever got anything of this which we call wisdom, poetry, virtue... (Emerson, from "Experience")

The Farewell Symphony seems to leave nothing out, although it has to, it's a composition, a book. Still, as I read it, I wondered what Edmund White might have held back, forgotten, suppressed or repressed. Nothing seems to be missing.

II

THE DEATH FROM AIDS of the man the protagonist/narrator loved most, Brice, frames *The Farewell Symphony*. "I'm beginning this book on All Saints' Day in Paris six months after Brice's death... Brice's ashes are stored in an urn." The novel is shaped by the narrator's trauma, and the narrator's loss of his great love immediately brought me into his state of mind, as if I were an intimate told something no one else knows.

White calls *The Farewell Symphony* an "autobiographical novel"; necessarily, it foregrounds his experience but not only his. It brings so many others' stories into it. And, its protagonist is no hero, except that he is determined to survive even himself. "Perhaps I should have just accepted my loathsome dependence on him [Sean] and recognized that nothing could be done with it." Most writers are kinder to characters who have been rejected by their first, great love. The protagonist comes in for frequent self-laceration and little praise.

The author's evaluation of his main character is not so different from his evaluation of others, and only a few characters, Joshua, for one, escape White's bemused wit or sharp knife. I attribute some of its acerbic tone to White's having written *The Farewell Symphony* during the devastation, before protease inhibitors arrived, and, though he records the time before AIDS, when life was, if not great, holding some hope, it didn't while he was writing it. The disease was taking no prisoners, and White was not only a witness, but also a surviving victim of the disease. It could be a mark of the trauma suffered that White gave no comfort and had little mercy to spare for himself and others who had so far survived. "There's no morality in my Catholicism and no hell except the one we're living in, this fiery posthumous existence I'm inventing." A "fiery posthumous existence I'm inventing"—a survivor's lament.

An autobiographical novel: what is this oxymoronic creature? White fictionalizes parts, as in a roman a clef, and sometimes uses actual events and people's names—Michel Foucault, for one. Famous names and public events interrupt a reader's fantasy, her imagination, and also augment a reader's experience of the novel—it becomes part of the actual world.

This movement, the flux, between so-called "reality" and fictive reality caused me to invest more in both the fiction and the "reality." That's hard to explain, although Wittgenstein cautioned, Don't explain, only describe. I jumped into this pool, *The Farewell Symphony*, floated, submerged, became suspended, treaded water, swam again. Staying afloat was often tough, because I was always aware that I was reading a tragedy, whose movement to disease and death was ineluctable.

Actualities beside and inside fictions, all these juxtapositions, felt uncanny, like cinematic jump cuts—shock, bang, shock. Freud's uncanny—making the familiar unfamiliar—suggests some of what White's novel effects. The familiar might be a writer's hopes; an insecure man's attempts to be included in certain circles and scenes, and his complicated relationships to a mother, father, and sister, their portraits like photo-realist works, warts and all. Next to these, he sets less familiar experiences, those less well represented and less representable.

White appeals directly to sensation, sensuality, lust, he writes of rapacious and rough, crazed sex, and also unreciprocated romantic love. He elucidates the demand and pressure of sexual need: the writing is flamboyant and excited, when adumbrating languorous or acrobatic intercourse, fucks of all kinds, and vivaciously describes men's bodies, their hands, the smell of their sweat, their penises.

> I felt lust playing on my solar plexus like a drum... Lust was also rudely flicking my nipples with the back of a fingernail, then injecting molten silver into my neck veins and forcing it to rise through my head... Sitting on the floor I could catch the sour, mildewy smell of his sweat socks and sneakers and after the idea that he wasn't impeccably clean repulsed me, I decided to like it.

I thought a lot about White's emphasis on the sexual act, and sexuality, about what it means, how it functions in the novel. White doesn't trust much, I realized, maybe only in actions that are taken freely, in the moment. He appears to trust sex, and what happens during sex and because of it, because it is as close to "truth" as he can get, or as life allows. The sentence—"after the idea that he wasn't impeccably clean repulsed me, I decided to like it"—suggests that his alter ego chooses to favor an accommodation in his taste in order to live in the moment, the moment of truth. Sex is the ur-existential encounter, and the sincerity White writes that he feared he lacked as a young man resides there.

The words "candor" and "candid" come to mind, reading White. He sets sex under bright lights, no shadows allowed, and also everything else he renders comes into the open, baldly. "I went to Rome because I was intimidated by Paris." "In my family I'd remained underdeveloped because unnoticed—a neglect, however, I'd come to like, since it permitted me to invent a simple, all purpose personality." There's a desire to shock, I suppose, definitely to surprise, but more a resolve to be honest. Honesty is stripping it down to basics, no adverbs, a very few adjectives, an attempt to write a truth, unadorned.

"I never stopped to wonder why I had to please everyone."

The protagonist doesn't want to please women, but feels compelled, forced. He might "act" heterosexual, up to a point, not to be embarrassed or humiliated by being gay, or unmanly. The novel's attitude toward women augments my sense of *The Farewell Symphony* as an important historical novel, historical in the way that the best novels are: It presents a sensibility and a consciousness in time, and, like a diary, expresses attitudes of that day. Some of these have shifted greatly in the years since White was born and came of age—gay marriage is legal, and the Stonewall Inn is a revered monument. Young gay and straight men's attitudes toward women have also shifted.

White writes about a psychiatrist, whom he saw as a teenager, that his "one big theory about human neuroses blamed Mom and he'd drilled me in it until I broke my dependence on her." Post World War II America, the 1950s, was an awful time for mothers, women generally—De Kooning's monstrous "Woman" series— and, of course, mothers can be destructive to their children. What strikes me as significant about this view from an earlier time, and not just among homosexual men, is the lack of recognition that, in a patriarchy, men police men. The Father, or the Law of the Father, regulates and punishes male behavior.

In *The Farewell Symphony*, the father has scant sympathy or support for his son. "My father had predicted my failure, and although I'd succeeded as a journalist for eight years, I'd failed until now to publish even a single page of fiction." His mother thinks the world of her only son, even as she suffocates him with a dependent love.

III

THE FIRST TIME I read *The Farewell Symphony*, in 2000, in Xania, Crete, White's recall and re-creations beggared my imagination. He described the feverish climb of orgasm; and, somehow he found words for ecstasy. I was dazzled. He described a pasta dish, its sensuous taste; the trattoria in Rome where he ate it; he observed perfectly how the light in Venice affected the color of a wall. There were many startling, lush elaborations. "... (I)ts slender ionic columns in the tiny salon that appeared to be made of lightly licked spun sugar and its courtyard fountain of a verdigrised Pan leering over his pipes while a drunken naiad embraced his hooves..."

Unforgettable and delicious scenes and portraits mount. But when AIDS strikes, one by one the portraits fall off the wall. White made the losses feel personal, as Rainer Werner Fassbinder did in, say, *Fox and His Friends*. I was losing friends, even some I didn't like that much. Or, that the protagonist didn't. They had been alive, now they were gone, just the way it had happened during the 80s and most of the 90s.

"Brice *had* become purer over the last few years, with the onset of his illness... After all, he'd been only 27 when I'd met him. Now, five years later, he'd aged by several millennia. He had to accept he wasn't going to live..."

Dead center in the novel, Brice is brought back to life, as the narrator relates the story of the couple's friendship with two Americans, Giles and Neil, in Paris. The two Americans, both aesthetes, invite them to a formal Japanese tea ceremony. "Giles was extremely attentive to Brice, who was now ectoplasmically thin... It seemed strange to me that Giles had never spoken of his own status and that of the five participants in the New Year's Day Tea, two were already dead."

The deft and sudden dropping of the AIDS bomb builds on the emotional impact of *The Farewell Symphony*. Things go along, much is told, and while the reader is thick in the midst of life and a fascinating world, death comes, harsh and awkward. Such a contradiction, and so like reality, such a shocking juxtaposition.

IV

READING *THE FAREWELL Symphony* in 2015, I thought again about an autobiographical novel. I'd written more, and realized how the conceit gave space for literary play. The precisely rendered and remembered sex scenes, and those meals, wines, interiors, and landscapes, might have happened or been exactly as White wrote them, or might have been fictionalized. An oxymoron serves memory's lapses, representing the gap itself. And, death is life's oxymoron, after all, so by now the contradiction was reassuring.

White's protagonist lives with contradictions. The character is irascible, sensitive, mean, sweet, harsh, gentle, generous, unfair, noble. He is decidedly shaped by the ironies of life, which include his goal of being a writer, so often self-defeating. A humanist would call him human or all too human. I question the terms by which people have named themselves "human," basically, giving themselves such a good rep. I follow, say, Kafka, Woolf, Barthes, Foucault, Freud, whose fictions and theories question our species' innate worthiness, and see human achievement, if it comes, more likely failure, as a result of struggle and compromise between and among internal and external conflicts.

Reading *The Farewell Symphony* in 2000, I had felt a despair greater than for just my life, but for life. What do I do now? I thought. I felt implicated in a story that spoke of a time just over, yet not over, and I had lived through it. Alone in Xania, I didn't have anyone to talk with about this opera, with its many brilliant, soaring arias and gruesome deaths. The novel's darkness overwhelmed the brilliant skies of Crete, and I was at a loss. I wanted to burn the book, have a wake for it, and scatter its ashes into the sea.

In June 2015, I felt a sadness muted by time. AIDS was no longer a death sentence for those who could afford the cocktail. I remembered some it had killed: friends Craig Owens, Gregory Kolovakos, Cookie Mueller, Keith Davis, David Wojnarowicz, Peter Hujar, and the actors and writers Charles Ludlum, Ethel Eichenberger, David Warrilow, Ron Vawter, to name only a few. AIDS wiped them all out, and their audience, too, as Fran Lebowitz once astutely observed. That special and particular sensibility, it was also gone.

I grieve that grief can teach me nothing, nor carry me one step into real nature. (Emerson)

Emerson wrote his essay "Experience" two years after his son died. He was grieving. I keep photographs of dead friends and my father nearby on my desk, on a bookshelf, or a wall. Maybe I'm a morbid character, but I don't want to forget them, and worry I will.

Edmund White's opus remembers so much. He was in grief, mourning, when he wrote it. It was an anguishing time. Most likely, many people will want to forget it. *The Farewell Symphony* is an act of willful remembering, and dares to be beautiful and also discomforting, pricking the conscience and reopening wounds. It acknowledges the past not as history but as experience, and I can think of no other book like it.

"What is crucial to underline is that at its very inception Proust thought of his book as several books, mostly essays. Only gradually did he see that he could bind all these diverse subjects together into a single work and that he could call it neither a memoir nor an essay nor a pastiche but rather a novel. Proust had always been drawn to writers who had confused genres: he was thinking admiringly, for instance, of Baudelaire's prose poems or the autobiographical side of Flaubert's novel *A Sentimental Education*.

But where Proust differed from all his predecessors was in the gigantism of his project, a first person narrative that would be not only the most penetrating analysis of several psyches but also a vast panorama of society--a book, in short, that would be as deep as it was wide."

—from *Marcel Proust*

MARCEL PROUST

SHEILA KOHLER

WHAT A DELIGHT and privilege to write about two of my
most favorite writers at once: Marcel Proust and Edmund White.
They seem both to be intrinsic parts of my life, threaded into the
memories of my own past and my present, and I hope I can say
my future.

In White's biography of Proust he uses all of his vast erudition,
his knowledge of France, its people, its literature and history, his
wisdom on the art of writing, the art of love and particularly homosexual love, his acquaintance with loss, suffering, and the
ephemerality of life itself to give us this brief, intimate, and ultimately touching portrait of Proust. He culls for us here the
information that we really want to know about this writer of genius: his world, his influences and education, his loves, the models
for his great books and ultimately how he went from being a
seemingly social climbing snob and dilettante to a prolific and
most applauded writer of the 20th century.

I first encountered Proust's work in what might be considered
rather adverse yet somewhat Proustian circumstances. He was a
favorite writer of my ex-husband and his Southern mother who
had discovered Proust on her own in the library in Kentucky

where she had taken out Scott Montcrieff's translation of *Remembrance of Things Past,* and read it by chance. (Scott Montcrieff, interestingly, led a double life and was apparently both gay and a spy during Mussolini's Italy.) A brilliant woman, my mother-in-law was immediately aware of what she had in hand, and Proust's characters soon became as dear—well, perhaps I should say dearer to her and perhaps more vivid than her own Southern relatives who seemed flamboyant enough in themselves to me (a father who was kicked in the head by a horse and dragged to death, for example).

She shared this love for Proust with her only son who, when I first met him, was just eighteen and in Europe to visit his adored and ailing Mama. She too suffered from asthma, and having divorced her husband, a Russian aristocrat, who had escaped the Russian revolution, traipsed through Europe for much of her life going from one European spa to another, looking for a cure. A long lean lady, she would lie languorously draped across a chaise longue, pumping her inhaler between breathless sentences, studiously ignoring me. She and her son talked of nothing but the Baron de Charlus, Swann, Robert de Saint Loup, the Verdurins, and Odette as though they were the people living next door.

"Doesn't she rather remind you of Odette?" she would say with a grin when some poor woman had just walked out of the door. Or dropping a French word or two, "Don't you think he's a bit *louche,* something of Charlus about him, no?"

Not having read Proust, and indeed at eighteen not having read much more than the 19th century English writers taught in my South African boarding school, I was decidedly and humiliatingly left out of the conversation. I did not know these fascinating people and longed to know them and join the conversation too.

During our honeymoon—we married at nineteen, a shotgun marriage—I attempted to fill this lacuna. It was spent in Paris in a one room apartment with blue walls on the Rue de Noisiel near the Portuguese embassy with our two grey Siamese cats, called Kochka and Minette, and my old and best friend who had come to visit.

I lay on one bed against one wall trying to read Proust in French, turning the fine pages of my Pleiade volume slowly, while my then-husband lay on his bed on the other side of the room reading a polycopié. He was studying French literature at Yale but doing his junior year abroad , attending Sciences Po. (Or the Institut de Sciences Politiques) and maintained that you didn't have to go to the lectures but could just read the polycopié, a written version of the lectures, which were the same anyway, year after year.

My friend, who I'll call Martha, a girl of German Jewish origin, was left to try and establish some sort of order in the apartment, organizing clothes and food in the one and only cupboard, sweeping up the straw which the cats clawed from the wicker furniture, and watering the azalea plant.

At first I think she tried to go out and leave us alone, but the truth was that when she did we fought. Finally she stayed home and she and my new husband would sit on the carpet and play Honeymoon Bridge for money and drink Champagne splits through the night. I think he mostly won. All three of us drank the splits of Champagne we had been given as a wedding present rather than the water from the tap which was still suspect in those days.

All of this was going on in the background, you understand, while I tried to follow Proust's meandering sentences through the Méseglise and the Guermantes paths of Combray and Swann's misguided but passionate love for Odette. Sometimes I would read in the *sabot* (shaped like a clog) bath. Mostly I confess I would fall asleep. Proust, I'm afraid, who had such trouble sleeping, had a soporific effect on me. Perhaps it was the warm water, or the Champagne I should surely not have been drinking, or because of my pregnancy. The baby would vanish as quickly as it had begun one night in my bed with a great flood of blood and Proust at my side.

Years later I would take up the great books again and read them in English and marvel at the scope of what Edmund White calls the consummate *Bildungsroman*, the apprenticeship novel. I would revel in the humor—I had not at eighteen realized how funny Proust was, the intensity of each moment conveyed with such precision and psychological depth, and yes, of course, the characters with all of our very human foibles and fantasies laid out so clearly for us to contemplate.

*

Many years later I was to meet Edmund White who was then a professor at Columbia University in the Creative Writing department. At that point I was separated from my first husband and in my early forties and had come to America to take up my writing seriously. I was doing an MFA at Columbia when I took Edmund's course. I did not take his Proust course but attended one he taught on Chekhov's wonderful story "In a Woman's Kingdom" where a factory owner, a woman, receives a large sum of money at Christmas and has to decide what to do with it. I will always remember and would later myself teach others what Edmund White taught us about the essential role of the question in a story or novel and how that keeps the reader reading.

Later he and I were to teach at Princeton where I am still teaching today and I have been at repeated moments the recipient of his generous friendship. We have done programs together for several of my books where he has questioned me so adroitly and with such wit, pleasing audiences and spreading the word so kindly and with such consummate erudition and the sort of seductive skill which we find in this biography, *Marcel Proust: A Life*.

White ushers us directly into Proust's world in his biography with a delicious first chapter of gossip: what the world has had to say about Proust: the good and the bad (Colette apparently went so far as to call him a *youpin* or yid). Yet, by the end of this initial chapter, where some of the essential details of Proust's early life have been slipped in almost unnoticed (the mother and the famous kiss, of course). White leaves a lasting impression of Proust as a brave and ultimately honorable man willing to stand up for what he believed, taking the part of Dreyfus (the Jewish captain who was accused of treason) and signing the petition for his retrial which he must have known would displease so many of the aristocratic friends he had fawned over and flattered in a desperate effort to ingratiate himself.

Then, having already seduced us from the start, White plunges us, with the novelist's necessary sense of place, into Proust's larger and nearer world: the bourgeois Paris he knew, rebuilt by Haussmann with its wide boulevards, new Eiffel tower, the new giant department stores, the Impressionists, and his own family's spacious apartment with all its "modern" conveniences and ugly furniture. Here we have Proust satisfyingly situated in time and place. We have all the places of Proust's life that reappear in *Remembrance of Things Past*, Illiers which becomes Combray, for example, and the cathedral so wonderfully described by Proust, St. Jacques which becomes Saint Hilaire. Proust is here placed amongst his childhood friends like Marie who would perhaps be transformed in his great book into Gilberte Swann, Swann's daughter, not to speak of the young delivery men transformed into girls in bloom.

From the start we have White's considerable insight into Proust's contradictory attitude toward his homosexuality which he seems to have condoned for children and with the "lower classes" where it was viewed as a sort of patronage. Inversion is indeed accepted but never named as such. Proust would indeed fight a duel with another homosexual to protect his "honor."

"Don't treat me as a pederast, that wounds me. Morally I'm trying if only out of sense of elegance, to remain pure," Proust writes so movingly.

At the same time White points out the relatively scandal free atmosphere for homosexuals in France (unlike England where Oscar Wilde was tried) where the laws dating back to 1791 had decriminalized sodomy.

White stresses the suffering of so many of these intense though ultimately ephemeral homosexual affairs. We have all of Proust's agony when he should have been enjoying his publishing success over the loss of his lover Agostinelli, for example, and his eventual and dramatic death as an aviator which White conveys with much poignancy.

And we can trust Edmund White, of course, to give us the intimate sexual details of Proust's life: the orgasm which needed to bring together many diverse elements: voyeurism, masturbation, and even perhaps profanation of the most sacred of objects such as the spitting on his mother's portrait during sex, elements that we find in Proust's work.

Perhaps the necessary mystery or camouflage that Proust's attitude toward his sexuality entails, his need to transpose recalled experiences from one sex to another, these strategies of disguise only added to some degree to the great subtlety of his work.

White gives us fascinating information about how Proust became the great writer he was: his early education at the Lycée Condorcet, despite his recurring bouts of illness, and the influence of his professor Darlu. We see Proust as the philosopher novelist, and his essential ideas are clearly expressed: Proust as the novelist who believed that life presents the author with only one book to write: one's own life translated.

White tells us what Proust read and who influenced him: Balzac and Ruskin whom he translated despite his lack of English. We read of what Proust saw and studied, Venice for example, because of Ruskin's book on that subject, and the great cathedrals which reappear in his book. What Proust listened to, his great love for Wagner and particularly Parsifal with its "fullness and explicitness"—the amplitude Proust preferred in literature as well.

We have such interesting, and for those of us who have had a book rejected, encouraging information about the history of Proust's publication of *Remembrance of Things Past*. The book was submitted first to a big commercial publisher, a house that had published Flaubert and Zola and was rudely rejected with the words, "What does all this mean? Where is it leading?" Next Proust tries the house that became Gallimard, offering even to underwrite the expenses just as Charlotte Bronte and her sisters had famously done.

Poor Proust feels obliged to explain his character, Charlus, to the editor, saying he believes he is original and a "virile pederast." Again the book is turned down and here even by Gide—a decision he was to regret all his life, and someone who should surely have been more discerning, though his style was so different from Proust's.

White gives us two wonderfully well-chosen and clear examples of these two writers' differences and states so succinctly. "Whereas Gide suggests, Proust spells everything out".

Apparently Proust was not discouraged by these failures but tried once again with Olendorff who wrote "I can't understand how a gentleman can use thirty pages to describe how he tosses and turns in bed before falling asleep."

It was Grasset who finally accepted the book (with Proust offering to pay). We have all the very satisfying details on the success of the book, the praise which ensues, though like Charlotte Bronte who could not enjoy her instant success because it was followed so closely by the deaths of her nearest and dearest: her brother Branwell and her sisters Emily and Ann, Proust is suffering from the loss of his lover Agostinelli.

This, of course, was followed by the coming of the First World War and the attacks on Paris, all of which with the death of Agostinelli were to change the second book where Albertine becomes the principal character and the theme of female homosexuality is introduced. Proust has the satisfaction of seeing Gallimard now perform a volte face and accept *Within a Budding Grove*, though it was not published until 1919.

Finally Gallimard, with the war over, brings out three of Proust's books, and Proust receives the Goncourt, France's most prestigious prize, though with some controversy, as it was supposed to be awarded to a young author and Proust was forty-eight, apparently considered old at the time. One journalist even wrote "a talent from beyond the tomb."

When in May 1921 *Sodom et Gomorrah* went on sale Proust was almost disappointed by the lack of scandal it produced, White writes.

It was only after Proust's death that the fifth volume of his work was published in 1927 and that the full impact of his work became known. Sadly by then Proust had succumbed to his many ailments. He died in 1922.

All the way through the biography there are moving passages on Proust's illness, written with understanding and empathy for his terrible suffering with asthma. We have detailed descriptions which bring Proust's physical sufferings to life: his dire asthma attacks and later his use and abuse of stimulants and then the use of calming substances such as opium.

All the way through the book, too, White brings the "minor" characters in Proust's existence vividly to life: all his social climbing amongst the aristocracy and attempts at seduction with men like de Bibesco about whom Proust says, "If I followed your example people would take me for an invert." We feel we know intimately many of his lovers, like Reynaldo Hahn the celebrated musician whom he meets in 1894.

We have an intimate portrait of the devoted Celeste, Proust's maid, and her life with him, in his last years, standing half the night by his bed listening to him talk, or making his coffee drip by drip, living in the gloom of the apartment where the curtains were kept drawn, unable even to attend mass on Sunday and told that her services to him brought her closer to God, and finally denying his homosexuality to his biographers after his death.

We find unexpected people in Proust's life: Walter Berry, Edith Wharton's American lover, the Prince de Polignac who was married to the Singer heiress, meeting Proust at midnight at the Ritz.

There are many of the presumed models for Proust's characters in this biography: Robert de Montesquieu (model for Charlus) who demanded and received from Proust excessive praise and recited his own poetry in his grating voice at length; Laure Hayman, who was perhaps the model for Odette the "grande cocotte" beloved by Swann; Gabriel de la Rochefoucauld, the liberal intellectual and Dreyfusard who would be the model for Saint Loup; his handsome secretary Albert Nahmias who typed up his words and probably was one of the models for Albertine, though Proust wrote that there were several, some of which he had probably forgotten. Proust writes, surely with considerable discernment, "a book is a great cemetery in which one can no longer read the names on most of the tombs."

There is the fascinating Agostinelli who drives Proust in his goggles and cap like a male pilgrim or a wimpled nun. He then becomes a sort of secretary whom Proust admires excessively and at the same time realizes that "love, boundless in its egotism means that the beings whom we love are those whose intellectual and moral features are for us the least objectively defined." When he wishes to become an aviator Proust pays for his lessons and just as the Narrator in his book accompanies Albertine to the flying fields around Paris, takes Agostinelli to his flying lessons. When he finally disappears he poignantly registers his name at the flying school as Marcel Swann.

And finally we have Rochat, the favorite waiter from the Ritz who eventually moves in with Proust and paints, who was apparently also a model for Albertine in *The Captive*, the only section where Proust interestingly calls the narrator, Marcel.

White clearly delineates Proust's most important ideas on memory: the important involuntary kind which the writer needs, and the willed act of remembering.

Perhaps though White is at his most brilliant in this book describing the transformation of Proust from a dilettante, who delayed writing his great book, writing only an unpublished novel, *Jean Santeuil*, some essays, and his translations, until he was well into his thirties and his parents were dead, to the great writer he became. It was only when his mother's "little Marcel" was gone that he would stop procrastinating.

He was now able to retire from the society he knew so well with a huge inheritance (that he mismanaged), moving from the large apartment into 102 Boulevard Hausmann where he would famously line his room with cork and take to his bed to write his book behind heavy curtains without light, dust or noise. It was here that he was able to bind together the essays he had in his mind into a book, "a vast panorama of society." It was here that he followed Christ's injunction: "Work while ye have light." It was here that he was able to juxtapose so fruitfully the personal essay and the novel.

White explains this transformation: what Proust had learned so brilliantly: the ability to reiterate his themes, to introduce a character through hearsay before he appears on scene, to develop a character by giving a series of successive and vivid "takes" bringing in the character again and again so that he seems to develop and change. He shows us how Proust was able to find a middle distance, using his own jealous rages and snobbism and also what he has observed so carefully and faithfully from life (sometimes using servants, who of course know all, to give him additional information). White describes how he would write a brief draft and then add and add, pages pasted into the manuscript.

He shows us how the whole of the first section of Proust's book, Combray is really an overture for the later volumes and announces all that is to come, the two paths that seemed so separate at the start of the book, the Méséglise and the Guermantes Way, are brought together like the tributaries of a great river by the end of the last volume, *Time Regained*. White writes: "developing themes and recurring characters spanning the whole long arc of the seven books give it an architectural solidity which the casual reader of the first two volumes could not have suspected."

The theme of what White calls involuntary memory, or what we might call the recall of unconscious material from the past sparked by something in the present, which occurs in Combray with the Madeleine, recurs in *Time Regained* with the two uneven stones in the Guermantes' courtyard which bring back memories of Venice; a spoon chinking recalls the noise of a hammer and a stiff napkin recalls a starched towel used to dry the narrator during a visit to Balbec. Art, Proust concludes, though he had not read Freud, can never be entirely under the control of our intellect or reasoning but comes from the unconscious mind.

White reminds us of Proust's precious ability to construct metaphor, something that even the great Flaubert was not able to do. According to Proust in order to find truth we need to find in two objects, or two common sensations, the same essence.

Certainly here in this brief biography Edmund White has captured what seems to be the truth about Proust, showing him to us with all his foibles and failures but at the same time with his courage, his great dedication to his art, and his sublime knowledge and certainty of the value of what he would leave behind at the end of his sad life.

"At about this time a punk interviewed me on television and asked, 'You are known as a homosexual, a writer and an American. When did you first realize you were an American?' 'When I moved to France,' I said."

—from *Skinned Alive*

THE FLÂNEUR: A STROLL

THROUGH THE PARADOXES

OF PARIS

WILLIAM STERLING WALKER

THE FLÂNEUR, WRITES Edmund White, quoting Walter Benjamin, the literary flâneur with whom he is most simpatico, "is a creation of Paris." Published in 2001 as part of Bloomsbury's "The Writer and the City" series, *The Flâneur: A Stroll through the Paradoxes of Paris* shows that Edmund White was still in that city's thrall three years after he quit his voluntary, fifteen-year exile there. And whether consciously or not, he attempted to "document every corner" of his subject as he describes in words what the documentary photographer, Eugène Atget, sought to create—a "visual record of a vanished Paris." Not quite a memoir, not quite a history, not quite a "sentimental" travelogue—though it contains elements of these forms—*The Flâneur* may be regarded formally as a monograph on what White, again quoting Walter Benjamin, calls the quintessential "Parisian Art Form:" *flânerie*, the art of strolling and sauntering in a sensual embrace of this city. In

six short chapters White alights on a plethora of places and personages, as we follow him glancing from left to right on a wide
boulevard of history, culture and memory. White not only focuses
his attention on the Left Bank habitués who haunted in their
times Les Deux Magots or Café de Flore in the St.-Germain-des-
Prés, Colette, Sartre and de Beauvoir, writing, drinking, smoking,
and gossiping. He also discusses Foucault and the two Jeans—
Cocteau and Genet. Significantly, White devotes considerable attention to the African American expatriates after World War I
who fled oppression in the States, delving into the hope and myth
of freedom in France. In extended sections White covers the stories of Sidney Bechet, Josephine Baker, Ada Louise Smith (also
known as "Bricktop"), and James Baldwin. Then White turns
away from the Second Empire Paris of Baron Haussmann and
wanders into the "teeming quartiers" of the Arabs, Asians, and
North Africans, the "strongholds of multiculturalism," with a
long foray through the Marais, the very heart of Jewish and Gay
Paris. In these chapters White emphatically declares his empathy
in the places and traces left by people on the margin—Jews,
blacks, gays, Arabs—and he succeeds in painting a vista of the
whole city, albeit in broad strokes, much as E. B. White does in
his equally slim volume, *This Is New York*.

His fascination with Paris should not surprise a reader, considering the duration of his exile. In his *New York Diary*, Ned
Rorem quotes John Ashbery, "Once you've been happy in Paris
you can never be happy anywhere else—not even in Paris." White
certainly endorses a subtle variant of the same sentiment when an
alternate of Ashbery's quip appeared as an epigraph to White's
most recent memoir, *Inside a Pearl: My Years in Paris*. "Having lived
in Paris unfits you for living anywhere, including Paris." The
proof, as it were, of the centrality of that city in White's oeuvre,
is in his literary production. To date, White has probably written
more words about Paris and Parisians than he has of any other
city or its citizens, including two memoirs, major sections of two
autobiographical novels, and biographies on Genet and Proust.

Years after I first devoured it, *The Flâneur* still remains one of
my favorite books by White because, for its brevity and simplicity,
it brims with feeling. For one of my first visits to Paris I re-read
The Flâneur, to glean a few morsels of useful information and secret tips. And while I did not carry my annotated copy of *The*

Flâneur around Paris quite like Lucy Honeychurch wandering Florence with her *Baedeker's* in Forester's *A Room With A View*, I had certainly used it as a resource. I had planned to take in two sites discussed by White—the Musée Gustave Moreau and the Musée Nissim de Camondo—museums I might not have seen or tried to see without White's book to pique my interest. But using *The Flâneur* as a travel guide is contrary to the spirit of flânerie. In the book, White warns that Americans, including me, are "particularly ill-suited to be flaneurs," because we are "driven by the urge towards self-improvement," the opposite of the true nature of flânerie. In the end I saw only the silent, intense Musée Nissim de Camondo near the Parc Monceau, for the Moreau was closed at the time for either renovations or because its workers were en grieve (on strike)—but I digress.

In retrospect, I came to an inkling of the true nature of flânerie on another visit to Paris a decade ago. One bitterly cold January day, I wandered the Île St Louis, stopping to browse in Shakespeare & Company, then strolling the Marais with one of my three traveling companions. Bristling under the yoke of a twelve page, single-spaced, hour-by-hour itinerary that two of my traveling companions had zealously devised for us, I had strayed off the plotted course into an arcade on the rue de Rivoli to see a fountain pen shop; my friend—the one who had not devised the strict schedule—was sent to corral me. More than once during that trip, I had been accused of being too enamored of "bright, shiny objects" to follow such a draconian itinerary. My friend, Vance, decided it was best to send them onward without us, and we veered off into a tangle of streets in the Second Arrondissement, sauntering aimlessly until we came into the rue Daunou, and I struggled for a second to recall why the address number five had been stuck in my mind—27 rue de Fleurus being the only other Parisian address I knew by heart. Realizing suddenly, miraculously, that we stood before Harry's Bar at "SANK ROO DOE NOO"—as I had remembered now from once reading a piece in *Esquire* mentioning Ian Fleming's short story "A View to a Kill"—we proceeded to while away the rest of the afternoon guiltlessly drinking too many Manhattans.

If Paris, as White writes, "is a world meant to be seen by the walker alone, for only the pace of strolling can take in all the rich if muted detail," then the ideal audience for *The Flâneur* is probably the armchair traveler who hardly ever goes anywhere geographically, but who has a keen mind and vivid dreams, perhaps someone like the great solitary Manhattan walker, Joseph Cornell. He never went to France. He hardly strayed from the five boroughs of New York City. He traveled exclusively in the mind, but Cornell "longed to build memorials to the feeling of wanting to go to France," wrote Adam Gopnik. A reader like Cornell would have no trouble imagining White on one of his grand perambulations, crisscrossing the city's arrondissements, enjoying their vitality, whether the cruisey hammam in Mosquée de Paris or the Tuileries Gardens. Ironically, though, *The Flâneur* is best experienced by readers in the plush comfort of a recliner and swallowed in a single sitting—the ultimate indulgence. As White writes, "The flâneur is by definition endowed with enormous leisure… [A] close rationing of time is antithetical to the true spirit of the flâneur."

In flâneur fashion, let us wander back to John Ashbery's quip and ask, how is one happy in Paris? White addressed that question in his 1994 BOMB magazine interview with visual artist, Alain Kirili:

> I relax more and I practice the art of the flâneur. I spend hours walking around looking at books and things like that, without worrying about wasting time, which I used to worry about all the time.

That remark contains a whole city's worth of thought. What White leaves unspoken is that he used to worry about wasting time, all the time, in New York, and what he left behind in New York was the city of his young adulthood, of his friends dead and dying of AIDS. White seems to have wished to escape less for the necessary solitude of the writer than for relief from the clatter of America's too many voices. Had we but world enough and time, would we not all live in Paris?

White proceeds from the premise that the most important way to understand flânerie "is to know Paris," not only on a pedestrian level, but to feel it as a completely immersive experience. "Flânerie is the best way to impose a personal vision on the palimpsest of Paris," he writes and indeed flânerie becomes his strategy for living in the moment. Of Charles Baudelaire's *The Painter of Modern Life*, an essay on Constantine Guys, White says that Baudelaire (whom White regards as the "consummate Parisian") "extols the modern artist who immerses himself in the bath of the crowd."

For the perfect flâneur, for the passionate observer, it's an immense pleasure to take up residence in multiplicity, in whatever is seething, moving, evanescent, and infinite: you're not at home, but you feel at home everywhere; you see everyone, you're at the centre of everything yet remain hidden from everybody.

One must have a near erotic susceptibility to the charms and inducements and unique pace of Parisian life, to be alive to its sense impressions. Interestingly, French grammar (as well as the grammar of Romance languages in general) distinguishes the knowledge or acquaintance of a city from the knowledge of a skill by the usage of the verbs connaître, (to be acquainted with, as one would know a person, or archaically, to know one sexually), and savoir (as one would know a skill), respectively. For White this idea is not merely metaphorical. The perceptual difference is hard-wired into the Latin language and temperament, as opposed to Anglo-American attitudes. Lest a reader miss the connection between eros and art, White raises the subject of flânerie and "amorous adventures." Cruising and flânerie, White offers, are co-joined, intertwined. In the first and penultimate chapters, White, as he has more than once in other works, considers cruising as a subject, with a focused discussion on the "amorous adventures" of the Surrealists. White finds common cause with the (mostly heterosexual) Surrealists and believes their biographies are instructive.

As throughout the book, White waxes elegiac, writing in this section, "Some of my happiest moments have been spent making love to a stranger beside dark, swiftly moving water below a glowing city." He continues:

When I arrived in Paris I was a fairly young-looking forty-three and when I left I was nearly sixty, snowy-haired and jowly. In the beginning I'd cruise along the Seine near the Austerlitz train station under a building that was cantilevered out over the shore on pylons. Or I'd hop over the fence and cruise the pocket park at the end of the Île St Louis, where I lived. There I'd either clatter through the bushes or descend the steps to the quay that wrapped around the prow of the island like the lower deck of a sinking ship.

To titillate is not White's sole purpose. The freedom to allow oneself to experience pleasure is for White the essence of what it means to be a flâneur and White offers cruising as the American corollary to flânerie. The essential difference between White and the other great flâneur-writers of the past, from August Strindberg, to Charles Baudelaire, to Honoré de Balzac, to André Breton, is the degree to which each writer balances the tension between being in the city but not of it, between the voyeuristic and the participatory. If Benjamin's model of the flâneur is an archetype of modernity, White adds his version: the middle-aged cruiser, with natural affinity for the street, a connoisseur of its theatricality, even at the risk of unfulfillment. Gay Americans of his generation saw through the prudishness and the work ethos, to cruising as a subverse revolt against standard mores. I am reminded by White's openness to experience of a favorite epigraph to Forster's *Howards End* and its powerful command, "Only connect."

The whole book is about how White interweaves this story, his story, his reading and personal history and how his personal history intersects with gay history. To read *The Flâneur* is to retrace the contours of White's own reading life in the "land of novelty and distraction." Books are coordinates on his mental map. *The Flâneur*'s rambling form becomes meaning—the text itself is flâneurable and this is one of the book's particular joys. The text moves at the ease of a casual conversation and a stroll. It ambles, it flows without middle and ends in a stream of consciousness with great wit. And the book is as much about the lost art of reading as a leisure activity—as attested by White's extensive, if eclectic bibliography, one that displays a singular depth and breadth of his reading. Every landmark White notes in the text calls to mind either a book or a historical figure. A friend once said to me that White has always turned "the lack of a plot into a stylistic virtue," and what comes across in this book is that White is a consummate stylist.

And for me, the narrative's breeziness and brevity, its warm, discursive tone, its confidence and candor, its lightness of touch, all belie a depth of feeling for the subject of flânerie and its concomitant solitude, a feeling all writers understand. For *The Flâ-neur* encapsulates, or rather attempts to recapture his fifteen years in the City of Light, and he means for us to know that certain city's "sadly gay" loveliness (to paraphrase the Douglas Cross lyric of "I Left My Heart in San Francisco"), that flush of nostalgia similar in feeling to watching for the umpteenth time Rick Blaine say to Ilsa Lund at the end of *Casablanca*, "We'll always have Paris."

White's vision captivates and seduces, yet it hints at the sadness and yearning for home that creep into the narratives of most exiles, no matter the reasons behind the decision to embark. Henry James wrote in his biography on the 19th century American expatriate sculptor, William Wetmore Story, "a man always pays, in one way or another, for expatriation," and implicit in wandering is detachment, loneliness and loss. To be at home everywhere is to be at home nowhere.

"They were ghosts who'd come back to haunt their former lives; some higher dispensation allowed them to inhabit this old apartment for just five days, but it, too, was ghostly—shabby without its soft lamps and bohemian throws tossed over the mammoth metal heater that no longer worked. The apartment was dusty and resonant. Given how small the rooms were, the resonance sounded off, as though they were in the antechambers to a mammoth cave. The windows were curtainless, the worn carpet denuded of the two sumptuous silk rugs Austin had brought back from a holiday in Istanbul, the kitchen empty of its dishes and cutlery."

—from *The Married Man*

THE MARRIED MAN

COLM TÓIBÍN

IT IS EASY to misread Edmund White's major novels *A Boy's Own Story* (1982), *The Beautiful Room is Empty* (1988), *The Farewell Symphony* (1998) and *The Married Man* (2000) simply as autobiography thinly disguised as fiction, or indeed merely fiction which uses the facts of the life of the author, and the texture of that life, as the basis of the narrative, and does nothing else. Such a reading ignores the stylistic differences between the four books themselves, and pays no attention to each of them as exercises in pure style, each with its own systems and cadences mirroring differences in the sensibilities that they portray and the worlds they dramatize.

Nonetheless, it is hard not to feel that the further apart the life of Edmund White is kept from the novels he has written the purer and more serious the fiction becomes. This is especially true with what I consider his finest novel, *The Married Man*. In this novel White dramatizes with considerable subtlety the conflict between two ideas, allowing his characters to embody these ideas and remain also filled with unpredictable and sensuously imagined life. The first idea is that the personal is political ("which," White wrote in 2002, "may be America's most salient contribution to the armamentarium of progressive politics"), that proposes before you join a demonstration for human rights you put your own house in order, that honesty and integrity in the domestic sphere are as important as large questions of public morality. This idea became important for gay men in the United States from the early 1970s onwards.

In *The Married Man* Austin Smith arrives in France all the more in possession of this idea because he is almost unaware of it. He meets Julien, a younger man, who is French, who believes, again almost unwittingly, in another idea: that the self is there to be invented, that evasion and deceit are fundamental to survival, and that full honesty in either the public or private sphere would make life impossible.

Both men have their charms, and they enjoy each other; but they come tragically to misunderstand each other, or at least Austin does Julien, as much as any Jamesian hero or heroine a hundred years earlier came to misread elegance for morality, or came to see style and presumed it contained goodness.

The less you know about the author Edmund White the more intense and rich the book *The Married Man* becomes, the more heart-breaking the final episodes, and the more complete the novel seems in its subtle moral shape. It is a work of art rather than another volume of autobiography.

Edmund White is in full possession of a prose style that is deceptive in how it functions. His writing can feel like conversation or someone thinking clearly and honestly or taking you slowly and effortlessly into his confidence. The cadences of his writing are close to the rhythms of speaking, but there is also a mannered tone buried in the phrasing, which moves the diction to a level above the casual and the conversational.

White's style, however, depends on a sort of candor, a strange knowing mixture of innocence and fascination with stripping the secrecy away from the story as it unfolds. As a writer of personal essays and biographies as well as novels, he has, it seems, no interest in hiding the sources of his inspiration or shrouding himself or anyone else in mystery. Since he was brought up in a time when many gay men kept their sexuality a secret, secrecy has little allure for him. He likes revelation, and the pleasure he takes in it adds great energy to the narratives he creates both in biography and in fiction. As a good mid-western American, he believes in plain, personal honesty; as a writer steeped in French life and literature he also loves intrigue, gossip, the spilling of well cooked and richly spiced beans.

It is possible to read *The Married Man* as a re-imagining a hundred years later of Henry James's *The Ambassadors*. In James's novel Lambert Strether comes to Paris in middle age with a clear task, which is to return the young Chad Newsome, who has been idling in Paris, to his mother in America. Slowly, Strether himself begins to idle in the city, allowing its beauty and allure to distract him from being single-minded. Slowly, too, he begins to spend time with Chad and his friends, attending a party in Chad's apartment and entering into the elegant and easy-mannered social life that Chad has created for himself in the city.

The Ambassadors is a paean to Paris itself, its street life, its social life, its architecture, its manners. Strether's first walk in the streets of Paris, his first taking in of the city's sensations, make clear that he is an American open to allure in the same way as Austin Smith in *The Married Man* is beguiled by the view from the windows of his apartment on the Île Saint-Louis. Smith could "lie in bed and look at the church's slate-covered roof, pitched sharply, and a huge volute of stone almost ten feet in circumference that had been carved to resemble a spiral closing in on itself and slightly squashed at the top."

Both Strether and Smith operate in a world of *belles lettres*, Strether as the editor of a review and Smith as a writer about 18th century French furniture, among other matters. This means they can be free to travel and move, to take their time, not to need, as other men do, to go to work each day and stay at work until day wanes. They are both, for the purpose of the novels, men of leisure. Neither is rich, but neither is especially preoccupied by money. Both are middle-aged, and in *The Ambassadors* and *The Married Man*, both become interested in people younger than themselves who seem to possess an energy, a vitality and an innocence which fascinates both men.

In Chapters Three and Four of *The Married Man*, we see Austin Smith's social world. Smith at this point is forty-nine. "Austin had invited six friends who were in their early thirties…The men were gay and the women straight and everyone loved to drink and joke and exchange stories and have a good time till one in the morning." In the next chapter he will attend the salon of the rich socialite Henry McVay and gossip familiarly with his host. Early in *The Ambassadors*, we see the social world of Chad Newsome in which Strether has been included, including a relaxed and elegant social event at Chad's own apartment and also a party at the studio of the famous sculptor Gloriani.

Strether and Smith are both men alone, socially secure enough to be included in many conversations, socially uneasy enough to notice everything, their noticing offering a richness to the texture of both novels.

"You could deal," Strether thought when he first saw Chad in Paris, "with a man as himself—you couldn't deal with him as somebody else." Both Strether and Smith see the world as it presents itself to them; they like what they see, and this pleasure taken in Paris and its denizens gives them both a sort of fictional density and complexity. It also allows them both, or induces them, to believe what they hear. Enjoying Paris has made them both even more innocent than they might be in America. Thus when Little Bilham, who is a friend of Chad's, tells Strether that Chad's relationship with the Vionnet mother and daughter is "a virtuous attachment," he takes him at his word. So, too, when Austin Smith meets a young Frenchman in a gym, he is inclined also to believe what the young man says.

"He was moving verily in a strange air and on ground not of the firmest," James wrote of Strether. What Strether was seeking was experience, the tender taste of life. In not seeking wisdom, he found knowledge instead, and he had no idea what to do with knowledge. He was ready to notice things, and wanted to notice more. As he moved slowly away from the rigidities of his background, he discovered, as did Isabel Archer in *The Portrait of a Lady*, that his only weapon was innocence, an innocence which became more exquisite as the novel proceeded, an innocence which was no use to him in this old world into which he had ventured.

When Austin asks Julien, the young man he had met at the gym, a number of basic questions, he finds Julien slippery and evasive. Like Strether, Austin's only weapon is his innocence, but his innocence puts him at a loss. "Austin felt he was out of his depth, facing an older culture than his own, one much harder to sum up. His own assumptions struck him as shoddy. He was sorry he'd revealed his West Village smugness; he had belonged to a

New York gay world for twenty years and it had left him with too
many ready answers."

As Julien becomes Austin's lover, he is all ambiguity, all
French sophistication. Simple questions do not interest him. The
story of his life that he tells is one of pain and loss and cruelty,
thus making Austin all the more certain that what he is in need of
now is simple comfort, ease, trust. Since he, as a younger man, is
an object of intense desire for Austin who believes that this may
be his last chance for love, then the question of full disclosure of
Austin's HIV status is pressing for Austin. He discusses this with
a French friend: "'I don't dare seduce him before explaining to
him about being seropositive. Or what would you say?' He was
half- hoping for some superior French worldliness that would get
him off the moral hook."

Just as in *The Ambassadors*, signs are given in *The Married Man*
that what the protagonist is facing is not old-world sophistication
but old-fashioned duplicity. Strether and Smith fail to see clearly
because they are dazzled by youth and by beauty, and they are in
a foreign country, but also because they are being most cleverly
and beguilingly deceived. Edmund White manages in the most
subtle way to make the most personal book into the most political
as post-Stonewall candor comes face to face with post-Vichy ambiguity, with what he calls Julien's "dandified distance from all
moral questions."

As Austin makes himself easy to read, Julien adds mask after
mask. It would be easy for Edmund White to make Julien's un-
masking into a large morality scene, and it is a credit to his artistry
that he slowly allows us instead to see Julien as fearful and desperate as much as mendacious and manipulative.

As *The Married Man* moves to America, it takes its bearings
once more from Henry James, but this time from the tone of condescension and barely-managed contempt which emerges in
some of the pages of James's book *The American Scene* (1907). For
example, James, who had become a connoisseur of European
beauty, disliked the new mansions perched overlooking the ocean
at Newport, Rhode Island: "They look queer and conscious and
lumpish—some of them, as with the air of the brandished pro-
boscis, really grotesque—while their averted owners, roused from
a witless dream, wonder what in the world is to be done with
them. The answer to which, I think, can only be that there is

nothing to be done, nothing but to let them stand there always, vast and blank, for reminder to those concerned of the prohibited degree of witlessness, and of the peculiarly awkward vengeances of affronted proportion and discretion."

Austin Smith, also returned after his own years in Europe, is equally affronted by Providence, Rhode Island. "Here he was in this cold, empty city with its boxy houses, their windows glowing dimly at night, this city with its abandoned, windswept downtown with the dark dangerous woods across the street... The house with its smell of mildew, its plastic poppies, its framed Polish lace... It was an outpost of an alien culture."

Alongside this dramatization of trans-Atlantic distinctions, delights and disapprovals, *The Married Man* begins to chart the slow physical disintegration of Julien from AIDS. Edmund White has managed with care to make us see and feel how much Julien fascinates Austin, and make us believe also that, despite moments of pure exasperation, Julien is the love of Austin's life. Now, in the shadow of death, Julien will try, with Austin's help, to live all he can, as Strether advises Little Bilham to do in *The Ambassadors*, as Peter, Austin's friend, who is dying, says in Key West: "Oh Austin, I'm determined to live as much as I can."

Thus the novel turns from being the story of a middle-aged man finding young love and trying to live up to it to the story of a young man, who knows he is doomed, setting out to find a protector who will look after him as he declines. Austin has been fooled. Once again, it is an aspect of Edmund White's subtlety that he does not make this discovery into a long night of the soul for Austin. He makes it merely another layer in a story of many layers, many motives and nuances and moments of truth and untruth.

By making Austin Smith a stranger in France and then, even more, a stranger in America, Edmund White can isolate and then intensify Austin's consciousness and his ways of noticing and thinking. Late in the book, Austin meets Rod, a fellow Europeanized American, at a reading in Paris and finds that they can laugh at the same jokes. Part of the drama of the love story at the core of the book is that although Austin and Julien are men and their sexuality makes them similar, their nationalities makes them totally different from each other. If Austin in this novel is a married man, then the marriage is to someone of the opposite nationality. They will never laugh at the same jokes.

In *The Ambassadors*, the recognition scene comes towards the end of book. Strether, still in search of sensation, travels out of Paris by train at random to sample the French countryside where, in an out-of-the-way place, he sees Chad and Madame de Vionnet and realizes the unmistakable relation between them. James manages to conjure up the scene in all its affecting and electrifying detail, as he did in a scene in *The Portrait of a Lady* when Isabel enters the room and finds Madame Merle standing close to the fire and Osmond, Isabel's husband, seated. "Their relative positions, their absorbed mutual gaze, struck her as something detected." So, too, in this scene in *The Ambassadors*, Strether's ability finally to see clearly becomes a way for his innocence to be darkened.

In *The Married Man* Edmund White is not interested in following the emotional structure of *The Ambassadors* to the letter, or doing a modern version of it scene by scene. He uses its contours and textures when he needs them, but he has his own novel to write. *The Married Man* is not a literary exercise. White charts the slow decline of Julien with both sympathy and care so that the novel becomes a drama about Julien's body itself and its defenses, or lack of them, rather than his moral sensibility, or indeed his soul. Julien is flawed in many ways, but these flaws serve to nourish the novel. Julien is also suffering from a cruel and slow disease and his bravery in the face of suffering, his will to live all he can, allow him or soar above mere moral questions, or at least evade them or exhaust them.

The other question then, the issue of his deceptions, is finally rendered almost as comedy. After Julien's death, Austin discovers that his lover's mother did not have a career as a concert pianist, but as an accordionist. "Austin realized that everything Julien had said about his family had been compounded of lies. His parents had not been aristocrats but a beautician and a shipping clerk, just as his maternal grandparents had been a railway man and a farm worker." He learns too that Julien had had many male lovers before him and that his bisexuality was an alibi, a myth.

It is an aspect of the genius of the novel that neither the reader nor Austin judges Julien harshly now. It is not as though Edmund White has waited until the end of the book to give us all a lesson in morality and make us re-think the book in the clear light of the difference between truth and lies. Instead, he allows Austin to miss Julien; he writes tenderly about grief in all its strangeness, all its unexpectedness: "Austin felt that an enormous thing had happened to him, Julien's death, and he wanted to share it with the most important person in his life: Julien. His frustration about Julien's silence made him talk out loud to him."

At the very end of the book, when all the facts have been made clear, Austin goes back to America, to Key West to see his friend Peter, who is now seriously ill, for the last time. In these scenes, Edmund White evokes, with tenderness too, moments of sweet loyalty and friendship and deep regret. He gives Austin Smith back his innocence, without undermining the sharpness of the experience he has lived through with his French lover in the pages of *The Married Man*.

"When I hold these essays in my hand I can feel the heat rising off them—the intense, baked terra-cotta heat of longing and desire, or the headachy, sobbing heat of grief writhing on the mattress, pounding it like a defeated wrestler."

—from *Loss Within Loss: Artists in the Age of Aids*

LOSS WITHIN LOSS: ARTISTS IN
THE AGE OF AIDS

PHILIP CLARK

I

EDMUND WHITE IS an appropriate editor for *Loss within Loss: Artists in the Age of AIDS*. From his introduction, it's unclear how much he did to shape his contributors' essays, but he has obviously done a great deal of thinking about what it means to be an artist, a gay artist, an artist with AIDS. AIDS is also the subject, spoken or unspoken, of much of White's fiction beginning with *The Darker Proof*. It is the subject that infuses so much of his later fiction with life and humanity.

II

THESE ESSAYS ARE also full of life and humanity. They don't always match the theories about AIDS and art that White himself has espoused, frequently contradicting his famous and oft-repeated line that such art "must begin in tact, avoid humor, and

end in anger." This line had already been critiqued by David Fein-
berg (who Sarah Schulman discusses in her essay in *Loss within
Loss*) in his 1992 OutWrite talk "AIDS and Humor," and the writers here continue to contradict it. William Berger's writing about
the composer Chris DeBlasio brims with laugh-out-loud one-lin-
ers. Ramsey McPhillips's ferocious essay about Mark Morrisroe,
the photographer who was his friend and lover, recounts in detail
the incident wherein a dying Morrisroe literally and intentionally
shit on his homophobic landlord. Is this humor, is this tactless-
ness, an appropriate way to address AIDS? Whatever works. And
perhaps best of them all, these essays work.

III

BESIDES, HOW ELSE should we write about these artists if not
with utter clarity? In the current age of AIDS as the much touted
"chronic manageable disease," where most people with HIV in
America quietly take their protease inhibitors and avoid the visible
markers of wasting and destruction, we are removed from AIDS-
as-crisis. I was born in 1980, just prior to the time AIDS first became known. How close can anyone my age or younger, anyone
who did not directly experience the waves of dying, get to understanding the magnitude of these losses? How close can we ever
expect to come except through complete honesty, in whatever
form, about these deaths? About these lives?

IV

What These Essays must do, then, is bridge a gap between audience and artist. A purist might say this gap is only crossed by
viewing the artists' work. If so, what do we do about Joah Lowe
when, as a dancer, only a few still photographs from his performances seem to remain? Or Robert Anton, the "fearsome
magician" of a puppeteer who Benjamin Taylor remembers in the
book's shortest and perhaps loveliest essay? Who will know, looking at Central Park's Strawberry Fields, that it was designed by
Bruce Kelly, another gay man who died too young? Marc Lida's
watercolors are mostly hidden in private collections. John C.

Russell's plays are rarely performed. As Taylor writes, "Once in a while…I do still meet someone who actually saw a performance of [Anton's]. It happens less and less, of course, and at some un-specifiable but roughly calculable point in time the next-to-last and last of us who saw the thing will disappear." How fleeting art can be—as fleeting as life—especially when the artist no longer lives to perform and to promote. These essays are often our scant inheritance, the most accessible remaining memory.

V

OVERT GRIEF HAS little place here; to compare this book with the poetry of AIDS, its essays are closer to the graceful, controlled verses of Thom Gunn in *The Man with Night Sweats* than to the emotional outpouring of Paul Monette's *Love Alone* (mentioned in passing in J.D. McClatchy's piece in *Loss*, "Two Deaths, Two Lives"). But they are rife with guilt, the guilt of those who survive. The most direct example is Alexander Chee's meditation on Peter D. Kelloran, an activist, musician, and poster artist. Chee captures the attitude of hero-worship he had for Kelloran, the kind of ad-miration and longing that very young artists can have for the glamour and talent of those just slightly older. And he captures what we miss from the artist taken too soon, not only "the paint-ings undone, the books unwritten," but "the imagination itself, the far richer treasure, lost." He is the one writer to ask directly, "Why should I survive on the earth where he didn't?" Unanswer-able, except as an epidemiological accident, but indicative of the despair that lurks beneath all this elegant prose.

VI

WHILE MORE THAN twenty individual artists are remembered at some length in *Loss within Loss*, the book is in no way only about the loss of the individual. In his introduction, White laments "a vanished sense of artistic vocation," which he pinpoints as disap-pearing at the same time that AIDS claimed so many artists' lives. "This world," he writes, "died out with AIDS. In the late eighties magazines liked to publish full spreads of photos picturing all the talent wiped out by the disease, but what these photos didn't suggest was that a way of life had been destroyed. The experimentalism, the erotic sophistication, the prejudice against materialism, the elusive humor, the ambition to measure up to international and timeless standards, above all, the belief that art should be serious and difficult—all this rich, ambiguous mixture of values and ideas evaporated."

VII

PART OF THE loss White identifies concentrates in the idea of bohemia and the concomitant role of the gay artist as rebel. As White argues, "the one social milieu that was open to the homosexual in the period before Stonewall was the bohemian—and this acceptance defined much of subsequent gay artistic history." To reject the gray flannel suit and be an artist in this era was largely to be poor and to stand outside society's mainstream. Gay men did not find it as difficult to enter a world where most were already marginalized.

VIII

BOHEMIA, THOUGH, THRIVES mostly in the urban. The vast majority of the artists of *Loss* led creative lives in New York City or San Francisco; others represent Los Angeles, Boston, and London. Those not born in urban centers found it necessary to journey to them and the haven they offered. (This rural-to-urban shift is such an archetypal pattern in gay lives, and in the literature reflecting them, that there should really be a term created for it.) As a key thread or a quiet backdrop—whether it is Joe Brainard leaving Tulsa, or Scott Burton leaving Alabama, or Bruce Kelly leaving Georgia, or...—the idea of escaping to the city to more fully pursue art permeates the anthology.

IX

IT WAS THESE cities that bred the circumstances artists needed to create: the safety of anonymity, and access to cheap rent, other artists, and endless stimulation. How incredibly connected artists could be in the city, absorbing each other's work; White—a New Yorker before decamping for Paris in 1983, as AIDS descended—lists his connection as acquaintance, friend, or lover to eleven of the artists whose lives are chronicled in *Loss*. He eulogizes the major pre-AIDS cities as home to "a time of interlocking love affairs and friendships, of a slowly emerging sexual identity, a time when gay bookshops were thriving community centers (instead of declining and disappearing porn dispensers as they are at the dawn of the 21st century). It was a time when intellect and accomplishment were *almost* as prized as physical beauty, when certain hot writers, painters, and filmmakers would cause a stir when they entered a bar or gay restaurant, when gay writers didn't yet teach on remote campuses (no university wanted them), when they lived in Manhattan where they supported themselves as advertising copywriters, as gallery employees, as magazine and book editors (even editors of porn magazines), as fashion models or actors—or with welfare and unemployment benefits they'd somehow scammed."

X

OFTEN, IN THEIR nostalgic evocations, eulogies elide thornier details—in this case, the exact ways that AIDS destroyed the city as a safe harbor for artists. Perhaps the issues have simply been thrown into higher relief in the decade-plus since *Loss*'s release. In her recent book *The Gentrification of the Mind: Witness to a Lost Imagination*, Sarah Schulman identifies AIDS as a factor in the destruction of the very neighborhoods White refers to. There, the death of gay men (and others) from AIDS led frequently to the loss of rent control; as Schulman characterizes it, "many of the gay men who died of AIDS in my neighborhood [the East Village] were either from the neighborhood originally, and/or were risk-taking individuals living in oppositional subcultures, creating new ideas about sexuality, art, and social justice. They often paid a high

financial price for being out of the closet and community ori-
ented, and for pioneering new art ideas…the apartments they left
were often at pregentrification rates, and were then subjected to
dramatic increases or privatized." To paraphrase Virginia Woolf,
it now requires a lot of money to have a room of one's own, if
that room is to be in the cities which bred the artistic world White
praises.

XI

A NOTE OF disenchantment colors the introduction, as when
White says "for the generation of gay artists of the seventies and
early eighties, the old bohemian ideal was still going strong, a spirit
that seems to have vanished from the world for good now. As
[Brad] Gooch points out [in his essay about Howard Brookner],
someone of his generation would have felt bad if he hadn't recognized the music of Busoni; today, a sophisticate rejects a
boyfriend for not having seen all of the episodes of *Rhoda*." Is it
fair, though, to criticize current gay artists in the way that White
does? He notes "the younger gay artists of the seventies and eighties had their elder statesmen"—without ever making explicit that
contemporary gay artists' elder statesmen were so often those
who perished. Less centralized than in the past, missing many of
the artistic teachers who could have guided them to a world with
deeper allusions than the latest TV shows, new gay artists have to
make a special effort to engage with the previous bohemian spirit
and learn from those older artists who survived AIDS. And we
do: creating art for little or no monetary gain, connecting to those
artists and writers who survived the deepest years of AIDS, and
learning from the work of those who did not.

XII

MUCH HAS CHANGED since 2001, when *Loss within Loss* was
published. The Internet allows for artists to discover each other
even when they don't live in the same cities. Some artists who
have died are now represented online. There has also been a surge
of interest in the effect of AIDS on artistic and social

communities, with a concurrent rediscovery of the work of at least some artists whose lives and careers were ended by the disease. Among only those mentioned in *Loss*, James Merrill, Joe Brainard, and Tim Dlugos's collected writings have been published or republished. Brad Gooch expanded on his relationship with Howard Brookner in his memoir *Smash Cut* about the 1970s and 1980s art scene. A full-scale biography of David Wojnarowicz, along with the scandal and subsequent protests surrounding his video *A Fire in My Belly* being censored from the National Portrait Gallery's *Hide/Seek* exhibit of gay portraiture, revived his notoriety; the Whitney Museum launched a full-scale retrospective in the summer of 2018. Mark Morrisroe's photographs are now widely available online and in an expansive catalogue raisonné. Organizations like VisualAIDS and the Estate Project for Artists with AIDS (which co-sponsored the publication of *Loss within Loss*) help promote the work of HIV-positive artists, both living and dead. David Groff and I published an anthology of poetry by writers who died from AIDS, *Persistent Voices*, and in 2016 I finished the late Reginald Shepherd's work editing the poems of Donald Britton, *In the Empire of the Air*. Additionally, documentaries like *We Were Here*, *United in Anger*, and the Oscar-nominated *How to Survive a Plague* (with its subsequent book) have refocused attention on what the world lost because of AIDS. But while these are just a few of the recent efforts to detail and memorialize the lives and work of those artists and writers claimed by AIDS, the picture is still sketchy, fragmentary. White's call for "a lively, detailed, multifaceted social history" of the gay arts scene in the 1970s and 1980s has, disappointingly, thus far gone unmet.

XIII

"AS I READ straight through the essays in this book as a totality and not in a piecemeal fashion, I am moved by the feeling and intelligence and the seriousness about bearing witness to those who have died. To my mind, at least, this is a tribute both to a vanished sense of artistic vocation and to the enduring and transforming beauty of friendship" —Edmund White.

Except in our memories and the work they left behind, these artists have, tragically, vanished. The sense of artistic vocation they cultivated has not. May both the beauty of the friendships chronicled within *Loss within Loss,* and the deep desire of artists to create and connect, long continue.

"Sexual passion is the strongest and noblest of human sentiments and the source of the best joys of our existence."

—from *Fanny: A Fiction*

FANNY: A FICTION

DAVID BERGMAN

FANNY IS A funny book, both peculiar and comic. I was surprised when it came out that so few of the reviewers understood that it was fundamentally a comic novel. Laura Miller in *Salon* claimed that it "does many things usually considered unforgivable in a historical novel. It indulges in anachronism, it subjects the past to the derision of the present." Another critic, who liked the book very much, took the whole thing seriously. "*Fanny* is wonderful historical fiction—intelligent and lively, moving and skillfully told," he said, omitting the one thing that seems obvious to me—that it is enormously funny as it deals with two very strange women—Frances Wright and Frances Trollope, both forgotten figures of the 19th century.

Edmund White says that he had been attracted to Fanny Wright for some time before writing the novel. And it is simple to understand his attraction. Born in Scotland into a very wealthy family with radical ideas, Fanny Wright and her sister were orphaned when Fanny was three-years-old and raised by a stuffy aunt. At sixteen (when she came of age) Fanny packed up her sister and herself and moved in with her philosopher uncle, who encouraged her to act on her own. She published her first book at 18. After a two-year-long visit to the United States, she wrote her most important work *Society and Manners in America* (1821), which was translated into several languages and published across the globe. As White puts it (in the voice of Fanny Trollope), "In 1829 she had been the most controversial and notorious woman in the country. . . She was the first woman in America to speak against slavery, the first woman ever to address a mixed [sex] audience, a notorious atheist, the first leader of the first labor party, the most radical journalist in the land." Then she fell out of sight, appearing only in the footnotes of pedants.

White's problem was how to address Fanny Wright. He wanted to write a novel, not another biography. And the fact is that Fanny Wright, although a fascinating figure, was an austere and abstract person, distant and humorless, not at all the kind of individual who would narrate her own story. The book waited on the backburner until White became interested in his other Fanny—Fanny Trollope.

If Fanny Trollope is remembered today, it is for two accomplishments. First, she gave birth to Anthony Trollope, one of the greatest novelists we have in English, but whom she pretty much ignored as a child. Second, she wrote *Domestic Manners of the Americans (1832),* a famous attack on America, written in a sarcastic, nobody's-fool tone that today is slightly campy. Indeed, as channeled by Edmund White, Fanny Trollope sounds like Charles Busch doing Eve Arden—practical, cynical, and yet ultimately romantic. Not without a certain self-awareness, she tells the reader, "I have never mastered the art of silence, I confess, nor of delicacy and beauty, but people do tell me I am vivacious."

White's Fanny Trollope is just a step away from a drag queen. Yet she claims our sympathy because, as in real life, White's Fanny Trollope is misunderstood. Not a great writer, she nevertheless wrote one of the first (if not the first) anti-slavery novel, one which influenced Harriet Beecher Stowe. She also wrote the first industrial novel and influenced Charles Dickens. Her nearly one hundred books of fiction and non-fiction indicate a strong social consciousness. Moreover she started writing only because her hapless but well-born husband sank them into crushing debt. Her writing saved them, and she turned her books out like so many meat pies in *Sweeney Todd.* Fanny Trollope was garrulous, hardworking and sure of her opinions. Robert Browning described her as "vulgar and pushing," an opinion shared by many. To tell the story of a high-minded and discreet Fanny Wright, White needed a narrator neither shy about telling all she knows, nor reluctant to speculate when she doesn't have a clue.

Bringing these two Fannys together provided White with both the means and the subject of a book. It allowed White to play with any number of post-modern techniques. The book we are presented purports to be Fanny Trollope's biography of her friend Fanny Wright. And it is supposed to be Trollope's very last book, written when her mind was going and when she was far away from the materials she had collected for the biography. In point of fact, after the first few chapters the book is more an autobiography, focusing on Fanny Wright's life only from time to time. White gives us the perfect unreliable narrator. But that's not enough. Trollope supposedly never had time to finish the book so the manuscript contains her notes to herself about editing a final draft. Her daughter-in-law, herself a writer, Theodosia Trollope, is reading the book over her mother-in-law's shoulder and makes various suggestions to correct her improprieties. (Theodosia regards *hatch* as in *hatch an egg* to be sexually explicit.) Finally there is an editor only too delighted to show his superiority. When Trollope opines that there will be no Civil War because "most Americans love money and money alone and a war would strike them as unprofitable," the editor cannot resist chiming in *"Here, of course, Mrs. Trollope was wrong on every count"* because they did go to war *"and it was ultimately profitable for the North"* (White's italics, 172). From the very beginning we are warned that the book will be a botched job, but Trollope must keep writing until the end. No thought must go unpublished. Writing had become as essential to her as breathing.

Although these two Fannys are very different—one rich, one poor; one high-minded, one gossipy; one idealistic, the other practical—they complement each other. They are two cheeks of the same fanny. White has Fanny Trollope say of Fanny Wright, "She needed me to be conservative that she might be the revolutionary," and this conflict between conservative and revolutionary plays out in White's other works. At the end of *States of Desire*, Edmund White tells us that "The most maddening fault that runs through these pages... is a peculiar alternation between socialism and snobbism." In *Fanny*, James Fenimore Cooper makes a cameo appearance, as a man for whom "democracy was a sacred mission, but even as he was energetically defending democracy, a more private, snobbish part of him, narrow but deep, was quite illogically insinuating that there was an American 'aristocracy,' refined, conservative, spiritual, to which he belonged." White also has his two Fannys comically enact this division. Fanny Wright represents the socialist element, and Fanny Trollope the snobbism. Yet that division is not so clear. As Fanny Trollope notes several times, Fanny Wright has a particular yen for famous men—Lafayette, with whom she toured America, and Thomas Jefferson, whom she met with Lafayette. As Trollope puts it, "Though [Wright] was among the first defenders of female rights she'd become so not in hoping to overthrow male authority. No, she wanted to be the co-ruler, the sharing monarch of a double throne." And Trollope, although she thinks "civilization, after all, amounts to nothing more than sufficient quantity of clutter" shows a spunkiness that is revolutionary. She was willing to participate in at least one utopian community, she wrote against slavery and child labor, and White gives her something that would challenge even Wright's radicalism—a black lover.

White did not invent the connection between Trollope and Wright. In real life they knew each other. Fanny Wright entered Fanny Trollope's life at a crucial moment—Trollope's near bankruptcy. Observing the Trollopes' diminished opportunities, Fanny Wright invited them to come to America and join her utopian community, Nashoba, where slaves could work toward their freedom and on the way acquire the intellectual and practical skills of making it on their own. It was a sort of grand work/study program, which failed in three years, because it was badly managed, poorly funded, situated in bug-infested, infertile land, and finally because Wright—believing that blacks should not live in the United States—told her slaves that once they earned their freedom, she would take them to Haiti, a place they had never heard of, whose language they did not speak, a fearful unknown they were reluctant to work for.

When the Trollopes arrived they found the cabins roofless, the communal kitchen periodically bursting into flame, and the atmosphere malarial. They almost immediately made plans to leave for Cincinnati, which they understood as the fastest growing city in the west. (It is also Edmund White's hometown. and Fanny Trollope's comments on the boredom, tight-fistedness, and insensitivity of Cincinnati may be as much a comment about the city in 1950s as it was in the 1820s.)

Fanny is a book about freedom and entrapment, that freedom can be a sort of entrapment. Fanny Wright is entrapped in her ideas, which she can never bring into concrete fruition. Fanny Trollope is entrapped by her concrete social and sexual condition as the poor wife of a foolish and hypochondriac husband, who can rarely rise from bed. America looks like a land of freedom and opportunity, but it turns out to be a trap for both of them. For Wright, it is a land that cannot live up to its founding ideals of equality and brotherhood, rationality and tolerance. For Trollope it fails to be a land of opportunity, for despite her heroic efforts, she leaves the States even poorer than when she entered. People are too ignorant, conventional, and cheap to pay for the magic she offers.

Fanny Trollope comes to the United States with her daughters, her son Henry and with Auguste Hervieu, a French painter exiled from his homeland for being part of an assassination plot against the Emperor. One of the ongoing jokes in *Fanny* is Trollope's inability to recognize that Hervieu and her son Henry are lovers. (This is all White's invention; there is no historical evidence to suggest that either was homosexual.) In fact, Fanny Trollope in her day suffered from rumors that she was having an affair with Hervieu. She is quite adamant in denying any amorous connection with the Frenchman:

> Auguste never once touched me in an ambiguous way. Certainly, he was attracted to me, but all this fascination was channeled into a chaste affection for my son Henry. Many a night Auguste would find himself too weary or *gris* after a long evening *chez nous* to make his way back to London and he'd stay with us in Harrow, sleeping with my son, and when I'd find them all tangled up together in the morning, Auguste's hairless white arm flung across Henry's hairless white chest, I could see in this filial embrace an emblem of a love for me that Auguste knew he could never live out."

After this passage, Trollope writes a note to herself "[Delete 'hairless'?]" She wonders whether making references to body hair is indiscreet, but she finds nothing improper in finding her son repeatedly in the embrace of another man. When Henry,

accompanied by his parents, goes off to Paris in an ill-fated attempt to become a banker, the good-byes are painful:

> August was distraught and clung tearfully to Henry, shaking him spas-
> modically. But Henry wouldn't relent and embrace Auguste. I knew
> secretly in my heart that Auguste was afraid to be separated from me
> and could not show it especially in front of my husband... I witnessed
> him sorrowfully as he kissed Henry's sturdy little chest in a wet Gallic
> pool of self-pity.

On Henry's return when he takes up ballet, she watches sym-
pathetically as August "very kindly" massaged "the strained
muscles in Henry's legs, working on the damage the boy had done
himself through overexertion." But if Trollope is blind to her
son's relationship to Hervieu (at least as White has invented it),
she is rather observant of sex in general and does not fail to note
that Jefferson is accompanied by "two brown young men who
were quite obviously his sons."

This running joke about Hervieu and Henry would get tiresome if it did not change register as the book goes on. White
expertly modulates the tone of these passages. For example, to
raise money—Frances Trollope is always down to her last
penny—she proposes to help out the suffering Western Museum
in Cincinnati by staging the "Invisible Girl," an act in which
Henry would "don a toga and veil" and utter a "mystifying mac-
aroni-language made of Latin, French, German and Italian." His
mother "padded him copiously [so] he'd have just the right ma-
tronly look for his contralto." She is delighted by Henry's
excitement over the idea. When she and Hervieu visit Henry in
New Harmony, the utopian community established by Robert
Owen, she curiously comments, "Auguste and Henry agreed to
share a room next to [mine] but we didn't hear a thing, not a
thing." What sort of thing was she expecting to hear? Why is not
hearing it so pleasing to her? In such ways, White suggests both
Trollope's awareness and her unwillingness to bring to consciousness her son's homosexuality. But slowly Trollope starts to
understand the criticism of the way the two behave. She agrees,
for example, that Auguste "did touch Henry too often by an Eng-
lishman's light," but such signs of affection, she argues, are
acceptable when one remembers that Auguste was an artist and
French to boot. But the tone rapidly changes when Fanny

Trollope confides to Fanny Wright that she is concerned about Henry's future, and Wright rather tactlessly responds, "Thank heavens he has Monsieur Hervieu as his lover." To which Trollope can only laugh "at her odd words." Dying, Henry takes up geology and is followed in his research by Hervieu, who drew every site they visited "though [Trollope] sometimes felt he spent more time studying the feeble Henry than the castle or the fortified town." What begins as a joke has now become a mother's way to protect the memory of her dying son from herself. When Henry finally dies, Hervieu throws himself into the grave. Trollope responds to it by telling herself that although "we English might learn the French language and even live in France... we could never permit ourselves these histrionic displays. They would always remain foreign to us." This is a remarkable passage. Even through the end, Trollope, like so many mothers of gay children, will not consciously allow herself to acknowledge the obvious. Her blindness is sacrosanct. Yet by calling Hervieu's behavior "foreign" and unknowable, she is allowing for something more than she is willing to recognize. The gesture is at once wonderfully comic and utterly tragic. Here is the one sustained love affair in her midst, and she forces herself to miss it. But White also seems to be playing with that old piece of gay slang in which *French love* meant *oral sex*, Mrs. Trollope.

White invented this love affair between Auguste Hervieu and Henry Trollope; it is hardly his only invention. More important for the novel as a whole, because the climax of this rather baggy picaresque novel, is Fanny's love affair with Jupiter Higgins, the black blacksmith who works next door to her in Cincinnati.

White builds up to this slowly. Although Mrs. Trollope candidly admits that "Rather quickly [she] had become used to the attendance of slaves," she was always bothered by "a nagging doubt about the propriety of slavery." These doubts soon get intertwined with her erotic feelings for black men, particularly when they are semi-nude. When she arrives in New Orleans, her first stop in America, she is held spellbound by:

> Black navvies, stripped to the waist, [who] were lowering the cargo into the hatches; even though the weather was mild they were perspiring profusely and crooning, 'De las' sack! De las' sack!'
>
> It was almost a song, certainly chanted in chorus. I thought they were lovely, though of course they were savages. And the white

Americans would have been horrified by my admiration, since for them, the blacks weren't even human.

In fact, Trollope's erotic interest in black men stands in contrast to Fanny Wright's disinterest in them as people (rather than as objects of social concern). Wright treats her slaves as servants; Trollope sees them as humans of admirable beauty. Trollope knows that not only must she keep her responses secret from other Americans, but from her daughter-in-law and from the reading public. When she comes to the point in her book when she will narrate her adulterous affair with Jupiter Higgins, she writes: "*Secret. Do Not Read* and *Destroy After My Death.*" The unnamed editor immediately rejects her request with the rather coy response: "*Here Mrs. Trollope is being disingenuous for no professional writer ever commits anything to paper that he doesn't want published*" (White's italics). White's literary executor take note!

Higgins makes his first appearance briefly in a list of neighbors, but it does not take long before he becomes a person of intense interest for Trollope. She goes to a camp meeting and attends the black service where Higgins is in attendance. His very "proximity and the possibility [she] might see him excited [her] unaccountably." When she finally does get to see him, she realizes that she "cared more for him than for" Wright. Things progress slowly—she brings him food, he finds her things she needs—even after she sees him stripped down and working at his forge:

> Mr. Higgins seemed greatly discomforted [by her coming unannounced] since he was working without a shirt on and he hastened to throw an old cape over his shoulders, but not before "I saw how powerful his upper body was—biceps round and black as cannonballs, a furry chest thick with muscle but burned free of all fat, forearms as tendoned as a horse's withers. He could have posed for an anatomical demonstration at a college of surgeons or artists.

Jupiter lives up to the name his slave owner gave him—a man of towering strength and physical beauty. The prurience of the passage is emphasized but how closely Trollope sneaks a look at his magnificent body, not even pretending to look away from what has always been hidden beneath overalls. Yet there is something comic in Trollope's attempt at light porn. The phrase "tendoned as a horse's withers" strives for a poetry it does not quite achieve. There is something very Chelsea gym about his "furry chest... burned free of all fat." The Victorians would have favored a little more flesh on their men. They would have looked at such a body as a sign of malnutrition. The obsession with the lowest possible body fat is a particularly late 20th century obsession, one of the comic anachronisms that dot the book.

White makes the romance between Trollope and Jupiter Higgins touchingly grotesque. Higgins calls Trollope "my little girl" although she's well into her fifties, and she calls him Cudjo, his secret African name. She sees herself as "big black Cudjo's little yellow girl" and later as "this elderly white Francesca and her burly black Paolo." She is candid about their lovemaking. She is fascinated by "Cudjo's irresistible sensuality, the whole hip-smacking, aureole-licking, ear-bathing thoroughness he brought to the job." This is not the most romantic or erotic way of discussing sex, but White is attempting to avoid the worst racial stereotypes. Cudjo is no "Man in a Polyester Suite" a la Robert Mapplethorpe, but a guy who brings erotic thoroughness to his job. We are allowed to smile at the thought of this elderly Victorian matron going at it hammer and tongs with the neighborhood blacksmith. The racial difference made it unspeakable in her day, but as she is reminded by a performance of *The Merry Wives of Windsor,* "any old person who dares to make love is always a figure of fun." And yet she admits though she cannot explain how "these convulsions [or] spasms of delight... restored me to myself."

In one of the last conversations that Fanny Wright and Fanny Trollope have in *Fanny,* they discuss sex. In the high-minded language she always uses, Fanny Wright declares "sexual passion is the strongest and noblest of human sentiments and the source of the best joys of our existence." To which Fanny Trollope smiles "thinking of Cudjo, until I realized every respectable woman would be shocked." The old friends are united by the memory of sex, not with each other, but with their various men. It is one of White's grandest and least qualified celebrations of the erotic, the power of sex not only to be noble but also to be joyous. *Fanny* comes at a particular turning point in his life and his career. The novels he had written immediately before were shadowed by

244 · CRASHING CATHEDRALS

AIDS and death. It is, I think, significant that he turned at this
point to a comic work, a hilarious *faux*-biography in which he
takes on the voice of a middle-aged Victorian matron, a work that
celebrates the nobility and joy of sex as well as the buffoonish
forms it takes.

"He [Vladimir Nabokov] must be ranked, finally, not with other writers but with a composer and a choreographer, Stravinsky and Balanchine. All three men were of the same generation, all three were Russians who were clarified by passing through the sieve of French culture but were brought to the boiling point only by the breezy short-order cook of American informality. Al three experimented boldly with form, but none produced 'avant-garde trash,' as Nabokov called it, for all three were too keen on recuperating tradition."

—from *Arts and Letters*

ARTS AND LETTERS

KEVIN KILLIAN

ARTS AND LETTERS is a salmagundi of commissioned pieces and articles that appeared first in a variety of slick and gay magazines. Take them together, and you get almost a readout of White's own irresistible personality, perhaps more so than in some of his celebrated autobiographical novels and memoirs. Plus, it's like being at the same party with some of the most intriguing personalities in the world today, as well as some dead divas, like Robert Mapplethorpe. When he profiles these luminaries White is never fawning—well maybe once or twice, but he does it so well you forgive him everything. He's fearless, and asks the people in question exactly the kind of questions you think you'd ask yourself, if you were there on the scene and you had balls of brass. Perhaps it is his insensate curiosity that made White the stylist we admire today, in every branch of his writing, because a novelist without tremendous interest in *how do other people do it?* won't hold the readers' interest for very long. Indeed he has always been a man with questions, the Curiosity Kid, the human interrobang, from the very first works of his that caught my eye in the 1970s, *Surviving Elena* (what is the structure of life?), *Nocturnes for the King of Naples* (how do we survive the absence of a particular other?), *The Joy of Gay Sex* (again, how do other people do it?). He grew up in an age, after all, in which the questionnaire

248 · CRASHING CATHEDRALS

began to proliferate through social sciences, big government and military, and pop psychology (like the famous *Cosmo* sex questionnaires, themselves cute, even absurd spin-offs of Dr. Kinsey's sex research), and during this age the floodgates opened, discretion died, and no one took advantage of the new potential more than our beloved Ed White. Societal changes can often be measured in the way verbs die, to be replaced by other verbs—the historic reassignment of the verb for orgasm, in Victorian days "to spend," replaced in our wireless days by the instantaneous "to come." In *Arts and Letters* White worries that Catherine Deneuve will "give" him nothing intimate, where any other writer would have used the old-fashioned, somehow more formal "tell."

When I was 30 or so I had a job writing reviews of "gay books" for a local radio station here in San Francisco. I'd write five hundred words on Alan Turing or May Sarton, and deliver my copy to the station, and then I would stay up all night to hear it mangled by a professional radio guy. He had trouble pronouncing "Foucault" and I was squirming inside, thinking, oh my God, what if Professor Foucault is up at this hour—*Bruce told me he stays up very late!*—and is somehow tuned in to this obscure college radio station and listens to this guy calling him "Fock-Alt." Why oh why did I have the name Foucault in the text so many times? I grew resentful of having to write uncredited copy for a professionally clipped, straight-sounding queen to massacre—and yet my press credentials got me into some cool events for free, never more so than the day my boss called me to say that my idol, Edmund White, was going to be speaking at Dominican College in San Rafael. Could I interview him?

"No problem, Chief."

New to the Bay Area myself, I had no idea how tough it was going to be to get to Dominican College, but I agreed hastily, before he could assign the job to a rival. Somehow I got to Marin, pretty good for a boy who had never been out of the Mission or the Castro, and showed some student my gay press pass, then tried to figure out which dapper gentleman milling in front of the podium was Edmund White, all the while trying to finish the last half of his then brand-new book *A Boy's Own Story* in the half dark that preceded the introduction. It was 1982, a signal year for LGBT writing, and though AIDS was menacing our citizenry it would be a little while before most of us had even heard about it.

White treated me as though I was a person with a real mind, as though my questions were all new to him instead of "So, what's *A Boy's Own Story* all about, Mr. White?" I could only speak to him for five minutes, for others took up his time, but I walked back to BART thinking, Kevin, you've started at the top. I could imagine no place more elevated on which to launch my career as the new Barbara Walters. On the train home I transcribed my hasty shorthand into actual sentences, even into paragraphs, and regretted even more that it would not be me who would get to speak them into a microphone for the world to hear. I still have the book Edmund White signed for me that day—of course I do, I could no more give that up than give up a tattoo, it made me *me*. And he remembered me in the years to come, or said he did, as my writing started to appear in similar places to his, and as I sent him so many dumb things once I obtained his address.

Arts and Letters is mainly "letters." There's just enough of a selection of White's writing about art to make you wish he'd jump in and write a whole book about the art and artists he admires. It's hard to come up with something new to say about (for example) Jasper Johns or Mapplethorpe, but after reading White's articles on both you will be viewing their work with open eyes. At the other end of the spectrum he provides wonderful introductions to artists whose profiles may not be quite as high as these guys--Rebecca Horn, perhaps, or Steve Wolfe. I hadn't heard much about the German photographer Herbert List, and reading White's tribute to him, I now see him as White does, as towering over all other gay photographers, an artist so subtle he didn't need to take the swimsuits off his gorgeous German boyfriends, he gave instead the suggestion of nudity without the unseemly colonialist hauteur of Baron von Gloeden, nor the aristocratic, or premiere danseur perfection of Platt Lynes' models. I find one characteristic emblematic of White's criticism of this period, that it manifests itself as a continual ranking or shading, as we can see in the List example—Gloedel's models dirty, underpaid, Platt Lynes' models not of this world, List's the boy next door, thus superior.

Another defining note of this criticism—one White perhaps borrowed or learned from his one-time friend Susan Sontag—is an energetic enthusiasm. Both writers can make you feel the raw thrill of the avant-garde, the sense of what's new in post-

modernity. One after another of these articles are stunners--
there's a fine piece on the late Nouvelle Vague writer Alain
Robbe-Grillet, which takes you back to the day in which he was
regarded as a wunderkind of depthless talent, and then shows why
he is still a writer worth studying.

White is not always Mr. Goody Two Shoes either. In one case,
the Ned Rorem profile, you watch in helpless delight as Rorem
gets skewered on the high kebab spears of White's erudition and
wit. I also thought that printing a brief review of James Baldwin's
1979 novel *Just Above My Head* and labeling it "James Baldwin"
leads the reader to think JB will be getting the full-blown profile
treatment and it rebounds and instead makes the review seem
skimpy. And in some essays the reader will disagree, perhaps vio-
lently, with White's assessment of this or that subject, and you
will still feel he has won the right to deliver it. I don't believe for
an instant that James Merrill is the equivalent of Cavalcanti
crossed with Noel Coward, but it's amusing to hear someone say
so.

Amusing, and more than amusing, for he writes with so much
knowledge and passion he just might convert you. Take, for example, the peroration to which White builds his memorable
profile of Nabokov, in which he places him at the topmost rank
of creators. "He must be ranked, finally, not with other writers
but with a composer and a choreographer...." It's a statement so
huge that it takes hours to unpack. First of all, look at how wonderfully the word "must" works in the sentence, a small word that
comes in the sentence so early that one doesn't even notice it, one
just swallows it as a step to some further verb, for had White put
his words in another order one might stop and say, "He *must* be
ranked? Why must he be ranked *at all?* Why the emphasis on rank,
except that it's your M.O.?" Like they say on *American Idol* about
"song selection," in magazine writing word order is all. Next
comes paradox. How bizarre, how delicious, how Wildean is the
paradox that there is no other novelist to compare Nabokov to—
thus lifting him right out of the profession he spent his whole life
following. Instead he is compared to two other categories of occupation that seem, according to the logic of the sentences, to be
more magical, ineffable, than one who writes a story—writing
music, making dances—creating in fact the wordless. And yet
White keeps the extended metaphor going long past the point an

ordinary mortal could push it. "All three men were of the same generation, all three were Russians who were clarified [! —but this is where it starts getting good!] by passing through the sieve [!!] of French culture [!!!] but were brought to the boiling-point only by the breezy short-order cook of American informality." Love that "breezy," the casual use of which makes this almost pass for an ordinary sentence. Tellingly, White fails to mention that all three nonpareils were severely anti-Communist and it was perhaps because of this stance that they became so beloved in the USA. Politics in general disappear, dissolve from White's description of his artists and writers, clarified by passing through the sieve of French culture, brought to the boiling-point by the breezy short-order, et cetera. This prowess with extended metaphor, which has made his fiction so memorable, the best of it so enduring, is on display here throughout. Sometimes you'll see three or four of them big motherfuckers on the same page! All of which combine to make *Arts and Letters* an astonishment from beginning to end.

"Lightness is a virtue in my scheme of things, rare and highly desirable."

—from *My Lives*

MY LIVES

ZACHARY LAZAR

WHAT I'VE OFTEN said about being a fiction writer is that, in its limited way, it has offered me an opportunity to experience other people's lives. I've always found it tragic that we only get to go through life in one body, as one self, in one moment in history, and so, for me, fiction writing has been an attempt to escape that, to try to inhabit other people's lives through the imagination. Looking over the notebooks I've kept over the course of the last decade or so, I find myself ensconced in the counterculture of the 1960s, real estate fraud in the American West, ancient and modern Israel, the Holocaust, organized crime, the lives of inmates at Angola Prison. What any of this has to do with my own life is hard to say. The notebooks and the books that have grown (and continue to grow) out of these jottings are something of a mystery, but what is undeniable is that they have made up a large part of my waking life, which is to say that much of that waking life has been given over to daydreaming.

There is of course another approach—a more glamorous approach—which is to live one's own life as an adventure, settling not just on one identity but burning through as many as one has the audacity to invent. Though he covers it up with self-deprecating humor, Edmund White is one of the most audacious self-inventors of our time. Early in *My Lives*, he gives us a small glimpse of what this has entailed in risk. He is a teenager on summer vacation in Cincinnati, borrowing his dad's car, and he uses it not to go to the movies but to pick up a hustler downtown, who, with an accomplice, robs him. White writes: "'Oh please don't' I said in an overbred, fluty voice, which revealed to me how much a victim I'd become… I was always reading novels, and I knowingly chuckled when a character was described as 'foolish' or 'naïve' but here I was: I was naïve, I was foolish, which until this moment I'd never suspected. The reader considers himself to be all-knowing, superior, but now I had to push this conventional flattery aside and recognize that cleverness is not a question of perspective but of accumulated experience in the world."

The accumulation of experience in the world is painful—it can't happen without injury, risk, embarrassment, misunderstanding. But when I first read this passage, I was struck by its comedy, the way it emphasizes the absurdity of the situation more than the angst or the terror. I remember this particularly well because at the time I first read it I was trying to write my own passages about a gay teenager picking up hustlers in the 1940s. The scenes I wrote were full of alienation and fear—they were the work of an unmarginalized straight guy trying to imagine his way into the experience of a marginalized young gay guy. White, of course, has a far deeper understanding of this realm of experience, but he also has a different kind of temperament, and along with that temperament comes implicit politics. While never strident or didactic, his project throughout his career has been to imagine a more enlightened view of "a subject, homosexuality, that (in his youth) was routinely labeled disquieting or tragic at best. I couldn't subscribe to this lugubriousness and wanted to laugh at everyone's solemnity." Like all his work, *My Lives* is marked by its brilliant, evocative style, but beneath that style is a transformative sensibility. "Lightness is a virtue in my scheme of things, rare and highly desirable," he writes.

It is that lightness I have often marveled at, the way it challenges my own tendency toward the solemn, the self-serious, the "dark." White has been called the American Proust, and it is true that he shares with Proust an understanding of the intricacies of the self, of social dynamics, and a descriptive virtuosity applied to the material world. Here, for example, (and I'm not being facetious) is a Proustian outpouring on his father's dog: "Ol' Boy, gorged on hamburger ground from prime beef, would doze beside his desk and wait for his morning walk outside in the hot, humid neighborhood. As he waited he drowned in Dad's oceans of Mahler or Brahms, which never made him lift so much as the tip of an ear, thought the slightest rustle from my father caused his eyes to fly open. He'd stand, excited, then seeing it was a false alarm and that Dad was still hard at work, Ol' Boy would cover his embarrassment by pretending to stretch and yawn, arching his back." This passage, like some of Proust's (or some of Nabokov's), matches an uncanny eye for physical minutiae with an equally uncanny eye for the image's emotional value. But the Proust comparison may place too little emphasis on White's Americanness: "If an employee got married, Dad would automatically give him a raise. These admirable guys had defended the country in both wars and now were holding the line against Oriental Commies in Korea. If only that little bastard Truman would have let a real man like MacArthur go all the way in after them and wipe them out!" This vernacular humor is White's vindication for surviving as himself in a world that didn't much want him to do so. He of course wouldn't put it this way, with so much solemnity.

My Lives is made up of other people, not just White in different mirrors, and its chapters are titled not after epochs in White's own development but rather after the significant foils and influences that have made him who he is—"My Shrinks," "My Father," "My Mother," "My Hustlers," etc. It is a charmingly conversational book, full of gossip and humor, but it also contains one of the most nakedly self-revealing chapters of any memoir I can think of: its seventh, "My Master," which is the story of a traumatic love affair that at the time of the book's publication was hardly even in the past. I remember when the book was first coming out and Ed—he insisted I call him Ed from the first time I met him—was worried that this was "Too Much Information." I remember being a little afraid to read it. I remember another friend telling me that he could barely get through it, and when I asked if that was because it was too revealing, he said no, it was because he loved Ed and it was painful to read about what he'd put himself through. "I'm writing this chapter now because my heart has just been broken by a thirty-three-year-old actor-writer-director named T," White, in his mid-sixties at the time, begins. "I met

him two years and two months ago." What follows is 40 pages of
heartbreak, obsession, despair, and sado-masochism, all of it still
so raw that it tests the limits even of White's formidable powers
of description. V.S. Naipaul once defined art as "chaos viewed
from a position of control," and in that light "My Master" is perhaps the high point of *My Lives*. It is not easy for me to read even
now, ten years after I read it the first time, for it is confessional
without being flattering, intimate in a way that is not romantic.
But it is candid and brave. "What I am trying to demonstrate is
that I had gone beyond the limits imposed on any self-respecting
person because, precisely, I did not respect myself," he writes. A
few pages later, he illustrates: "He pissed all over me, and when I
turned my face to feel it on my cheek, he said, 'In your mouth.
Take it all in your mouth. Swallow it.' He said it in a confidential
tone, like a father saying, 'This is for your own good.'"

This is just the beginning, not even close to the painful end.
White describes the end: "Nothing really explained the panic and
despair that took hold of me. My heart beat so hard and fast that
I feared it would knock its way through the thoracic cage. I could
think of nothing else and if for a moment I did, I'd feel my way
back to my unhappiness just as a tongue seeks out a cavity." He
goes on: "It was as if T had kept me suspended in a bubble, im-
mune from the contagion of age, but now I'd been expelled and
I was shrinking and withering visibly...My two months of suffering over T were the most lacerating of my life."

Lightness is a virtue in my scheme of things, rare and highly desirable.
For anyone tempted to take lightness as a synonym for shallow-
ness, "My Master" shows why it matters to White, why it is so
desirable.

"Psychoanalysis did leave me with a few beliefs," he writes
earlier in the book, "including the conviction that everyone is
worthy of years and years of intense scrutiny." *My Lives* is not a
memoir in the conventional sense of someone taking stock of his
whole past from a high peak of objectivity. It is more like a snap-
shot of the moment of its own composition. What it focuses on
are the episodes and people that mattered most to White at the
time of its writing, and so it is implicit in the book's design that
ten or twenty years later he might choose to emphasize entirely
other episodes and other people. What makes it cohere, and what
binds it to all of White's other work, is its openness. In another

person's eyes (perhaps mine), T would not be worthy of so much real estate. But White is less interested in such distinctions and more interested in the thing in front of him at the time, which is life itself.

Last time I talked to Ed he was hosting a Danish couple of "cagers and feeders" (I think), where one likes to be kept in a cage and force-fed by the other. The one who likes the cage is hugely fat and worth zillions. Ed had a new twenty-something boyfriend in Madrid. My life is colorless by any standard, but by that standard I might as well be Lawrence Welk.

I found this in my email just now, a note I wrote to a mutual friend a few years after *My Lives* came out. Ed would have been 69 at that point. There is always a lot of talk about freedom in America, but those who talk about it most fervently often seem to be those who are least in favor of its actual expression. So many people are too lazy to lead even one life, much less many.

"In my pursuit of lightness," Ed writes, "I sometimes feel like a spider monkey swinging through the trees in a world that is more and more deforested. If I look hard I can still find moments of frivolity, of silvery silliness, of merry complicity, even of pure cross-eyed joy. Till now I usually can spot the next branch but sometimes it's quite a stretch."

"Whenever I become snobbish about my native land it's a sign that it's making me tense."

—from *Terre Haute*

TERRE HAUTE

TIM TEEMAN

OF COURSE, IT ended up being a tricky relationship—how could it be anything but? Both well-known writers, and one—Edmund White—out and gay, who wrote about sex, politics, desire, and AIDS; the other, Gore Vidal, an American literary lion from a previous age who proudly rejected categories of all kinds, including defining himself as gay.

Vidal said he was bisexual, even if his relationships with women had been limited to his youth, and he had been in a relationship with a man for 53 years, as well as the many male hustlers they enjoyed. For Vidal "gay" meant a sexual act, not a sexual identity.

There was a professional contrast between the men, again rooted in sexuality: Vidal had written one of the first contemporary novels to deal with homosexuality, *The City and the Pillar*, in 1948. *Myra Breckinridge* (1968) featured literary fiction's first transgender character. But Vidal's sexual radicalism on the page was outpaced by the times, and by writers like White, who wrote openly about homosexuality: sexually, politically, and culturally.

Vidal was a renegade for sure, but one whose expression of sexuality was inhibited by the generation he came from, a complex hangover of shame, and his own intellectual distrust of categories. He was proud of *The City and the Pillar* while knowing it had marked his card—he never achieved his ultimate dream of being President, and even failed to achieve political office on the two occasions he attempted to.

The men met for the first time at a cocktail party at Peggy Guggenheim's Venetian palace in 1974. "She was very cheap, you know," says White. "She never served *hors d'oeuvres*, but might have some Prosecco. She was the kind who would count the apples in the fridge to see what the servants had eaten."

Vidal was "handsome, frosty and nice. He was definitely cute, but I was sort of an ageist. I was thirty-four years old and he was almost fifty, just enough older not to make me interested. There was no spark there. I was sure he didn't know who I was, I'd only published one novel, *Forgetting Elena* (1973), by then."

White had heard stories about Vidal as they lived a few blocks away from each other in Rome. Vidal and his partner Howard Austen had moved there first in the age of La Dolce Vita, living part of their year there, and part in the U.S. Later they would move to their dramatic cliff-side home in Ravello.

"The main story I would hear is that he was irritated by his friends cruising for guys, he would hire hustlers in the afternoon," White says. "In Rome in those days you would eat outside on the Piazza Navona on a big table with ten to twelve friends. It was very cheap and you'd look at all the trade going by and there were these really cute but preposterous-looking boys who would be swinging Maserati keys, but they didn't have a Maserati. Everybody could be had for money."

On one occasion, an American friend of White's, indicating a cute guy on a Rome street, asked how he could "get" him. White said it was very easy: find two blonde women, go over and say how lonely-looking the guy is, why doesn't he join you. Go from club to club, get drunker and drunker. At the end of the night, say, 'Why don't you stay at my house tonight?'" White smiles: "Then you get to suck him."

People of Vidal's era, and even "somewhat" his own, says White, "weren't interested in sleeping with gay people, but just into sleeping with straight trade. You might say, 'Why don't you go out with my good-looking gay friend Bob?' to someone like Gore, and he'd say, 'And do what—bump pussies?'"

White sighs. "I have never met so many weirdos as the gay men in Italy. They lived with their mothers, they had to be home by dawn, they never had affairs, just one-offs. When I lived in Rome in 1970 people went to the movie theater, sitting with their raincoats on their laps, jerking each other off, or they went to the Coliseum late at night, when you could still get into it, and have sex. Nobody was 'out.'"

White believes Vidal was "genuinely bisexual," pointing to Vidal's friend of the late 1950s and early 1960s, the author Elaine Dundy, who wrote in her memoir that "once, and once only, Gore and I went to bed together. Next day everything was back to normal. Let us say we chose to bathe in the pure, refreshing streams of friendship rather than shoot the perilous rapids of physical love. Which is not to say I wasn't in love with Gore because I was. I saw nothing odd about this. If platonic love is not based on passionate feelings, how can it sublimate itself and ascend the heights?"

Vidal quotes this in *Palimpsest*, his first memoir published in 1996, without confirming if it is true or what his thoughts were about it. Dundy told Vidal's friend, the actor Jack Larson, that she and Vidal had a "major affair."

Dundy was married to Kenneth Tynan, "so she liked sardonic men," says Larson. In 1955, Vidal told Tennessee Williams that he was thinking of getting married, but to whom it is unknown.

As his fame grew, so did Vidal's propensity to feud and fight. After very public confrontations with William Buckley and Norman Mailer his sexuality was at the heart of his last significant contretemps, with White who wrote the 2006 play *Terre Haute*, imagining an intimate relationship between Vidal (named "James" in the play) and Timothy McVeigh ("Harrison").

Terre Haute is the Indiana federal prison in which high-profile Death Row prisoners such as McVeigh are incarcerated. The huge loss of life, indeed McVeigh's act of mass murder, goes unmentioned by Vidal in the play.

"He was a true patriot, a Constitution man," Vidal claimed of McVeigh, when I interviewed him for *The Times of London* in 2009. "And I was torn, my grandfather [the Democrat Senator Thomas Gore] had brought Oklahoma into the Union." McVeigh said he had carried out the bombing as a protest against tyrannical government.

White wrote the play for "T," a younger boyfriend for whom White was a sex slave. "I said, 'You know, you are my master and you could command me to write you a play.' He suggested I do something about McVeigh, whom he resembled."

Initially Vidal, who admired McVeigh's anti-government beliefs, "didn't mind" White writing it, White says, but said he would never be interested in a 'piece of rough trade' from upstate New York."

Vidal had corresponded with McVeigh for a long period of time. "I put into the roles the anguish I was feeling about the thirty-year age difference between T and me," White told me. "When he finished with me I felt wretched. T was a fan of my work, just as McVeigh was an admirer of Vidal's."

In real life Vidal never met McVeigh, though they did correspond and Vidal wrote several articles defending McVeigh. McVeigh invited Vidal to attend his execution in 2001.

Sean Strub, the founder of *Poz* magazine, who optioned and developed White's play, recalls that on the day McVeigh was originally scheduled to be executed, May 16, Vidal was planning on attending. "But at the last minute, there was a stay for two weeks, so Gore canceled his trip and, instead, took me to lunch at [New York showbiz restaurant] Sardi's. It was my birthday."

The play imagines four conversations between McVeigh and Vidal, interrogating the parallels between two men who believe passionately what they believe, what it means to be American and what that leads them to do in their lives.

The play focuses on the men's evolving intimate relationship: in Harrison's cold dismissal of James and the latter's unmet sexual needs, White told me in 2006, "When you're old, if people like you, they see you as venerable; if they don't, you're invisible. Sexually and romantically, you're turned into a eunuch."

At the end of the play Harrison/McVeigh asks James/Vidal what he would want if he could hypnotize him. "Just to see your torso," James replies.

The character of James in the play was not purely Vidal, White says. "I made him an amalgam of me and him. His own agent said, 'I don't know why Gore objects. Your character is much nicer than he is.' Gore felt I'd made my career out of being gay. He didn't like that label. He felt my play had muddied the waters. Since he admired McVeigh's actions, I was diluting the whole thing by making it into this crummy sexual thing. I felt I had represented the ideological positions faithfully."

If McVeigh was a hero to Vidal, he was a "bitter person unable to make it as a marine" for White. He gave Vidal a copy of the play and said the BBC wanted to produce it. "Gore predicted it would be a success. I said that I didn't think I'd ever had a big success. He said, 'Well, maybe because I'm in it, it will be a big success.'"

But Vidal wasn't happy. "He was mad, he felt I hadn't represented his arguments fairly, he accused me of not reading his books," White says. "I was never a fan of his writing, I really hated his historical novels, which I thought were pure taxidermy: no life, no style. I read a few of them: they're all pretty horrible."

Vidal gave permission for the play to be produced by the BBC; then it was performed in Edinburgh and New York. White received word, not from Vidal directly, that Vidal was threatening legal action, after a producer mentioned her desire to make it into a Broadway production.

"I was so tired of this," recalls White. "I really took the high ground. I sent him a very obsequious letter making him sound like a mentor, which he never was. I mentioned he'd already given permission for it to be produced by the BBC. I think that kind of shut him up. I never heard another word from him. He could see I was not going to squabble with him, and I pointed out that I was very poor, so it was pointless to sue me anyway."

When I interviewed Vidal for *The Times of London*, he said of White: "He's a filthy, low writer. He likes to attack his betters, which means he has a big field to go after." Had he wanted to meet McVeigh? "I am not in the business of meeting people," Vidal said. "That play implies I am madly in love with McVeigh. I looked at his [White's] writing and all he writes about is being a fag and how it's the greatest thing on earth. He thinks I'm another queen and I'm not. I'm more interested in the Constitution and McVeigh than the loving tryst he saw. It was vulgar fag-ism."

To Strub, Vidal appeared to find White's sexual openness, both on the page and in life, "distasteful," a clash of gay-generational sexual mores. For Strub, the final draft of the play "depicted a more sexualized relationship between the characters and trivialized Gore into a panting old queen trying to get his rocks off with McVeigh. Gore was offended. If there is one thing Gore Vidal wasn't, it was one who longed for the unattainable boy across the room. I never saw him convey a lecherous persona."

Vidal's animosity towards White continued: over lunch with Jonathan Burnham, White's publisher at Chatto, he accidentally swigged what he thought was wine but was olive oil. "He spluttered it all out and claimed Jonathan deliberately hadn't stopped him. He said: 'You want me to die so your writer Edmund White will be King Fag!'" Vidal may not have liked to have been known as gay, but he didn't want to be deposed as "King Fag" clearly.

Maybe it was White's self-definition as gay, and his success as an author of gay-themed books, that angered the anti-category Vidal. In an interview with the publisher Donald Weise, Vidal, while not dismissive of White's work, was dismissive of his self-definition.

"There are certainly people who call themselves 'gay novelists' like Edmund White," Vidal said. "I think he's out of his mind. Why limit yourself any more than literature has limited you? In a world where people don't read, what are you going to make of a man who calls himself a 'gay novelist'? What's that supposed to mean, that he only go to write about cock? He's a quite good writer, but I didn't think he was that dumb to characterize himself."

How much of that scorn is internalized? Vidal had categorized himself when *The City and the Pillar* had been published, and his career and political ambitions were skewed after that, he felt.

By 1999, in his interview with Weise, he claimed defiantly, "With my temperament I didn't give a damn. It didn't mean I didn't get irritated. I didn't care what people thought of me. I was too busy judging them. I just let it all go."

Vidal said he had rejected his election to the National Institute of Arts and Letters in 1976 on the grounds he "already belonged to Diners Club. This is how I treated the literary world, with the same disdain as they have treated the fags over the years. They don't mind apologetic meek little fags passing with one point one children and a wife who drinks, and they don't mind the caricature fag like [Truman] Capote, that's how fags are meant to be."

Vidal said he was among the first of the "war novelists" who were "rather tough." Vidal was suddenly playing the proud gay freedom fighter, but on his own terms—never as a "fag."

For his part, White doesn't rate Vidal as a significant figure in gay-themed literature. "What's the young gay man of today going to read? *Myra Breckinridge*? It's fun but I don't think he's widely read like Alan Hollinghurst, or even Christopher Isherwood. To me, Isherwood was a great man and *A Single Man* the first really good gay novel."

What did Isherwood, who was close to Vidal—even if their friendship had its own dramatic peaks and valleys—find so warm in Vidal, I asked White. "Intelligence and worldliness," White thinks. As for *Terre Haute*, White says "it's too complimentary as a portrait of Gore. James has a lot of my own pathos and sweetness. I don't think he had any of that."

For instance, Vidal—throughout his life, even though he was with Austen—maintained his enduring love was Jimmie Trimble, a childhood sweetheart who, later as a Marine, was killed at the Battle of Iwo Jima. Whatever romance there might be to the story Vidal crafted, many, including White, are more circumspect.

To White, Vidal's loving enshrining of Trimble "sounds like an alibi. 'This is why I haven't had a love affair, because I was so in love with a boy who died in the war.' Don't you find something lightly putrid about that, like (William) Faulkner's story 'A Rose for Emily' [in which the dead body of the female protagonist's lover is found in her bed after she has died]. I just think that anyone like Gore would have gotten on with things, met people, especially someone as rich and good-looking as him. It's such a weird fixation you feel he doesn't really believe it himself."

Vidal also said he and Austen had stopped having sex shortly after beginning their relationship. For White, "I think it was cruel of Gore to say that he and Howard didn't have sex. That's like denying in any real sense he's your partner and again characteristic of that generation to be evil like that and an awful betrayal of Howard's public role."

White recalls reading an interview with Marguerite Yourcenar, the novelist and essayist, in which she was asked about Miss [Grace] Frick, the person she lived with. "She's just my secretary," Yourcenar said, whereas, says White, "in fact Frick was her partner, supported her, typed her manuscripts, and probably licked her pussy."

Vidal's public disavowal of intimacy with Austen "probably meant quite a lot to Howard, I would have thought," says White. "It's like, if you're the King of Hungary, saying, 'The Queen and I have never consummated our relationship.' How is she expected to reign after that? What position does she have? Why say it? To pack his heart in ice. Men like Gore have companions like Howard who do everything for them: if they can't sleep they stay up all night with them, if they have to have their wisdom tooth pulled they go to the dentist with them."

White thinks Vidal, despite his public disavowal of Austen's role in his life when he was alive, "probably had a very intimate relationship with him and was probably very devoted to him. He was a bit like Tennessee Williams, who fell apart after his man-friend [Frank Merlo] died. Both men were kept reasonable by their lovers and fell apart when they died."

Indeed, years after Austen's death in 2003, in his second memoir, *Point To Point Navigation* (2007), Vidal devotes a number of moving passages to Austen, his decline and death, and to dreaming about him.

For White, Vidal had "separated out friendship, companionship and sex, which many people did in the 70s. You would assign those roles to different people—fuck buddies, the lover you lived with, friends, friends with benefits... all before AIDS. There was an eagerness in the gay community to find lots of possibilities, but I'm giving Gore too much credit to say he did that."

If Vidal wasn't gay, but mostly, if not exclusively, had gay sex, why did he believe in the model of sexuality he constructed, without defining himself in any terms? How did he see himself and the world around him?

White believes that Vidal's "no such thing as being gay, only gay sexual acts" dictum matched the theories of Michel Foucault, the philosopher and literary theorist and friend of White's. "He was against the same thing. I think Gore was deeply grounded by research in the classical period: in classical Greece the men really were bisexual and weren't definitely one way or another.

"But in his case it was muddled. He wanted to run for office, he was from a very political family. Perhaps his rejection of labels also came from how bitter he felt about *The City and the Pillar*, which was crucified by many critics. He felt the *New York Times* wouldn't review him for years after that. I think that affected how he saw homosexuality generally."

In a friendly gesture, White called Vidal on one of his last New York visits. "You should come by and have some dinner. I'll invite some cute boys around," White told him. Vidal replied, "Oh, cute boys, that's the last thing in the world I want."

"I don't know what that meant," White says today. "Was he bidding a farewell to sex altogether, or he had enough cute boys around him anyway? I had the feeling he wasn't interested in sex at all: one more reason why he was so bitter perhaps. He was mainly into booze and revenge."

Indeed, Vidal's awful decline—encompassing excessive alcohol consumption, dementia, and the severance of many friendships with loved ones and friends—ended in his death at his Hollywood Hills home from complications of pneumonia on July 31, 2012. He was 86.

White sallies on, with new books, and—despite himself being assailed by illness—his innate sense of mischief and open-hearted interest (including sexual interest) in the world. Somewhere perhaps Vidal is raising a glass, with a lugubrious smile, to the man who supplanted him as "King Fag."

"And honestly Jack didn't know what he was doing or why. Was he paying out a hundred twenty dollars three times a week just to exercise his skills at reassuring others? Did he crave this contact with another human body as monkeys need their real or terry-cloth mothers? ... All his life he'd pursued lovers or had them pursue him, and this was an activity familiar to the point of necessity, a focus for his days, even something like a luxury if le luxe is defined as useless but highly conspicuous and necessary consumption."

—from *Chaos: A Novella and Stories*

CHAOS: A NOVELLA AND STORIES

ALDEN JONES

BEFORE THE AMERICAN memoir craze there was autobiographical fiction. Some fiction writers have been coy about the autobiographical elements of their fiction, but Edmund White never was. *Chaos*, like so much of his other work, veers between straight-up autobiography and stories that stay close to White's experience. But if you run into Ed at a party and ask him how much of a work of his fiction is true, chances are he will tell you. Chances are he will say something along the lines of "All of it. Well, mostly all of it."

Which raises the question of what distinguishes autobiographical fiction from memoir, aside from the leeway to invent. One of the benefits of fiction is the latitude offered to the protagonist, or primary character. Memoirists are generally preoccupied with how they come across on the page. If a reader doesn't like the narrator—who is a version of the writer—they won't like, or even perhaps read, their story. A memoir by a pedophile like Humbert Humbert would be greeted with contempt. But because *Lolita* is fiction, and we assume Nabokov is exploring an *idea* by researching and inventing Humbert Humbert as a character, many good people have allowed themselves to spend time in the head of this pedophile—to enjoy his company, even—and Nabokov carries on, admired.

There is freedom in fiction, including autobiographical fiction, to take more risks related to likeability. And indeed, likeability is one thing Edmund White never seems to care about on the page. He is interested in recording psychological authenticity, and our inner worlds are not orderly spaces. Our thoughts, desires, and urges are not always admirable—and sometimes they are. Edmund White is interested in intimacy, both between lovers or friends and between the writer and the reader. As he wrote years earlier in *The Beautiful Room is Empty*, "the most important things in our intimate lives can't be discussed with strangers, except in books."

In the novella *Chaos*, our narrator is Jack, a writer, a sex-obsessed older man who pays for sex regularly despite his constant financial anxiety: "The more he had money problems, the more he prowled after men and boys online." The novella becomes itself a meditation on Jack's two primary activities, sex and writing. "If sex was an immediate rush so intense it became the only here and now and crowded out past and present, fiction was always written in the past tense and was lobbed like a paper plane over a cliff towards an unknown destination." But both his sex life and his writing life have a sad, almost desperate tint in *Chaos*. His published works aren't bringing in the money he needs to support his basic living needs. The novel he wants to write about the life of Nijinsky isn't well received by his agent, who crushes the project. And dating in the Internet age, while aging, offers Jack no end of frustration and humiliation:

All the New York hustlers now worked online and by cell phone; actual spontaneous encounters in the flesh had been eliminated, as if no one could bear the uncertainty anymore or the possibility of rejection. All the hustler bars had been closed. Nor did anyone want to stand on an icy corner in a T-shirt and Levi's jacket while the paired passing headlights picked at his body like chopsticks. The photographic portrait had become the only physical reality; erotic photographers available to do sexy pictures for clients' online profiles advertised in all the gay magazines…As soon as one made contact with someone online he would flash back, "Stats? Pics?" Jack never bothered to reply since his disastrous statistics revealed an outsize waistline, a meaty, sagging chest and a body that outweighed by at least a hundred pounds anyone he would consider bedding.

Jack begins to meet, and regularly pay for sex, a young ex-Mormon named Seth. Their sexual relationship is clear: Jack pays to provide Seth pleasure. Jack's "idea of sex had very little to do with his own penis…Seth's dick belonged to both of them and Seth's climax was something they shared. Sometimes Jack said to himself that only Seth could keep up with him and only he had as strong a sex drive as he did, but that was true only by courtesy. If Seth came five times a day, Jack could swallow semen just as often, but sometimes Jack barely got hard, much less had an ejaculation."

There is very little literature even on the fringes of our American canon describing sex in old age, and even less willing to explore the complexities of what motivates us sexually beyond the simple goal of orgasm-related satisfaction. In *Chaos*, the other stories in this book, and much of his later work, White gambles on his reputation as a "famous gay novelist," a literary icon, in order to describe something real about what is difficult about aging, financial struggle, and incessant, complex emotional-sexual desire. This is exactly what earns White his icon status, when combined with his masterful sentence-making and roomy intellect. Throughout his body of work, his devotion to an authentic self-examination, and the degree to which he offers himself up to his readers, is ground-breaking.

Chaos is not without redemption. If you are tempted to feel sorry for Jack (Ed?), the novella ends in the voice of Seth, who has just finished reading—as you have—Jack's missive and writes his own letter in response ("Dear 'Jack' since that's what you want to be called"). "I guess you'll put this in your book, too," he writes.

I won't spoil it for you if you haven't yet read *Chaos*. But love comes in unlikely forms. Sex is never the same experience for the people having it together. We might have fears and doubts about our lives, but others see us differently. Edmund White's dive into the psyche is a gift to any reader who values self-knowledge, and the rare moments, only in books, we are allowed this close to an unvarnished stranger.

"He counted for something and his story as well."

—from *Hotel de Dream*

HOTEL de DREAM

TREBOR HEALEY

I FIRST HEARD OF *Hotel de Dream* during a reading in a dark
East Village bar and former massage parlor called Happy
Endings, where all the poets were reading tales of lost love as sad
as my own under the muted light and minimalist decor. I was
touring my poetry book, *Sweet Son of Pan*, which is full of elusive
liaisons with satyrs and the like, and I'd just read a poem, "My
Antinous," about a guy who loses a young lover and, Emperor
Hadrian-style, commissions statues of fauns to be built and
mounted throughout the city of San Francisco. Someone in the
audience mentioned Edmund White's book about a 19th century
New York hustler who was also the subject of a similar passion,
and I jotted down the title and soon discovered *Hotel de Dream*.

I'd read *The Beautiful Room is Empty* of course, and *A Boy's Own
Story*, both seminal works of the coming out process, but had not
revisited White since. I'd been on a bender back then, reading
every coming out story then available in that first wave of such
books, from White's aforementioned novels to John Fox's *Boys on
the Rock*, Aaron Fricke's *Reflections of a Rock Lobster*, Jeanette Win-
terson's *Oranges Aren't the Only Fruit*, and Patricia Nell Warren's
The Front Runner, among others. Then I ventured into the darker
recesses of queer life with Rechy's *City of Night*, Genet's *Our Lady
of the Flowers* and Wojnarowicz's *Close to the Knives* and was soon

captured by the historical gay underworld, drifting far afield from modern American gay fiction to Charles Warren Stoddard's *South Sea Idyls, Teleny, The Sins of the Cities of the Plain,* Camina's *Bom Crioullo, Sodomy and the Pirate Tradition,* Mishima, Purdy, Cocteau and the like. Suffice it to say, White's exploration of gay life in 19th century New York immediately grabbed my attention and brought me back to his oeuvre with a renewed appreciation for his brilliance and skill as a novelist and writer.

Hotel de Dream became my favorite of his books, not only for the poignant story of the faun-like young Elliott and the "middling" banker who falls in love with him, but for the interwoven tale of the tragic early death of Stephen Crane who, White postulates, had begun to write a novel about just such a boy (evidence exists in Crane's letters that he'd begun but later destroyed the manuscript). Crane's own story turns out to be just as poignant and original as young Elliott's, as he struggles futilely to finish his final novel in a country house in England, cared for and aided by his much older girlfriend and caretaker, Cora, as he slowly succumbs to the consumption that will finally kill him at the young age of 28.

These are stories of lives cut short, and so the shadow of AIDS looms. Both Elliott and Stephen are young men living on the edge—one by choice and one by necessity. Elliott, driven from his home by abuse and violence and the denigration of his sexuality by his father and brothers upstate, sets out for New York City and has no real choice but to pursue prostitution. Crane, on the other hand, is a struggling writer, with a sincere and righteous interest in the underside of the American experiment, its injustices, indignities and lack of humanity—all so grossly expressed in a truly brutal era of New York's history. Crane wrote an important book about this epoch, sadly not well-received at the time (1893), called *Maggie, A Girl of the Streets,* about a young prostitute (it's brilliant and raw and feels bluntly authentic—I picked it up while reading *Hotel de Dream*). In fact, so interested was Crane in New York's underbelly that he even risked jail time when he was accused of soliciting a prostitute—in fact, he'd been interviewing her and ultimately had been forced to defend her against yet another case of all too common police abuse.

White imagines Crane interviewing a boy in similar circumstances and sets out to describe a fictional account of the two young men meeting, as well as Crane's subsequent obsession with finishing the conjectured novel that grew out of that meeting. White has Crane dictate the story between coughing fits and much-needed rest to the loyal Cora in what can only be described as a brilliant technique to not only draw us into the story of Elliott, but also into Crane's story and that of his unconventional relationship with Cora, several years his senior and the ex-madam of the Hotel de Dream. White titles Crane's never-realized novel *The Painted Boy* and proceeds to conjure up the precarious life of a living-by-his-wits androgynous youth plying his gay trade in 19th century New York City. White's description of the gay demimonde of the era is well-drawn with its rouged-up old queens, secret haunts, the sailors, the violence, the endless bitchy banter and the aptly named bar, The Slide. And, he just as deftly depicts bourgeois homosexuality with its closeted "gentlemen" like Theodore the "middling" banker, compromised by secrecy and self-loathing and, when discovered, ironically mocked for their coded language: "Last year, he was *my* nephew."

To learn that all those little boys hawking papers in the afternoon—the "EXTRA! EXTRA!" sentimental trope of *Saturday Evening Post* America—were quite likely delivering newspapers to select gentlemen and turning tricks to make ends meet was as shocking to me as it was suddenly obvious. Well, of course! Extra, Extra indeed. How could I have been so naïve? White's portrayal of the Fagin-like Silas recruiting Elliott from right off the train platform to join his crew of newsboys to the later street adventures with the young redhead Mick has the ring of truth. Friendly, streetwise Mick not only trains Elliott in the ways of hawking the news—lies work best: "War Declared!" "President Assassinated!"—but he insists on instructing him as well about taking care of other business, such as "his knob, which he'd extricated from his trousers for the occasion…and Mick had his way with the frail boy."

White's attention to the sights and sounds of late 19th century New York brings the city to vivid life: "Elliott loved the populous city, with its miles and miles of slums, those mephitic tenements spread out everywhere and quick with noise and drunken brawls, banging doors and rank cooking smells, unlit passageways and rickety stairs, the sense that every wall and door was just the thinnest possible membrane holding back a boiling larval mess soon to explode and metamorphose into more and more sticky life." I thought of the film, *Gangs of New York*, and Whitman's ebullient descriptions of Manhattan's teeming masses; Melville's *Pierre* and its rendering of the darker, seamier side of the great metropolis.

It's in these passages that White most fully enters into Crane's literary vision. His extensive research into Crane's career and the mystery surrounding the alleged manuscript, as described in the book's postface, clearly inspired and informed the story, and the result is historical fiction of the first order, painting a picture not only of a particular time, but taking it a step further by exploring what might have been and what's been left unsaid in the historical record—both Crane's and boys like Elliott's. As a writer, I am of course—like White and likely every contributor to this book— fascinated by the lives of other writers and how they make a go of it, as well as what drives them to glory or ruin—or both. White did his research, not only on Crane—who he renders so convincingly I feel him almost as a contemporary—but on the flavor and street slang of 19th century New York. When Mick, who ultimately turns to pickpocketing, recruits Elliott, the scene is both funny, brilliant and wholly believable, rife with period pickpocketer slang: "...We're all engaged in breach-getting...throwing the mitt...a touch...the dipper wires him." A "moll-buzzer" robs women, and when they steal money from the church collection plate it's called robbing "the Dago." White also makes liberal use of the gay slang of the period: "finger in the honey pot... kiss the worm...does your son robin wear a low neck and short sleeves? (circumcision)... chopsticks (mutual masturbation)... boy-simple (someone wild about boys)."

White clearly revels in as well as admires Crane's pursuit of the harsh and naked truths of 19th century American urban life, and I think it inspired him to do the same in rendering this fantasia of a Crane novel. Crane was a brave and adventurous writer, as evidenced by his most famous book, *The Red Badge of Courage*. He was not afraid to confront unpleasant realities like military desertion and child prostitution. He traveled to Cuba twice as a journalist to cover the Spanish-American War, and ended up with both yellow fever and malaria. On one such trip he visited the Hotel de Dream, a renowned Jacksonville, Florida whorehouse where he met and became involved with its madam, Cora Taylor, who, though several years older than him and still married to someone else, afterward became his life companion. White doesn't pass up the chance to show Crane's boyish character in relation to his older girlfriend and even to his elders in the literary community, including Henry James and Joseph Conrad, both of whom make cameo appearances in the book.

These introductions of other arguably "queer" authors of the period add a breadth and depth to the story and allow White to explore the whole queer/sexual reality of fin de siècle America. James dedicates a story, "The Great Condition" (a hilarious title of Jamesian abstracted understatement in the context of the raw candidness of White's story) to Crane, featuring a love interest who is saddled with a "dishonorable" past, reminding us of the prudishness, classism and repressed sexuality of "the Master" so skillfully examined by Colm Tóibín in his eponymous novel written around the same time that White penned *Hotel de Dream*. Cora is insulted by the story, of course, and tears it up, unimpressed by James's "English polish," "discretion" and "beardless sentences," all of which serve to remind her of what she loves so much about the unaffected and earthy Crane: "How she loved his bantam arrogance, that hard, nagging core of primary masculinity that kept throbbing inside him—an assertiveness that Mr. James would never know and could approximate only through a eunuch's sly attitudinizing. She could tell by the way that James lit up around her husband that he was queer as a football bat. But Mr. James never gave in to his impulses—he wouldn't hug or kiss the poor thin sweating Stevie." Later, when Joseph Conrad, author of such homoerotically-charged novels as *Lord Jim* and *The Secret Sharer*, pays a visit, he visibly stiffens as Crane inquires as to whether he's ever known "any inverts." Conrad answers predictably that "as a sailor I heard about such abominations," and when Crane mentions his story about Elliott, Conrad responds that "you'd have trouble getting it published. Ever since poor Wilde's trial, society has grown even less tolerant." And so enters Oscar Wilde, the specter representing the very real danger of being fast and loose and unabashedly homosexual. Crane does not so much judge Wilde for that, but rather for his being "a dreadful cad," hinting at his own effort to render the homosexual life of young Elliott with sensitivity and respect, offering a lens on the very different dangers facing the unprivileged queer nobodies like Elliott, who contrasted with Wilde, James, Conrad, et al, have—like the prostitutes Crane knew and loved—a dignity borne of their humble station, which necessitates honesty and self-acceptance. He comes to even admire Elliott, who "kept himself clean. He spent most nights at a newsboys' home where he rented a bed for six cents, got a free bath and occasionally a haircut for three cents from one of the older boys. Now that Stevie knew him better he realized that there was something cool and elegant about Elliott, as if he were the lost Dauphin."

And so, far from being discouraged by Conrad's admonitions, Crane returns to the manuscript with renewed vigor, putting aside *The O'Ruddy*, the book under contract that he was supposed to be writing, but which he felt in truth was just another—and paler—version of *The Three Musketeers*, a swashbuckler's picaresque trip through the demimonde instead of an authentic examination of it. Because Crane's strength is empathy and raw truth, and getting down into the messy entrails of life without romanticizing any of it. He doesn't set himself at a distance, nor does he patronize: "If Stevie could advise Elliott about the ways of the world, Elliott could teach him how to decipher the city around him." Together the two follow fire wagons and go to bawdy plays. Elliott takes him to meet his "queer mother" who'd "taught him how to be queer. She's just a friend. She takes care of me." And Crane doesn't spare us the sadness of these 19th century queer lives—the abuse, the disrespect, the violence, the tragic love affairs and sexual escapades, the deforming effects of being an outcast and a pariah. Crane's virtue is in not seeing them as "other." He's like the best kind of investigative reporter. Or maybe, it's just that he's a down-to-earth dude, which is why White's depiction of him seems so contemporary. Crane "liked people with a canine friendliness and an acquired amused skepticism." He seems unthreatened by the tribulations of life—or, more to the point, even drawn to them—which seems so refreshingly uncharacteristic of the 19th century middle class. Succumbing to a coughing fit and sitting down on a park bench near Madison Garden, he catches his breath long enough to say to Elliott: "What a fine pair we are, you with the syph, me a lunger!"

And I think all this says just as much about Edmund White as it does about Stephen Crane. White is as generous—in this book as in all his others—with his characters, refraining always from judgment or moralizing. White too seems to like people "with a canine friendliness and an acquired amused skepticism." And I'd guess he sees himself in Crane, just as Cora muses that Stephen "saw himself in the painted boy as in a distorted mirror," and that the story itself represented his "dying self revisiting the vital kid he'd once been." In some sense, in *Hotel de Dream*, White seems to be doing something similar.

Which brings us back to the faun in my own mirror. How do we capture our lost selves, our lost histories, and the elusive objects of our affections? Is it through poetry and fiction, or as in the case of the banker, Theodore (or the protagonist in my own poem), having it rendered in marble as an idealized being. "A distorted mirror" indeed. But such is art, and it's the best we've got to see what those who came before us saw.

The strength and uniqueness of White's novel is that it does not just this, but something of the opposite as well, taking some of the distortion out of our view of the past by unearthing the stories and voices that have been silenced or never fully explored. This is what Toibin has done as well with *The Master*, and I'd guess he must have seen something of himself in James. I certainly see something of my young self in a faun, and thinking about the few times I've attempted historical fiction, I guess I do identify with Constance, the Irish immigrant girl I wrote about who falls for the butch lesbian, Captain Jinx, herself passing as a cowboy in 1890s Los Angeles; or, my own private Jack Kerouac as an out gay man in the 1990s, still as stuck on Neil Cassidy as the closeted straight version, but enjoying a little more consummation and certainly drinking a lot less.

And so, if empathy is the work of the novel, it actually goes both ways. We learn to empathize as we write our characters just as readers empathize with those same characters as they read them. Though it may truly be that we can only see the past and the souls of others through a distorted mirror, I pretty clearly saw myself in each of the characters of *Hotel de Dream*—from the restless adventurer and man of integrity Stephen to the pathetic broken down banker Theodore, lost in a tragic and doomed love affair; from the caring bohemian Cora to the devil-may-care Mick, and to each and every one of the queens, sailors, rentboys and elderly gentlemen of 19th century New York. And thanks to my queer writer elders like Edmund White, I didn't see a lot of *myself* in James or Conrad, and yet I did see *them* more clearly—in that

288 · CRASHING CATHEDRALS

social isolation we all knew when we couldn't conceive of how to
come out, endlessly dodging our own nature and attempting to
navigate through a world that required we hide the most essential
truth about ourselves. If dreams mirror our lives, and if the best
way to understand the past is to see it in your own reflection, then
White has done something extraordinary with this spare little
dream of a novel. He's given us a perfect little portrait of our own
past as a people, and something more—he's enriched our present
as only an understanding of the past can do. I am forever the
richer for it, as are all who check in to the *Hotel de Dream*.

"Now the boat is stripped of its crew and indifferent to its cargo—it is free to travel wherever chance and the currents might take it."

—from *Rimbaud: The Double Life of a Rebel*

RIMBAUD: THE DOUBLE LIFE

OF A REBEL

KATHE KOJA

A WRITER WRITING ABOUT a writer writing about a writer: and one a poet. One by one, we climb into the small, sufficient, drunken boat, we find a way to seat ourselves without toppling, we bob and drift and swirl away from shore.

MY OWN, MOST lasting and definitive readerly relationship with Edmund White (though I knew his work before, of course, knew *A Boy's Own Story* and *The Beautiful Room Is Empty,* and most recently, as I write this, *Hotel de Dream)* comes through his examination of that most definitive bad boy, the madman's poet, the teenage genius brat Arthur Rimbaud, in *Rimbaud: The Double Life of a Rebel.* I'd been researching Rimbaud for a project of my own, looking to gather every useful text I could find—but in that process I learned that some of the "best" were actually surprisingly obtuse, either too distant by design, or from dismay (look out for the lice and the gunrunning), or too flutteringly worshipful (oh, those amazingly blue eyes!) to be of lasting use. In White's work, I found a different sensibility.

His own literary friendship with Rimbaud developed early. As a fellow teenage boy, immured in a snowbound boarding school, mute with growing frustration and longing, White writes of discovering Rimbaud at age 16, and "[b]eing buoyed up by the sensual delirium of... 'The Drunken Boat,'" and the subsequent dreams the poem and its author engendered, of escape and freedom and success, his own dreams "to run away to New York and make my mark as a writer; I identified completely with Rimbaud's desires to be free, to be published, to be sexual" —dreams born side by side, like a cold conjoined twin, with the tangled fear of their success, of being called upon to truly "live out all my fantasies—and the notion of answered prayers I found even more alarming than a continuation of my dependence and frustration." Because our dreams, those authentic dreams, *are* dangerous; they tug and eddy like the current that leads to the tide; they make us real, whether we will be so or no. And once the poem has found its reader, the voyage has begun.

The process of attraction, why we read who we do, whose words speak to us as if they were written with our reading in mind, is its own kind of poetry: why this voice and not that, why him, why her? Why me? The way it scans, that living poem of attraction, is entirely mysterious, and to try to parse it is as pointless as counting the shadows of the leaves on water, trailing willow, sturdy beech, all of them moving and changing as that current moves us, as we forbear to use the oars and let ourselves go where the boat goes.

White accompanies Rimbaud, half a pace to one side, as he makes his own circling, elliptical journeys: from the buttoned-down schooldays in Charleville, to a wild tyro's on-the-road joys, ones that come alive in poems like "My Bohemia," that White describes with a comrade's approval as "vividly render[ing] the thrill of being a teenager on the road." "With his 'fists stuffed in pockets full of holes,' he marches along and dreams...There is something delightfully cartoonish and indelible in this picture of the boy 'playing' his shoelaces—all the pleasures of art, daydreaming, masturbation, and freedom coming together in one electrifying image."

And then the road turns, at last— "at last"? So young! —to the great metropolis, Paris, where Rimbaud hopes and plans to mingle with the august Parnassian poets, and to the fateful, funny, awful meeting with Paul Verlaine, fellow poet, tormented lover, moony and labile being whose best care for Arthur came only after their final separation. White turns that comrade's honest and diagnostic eye on Verlaine as well: "a homicidal alcoholic…[and] also an extremely gentle, sensitive poet with a distinct tone and a remarkable musicality. These two aspects of his character had set up a pitched battle over his anguished destiny[.]" White's examination of this fraught and violent, passionately creative relationship is encapsulated by his description of Rimbaud's arrival at *chez* Verlaine: "Into this snug, middle-class world Rimbaud entered like an invited catastrophe. He arrived with what would prove to be his greatest poem, 'The Drunken Boat,' a poem to the sea by someone who had never seen it… There in the small cosseted salon they found the young belligerent poet with his sunburned face and large hands, his piercing blue eyes, unsmiling mouth, uttering monosyllables in his heavy Ardennes accent." Verlaine had even financed his train fare into town.

There is no conversation; that congress is unneeded on this trip. The bounds of chronology have dissolved like sugar in water, like brick crumbling into sand, as the boat rides the currents, passing through on its way to wherever it will fetch up, find ground, or finally flounder and sink; and if the boat is drunk, what of its passengers? Or captains? Who wants to steer this thing, anyway?

No reply, or replies, just the sound of the water cupped and clapping against the small warped hull. Someone sighs. Someone laughs. Someone scans the grey silk of the horizon, as far as the eye can see. We all chose to be here, where the weight of choice falls away. We all know what it is to be lost.

It's tempting to speculate on Rimbaud's possible continuing influence on White's own body of work, beyond the example of the man with "soles of wind" fleeing forever a step ahead, up the path, into the world, following no one's lead. Can we extrapolate from the 16-year-old reading the 17-year-old, two boys communicating through words on a page, to reach that author who was inspired to write this brief biography; how far, through chronology and sensibility, do the echoes really reach? If nothing else, *this* boy's own story—of a "precocious adolescent who has already lived hard, who has defied society, who has staked everything on his genius but isn't sure of winning, and who is already bitter"— could, may, have served as its own kind of cautionary tale.

Certainly White keeps his eyes open—there's no hagiography in *Double Life*. He clearly communicates Rimbaud's cruelty and emotional aggression toward the hysterical, lyrical, exasperating Verlaine, as the brutal energies of that lovers' voyage devour Verlaine's teetering marriage and responsibilities to his infant son. He details the increasing fury of that swung pendulum's trajectory, Paris to Brussels to London, the relationship cannibalizing itself again and again, using whatever came to hand—a pair of knives, a herring, a handful of poems traded off for cigars and absinthe— to set the doomed table, day after day. And when the bill eventually, inevitably comes due, in a frenzy of alcohol, tears, and two fired pistol shots, White details the collapse of that relationship as honestly and unsparingly—along with Verlaine's humiliating, invasive, instrument-aided examination at the hands of police doctors, to "see if he was a homosexual"—before Verlaine's incarceration ended his seasons in hell and joy with Rimbaud.

And always, like a compass needle, White returns to the life through the lens of the poetry: "Though these two books were written almost back to back (as can be said of any two works in Rimbaud's oeuvre, since his writing life was so short), they explore two opposing poles of inspiration. *Illuminations* is often glacial, futuristic, and impersonal, whereas *A Season in Hell* is— starting with its title—retrospective, post-Christian, and autobiographical." It's where he, and we, see Rimbaud most forcefully, where Rimbaud's own fierce force is concentrated, in this life's work that he is, after all, so soon to abandon: "At twenty-one he evidenced a strong urge to change his life entirely—and to avoid the literary world where he'd earned nothing but a detestable reputation. We think of him as a powerful and successful poet, and yet he thought of himself as a failure." No hagiography: but a fellow writer's understanding, the knowledge that how we see ourselves and how the world sees us can hold an ocean's breadth between them.

Many sights can be glimpsed from the prow of this vessel, some dangerous, some mundane or serene. A certain quantity of notes are taken on the journey—it's a boat of writers, after all—but most, if not nearly all, end up discarded, grey paper flowers soaked in spatter and bilge. That's not what this journey is for, to create a brisk and sharable examination of the passing sights. It's not what writing is for, poetry, fiction, non-fiction (and what a curious term that is, "non-fiction," as if the truth were really just a lesser version of make-believe)—all of it produced by those who write, did write, will write to make a sort of sense, private or public, of the worlds we saw, the roads we traveled, the rivers we crossed or rode upon. In vino veritas is the maxim, so let this boat's intoxicating trajectory tell that final, fictional truth—isn't that why we read in the first place? To go somewhere else, somewhere exotic or achingly familiar, and find our truth is waiting for us there?

In the last third of this brief book—fitting, sadly, for this brief life—White follows a trail of constant, almost obsessive journeying. Post-poetry, post-Verlaine, he tracks Rimbaud through a series of landscapes, detailed through infrequent letters to associates and family—in thigh-high snow through the mountains, at the house of a Milanese widow, on a Dutch naval ship bound for Java; and the Cape of Good Hope, and Ireland, and Stockholm—trips undertaken with varying stated purposes, but truly because "Rimbaud longed to travel, and once it was in his blood that was all he could dream of doing."

But if the map enlarged beneath the traveler's feet, the world of letters abruptly constricts: White narrates this ending without sentimentality, without long sighs for what we, Rimbaud's readers, might have missed with his departure from poetry along with his final departure—until his life's end—from Europe and its discontents. White notes that "Although Rimbaud had turned his back squarely on literature, he remained obsessed with books….He who had hoped to reshape the world through the alchemy of language was now reduced to the study of actual practical techniques. And yet the goal—to know everything and control everything—remained the same." In an interview with David Velasco, White notes that "Rimbaud had a very exalted notion of what poetry was and what it could do to the world. I think he really thought it had transformative, magic powers, and when it turned out that it didn't, he gave it up. It was easy for him to give it up, because he was so deeply disappointed."

Does White perhaps feel some silent solidarity with this turned back, these firmly-folded arms? Do I? All our lives contain lacunae and pockets of despair, where we cannot imagine the fulfillment towards which our desires drive us, our talents, losses, and energies: it all seems like an icy slog through the mountains in snow, it looks just like the desert. And we, all of us, might escape, or dream of escaping, that place, or anyplace, or an occupation, a lover or our family, in this way, with firm despairing purpose and without a backward look.

But the escape from being a writer—not possible. If Rimbaud's life has lessons to teach (and what a burden to put on anyone! Only the posthumous can survive it), that must be the foremost: we are who we are. No matter our gender, our sexuality, our gifts or infirmities, we can transcend—sometimes, and with effort—what outer circumstances may create; but in doing so we only become, can only become, more deeply who we are. And he was still Arthur Rimbaud.

And White follows him still, on that road leading to Africa, to the years as a trader and exporter and gunrunner in Harar, where Rimbaud's stated dream was to become a successful businessman, a married man with a son whom he would train to become an engineer—how much of his own absent soldier father did he project onto that ambition? None of it came to pass: more disappointment, as White notes.

And when the last journey to Europe was made, as a man desperately ill, his mobility destroyed by a tumor that began on his leg and moved relentlessly to consume him, as he fled it from Harar to Aden to Marseille and then, poignantly, grotesquely, to his mother's farm in the Ardennes, White keeps pace beside him all the way: through suffering, amputation, final family estrangement, and the death that released "this troubled soul" to whatever road might open for him afterward.

Meanwhile, of course, his poetry was very much alive, its reach and reputation growing more and more robust, thanks in no small part to Verlaine who remained "faithful to [Rimbaud's] genius," White giving credit where it's due in this last chapter of *Double Life*. We're allowed, we readers, to find some comfort there, like the claimants and ardent squabblers who each see, in this prickly, solitary, ferociously talented individual, a mirror or a comrade or a guide. As White says, "[Every] important thinker and artist of the last hundred years has had an opinion on Rimbaud, who continues to elude us[.]"

But here I'll disagree with White: I think we may still see Rimbaud as friends might. An unknowable friend is no less a friend, if we choose to sustain company together, whether it's in a café, on a bright anonymous boulevard, a trader's track through the dust, the pages of a book; in a boat. That striking blue gaze may stay unfathomable—are ours any less so? "I" *is* another, we all are strangers to ourselves.

That Rimbaud was able to offer through his writing so much of his mind and his life's philosophy, is the much greater mystery, at least to me: that he could *see*, and say what he saw, in poetry engendered in struggle and obscurity; that Edmund White (and I) could read it, and feel its audacity and weight; that White could then write a book that I would read—all the mysteries of affinity and friendship commingle on those pages, and will every time we read them. And others will read them, too. The double life will begin anew, the boat never stops slipping the shore.

If every journey is really the traveler's life in miniature, if everywhere we go, there we are, then this boat brings us back at last to a cloudy little puddle in Charleville, a chilly boarding school dorm room window, an old school-teacher's desk where both these writers were met by this third. And if poets and rebels live doubled lives, my own real life began the day I learned that putting one word next to another could strike sparks and make light, and that certain fellow travelers—like Arthur Rimbaud, like Edmund White— were finding their separate ways in that light, a step or two ahead on our road.

"All this adolescent tomfoolery has given way to a description of a voyage that is both an actual odyssey and a spiritual saga... The poem ends not with a triumphant crossing of the open seas or a shipwreck, but rather with a little boy crouching beside a puddle and sailing a toy boat." (White, *Rimbaud: The Double Life of a Rebel*)

"What we desire is crucial to who we are."

—from *City Boy*

CITY BOY

FRANK PIZZOLI

THE CRUX OF the matter lies in the first two sentences of *City Boy's* book flap: "... after college he had the chance to pursue a Ph.D. at Harvard. Instead, he followed a lover to New York City." In looking back on my own life, I've often remarked that I have no serious regrets save one: that I didn't move to New York City the morning after graduating college. That shared, had I done so it's possible I would not be here to write this chapter.

I was 18 in 1969 when Stonewall erupted and I didn't miss a thing—hitting New York City as often as possible, I had lots of freelance sex, failed miserably at relationships because I didn't have a clue about what a relationship between two men was about or could be like. Early on neither did Edmund White, so I learned from interviewing him three times for *Lambda Literary Review*, two times in person and a third time via conference call with Felice Picano and Andrew Holleran as surviving members of The Violet Quill.

In our Violet Quill interview White said: "... I remember that when I first came to New York in July, 1962, the second or third night I was here, I was invited to the gay restaurant, The Finale. A gay restaurant? Why would gay people want to eat with each other?" He said right before that: "I think that when we were hearing the phrase "gay culture" I thought what on earth are they talking about? We're just a bunch of cocksuckers, you know. Where is this culture part?"

Even though we're still asking if there is or is there not "gay culture," assimilation moves large segments of the LGBT demographic into two spheres John Waters joked men of our generation happily avoided—marriage and the army. In that respect, we have become our parents. But in the preceding years, when we and White were city boys, our expressions of love and liberation were unparalleled. Our sexual culture evolved into an art form, our bodies the canvas, New York City a gallery open 24/7.

In White's city, as elsewhere, homophobia had a great deal to do with the spread of AIDS in the epidemic's early years. Until recently, and certainly before and immediately after Stonewall, the Heterosexual Dictatorship was in full control of the culture. Circumventing this oppression, gay men went underground and created an elaborate and efficient system of establishing a mostly sexual community. Post Stonewall, we moved the underground labyrinth into daylight and defiantly defined our liberation as sexual liberation. Since nothing happens in isolation, these twin forces—the sexual dictatorship and our response to it—created the perfect circumstances for a public health storm. We did in closed and open spaces what our oppressors defined, as does White and Jean Genet before him, as a criminal act, a mental illness, or a sin. We fucked with pride. In his Genet biography, White describes how he began "to question the official versions of normal behaviour." In 1949, Genet's published essay "The Criminal Child" notes the public's admiration of art glorifying criminals but that same public despises criminals themselves. For his own sexual life, Genet preferred the label of "criminal" to sinner or illness. Working with her now famous illness metaphor, Susan Sontag summarized post-Stonewall as a time when "many male homosexuals reconstituted themselves as something like an ethnic group, one whose distinctive folkloric custom was sexual voracity, and the institutions of urban homosexual life became a sexual delivery system of unprecedented speed, efficiency and volume." White's relationship with Sontag is legendary. He cooked dinner for her in his one-room apartment where she would find Robert Mapplethorpe or Fran Lebowitz. With her recommendation for a Guggenheim Fellowship, he moved to Paris in 1983. Sontag wrote a blurb she later rescinded for White's *A Boy's Own Story*. Their falling out centered on his fourth novel, *Caracole*, which "could be read as an attack… on Susan," White admits. He said during an interview, "If she'd have kept her big mouth shut no one would have known it was her!"

For many, participation in the gay sexual revolution was the first time they felt connected and loved. When AIDS first hit and activist groups formed all across the nation, many of those same gay men said the same thing—they finally felt connected to a community. That sense of community outside of sexual venues happened here in my adopted city, Harrisburg, PA, where in my living room, and the front room of a friend's home, we met fueled by fear to discuss what we might do and eventually formed what is today Alder Health Services. Gay Men's Health Crisis formed in much the same way. White retold in one of our interviews how "Larry Kramer got us all together in his living room. There were about 50 to 70 guys, I don't remember exactly how many, but we were all standing and it was a very big room. We heard Dr. Freedmen Keen talk. He was an NYU specialist, a straight man, and who ended his talk with the chilling words, 'if I were you I would just have no sex.' We knew the disease was sexual in origin but we didn't know what aspect of sex causes it. 'If I were you, I would just become celibate,' he advised. This he said to a room of fast lane New York men. And we were going out that night too."

With Gay Men's Health Crisis now 37 years old and ACT UP 27 years old, we are in the midst of canonizing AIDS with books and film. The process has begun; it is not complete. There remains much history to think through, honestly, and with the inconvenient candor of political incorrectness. Perhaps Sontag said it best—"Martyrdom is a hard legacy to disown."

White is anything but a martyr and he is honest. In thinking about his own life, White expressed in an email exchange that in trying to decide what influences our lives: "It's hard to be consistent or reductionist." He was in Maine writing a novel about a gay male French fashion model who comes to New York and never ages. I'd noted that writer and John O'Hara biographer Frank MacShane, while trying to frame O'Hara's *A Rage to Live*—a novel about my adopted hometown of Harrisburg—was influenced by Jules Romains's immense novel in 27 volumes called *Men of Good Will*, a panoramic view of French life from 1903 to 1933. In his portrayal of France, Romains takes up individuals and groups, tells their stories and then moves on to others, so there is no central character or necessary link between one and another. "I face the fact that this life of ours is very difficult to group around any central character," Romains explained; "that, indeed, it obstinately refused to be so grouped." This observation is similar to White's treatment of his own life in *City Boy*. His close friend, novelist John Irving, quotes White in his *Introduction*: "What we desire is crucial to who we are." What White desired in those years reflects who he was, the same as our desires those same years, and now, reveal to each of us who we are. If to victors go the spoils, so too to survivors goes the writing of their history. As we construct our AIDS history from these years will we be honest about who we were? (I'm not claiming to have the honest answers.) Will we resist easy reductions?

White himself said in an interview: "It's like the history of Syphilis or Tuberculosis in the 19th century, everybody had it and some wrote about it... What did AIDS do for us? I think it gave us a good subject. Yeats said there are two great subjects for any writer—love and death; and AIDS had both. Some of this comes through in White's *The Married Man*.

White's been with Michael Carroll since 1995 in a relationship he describes as based on "esteemed love," not necessarily monogamy, a theme in discussions of contemporary men's relationships that resonates especially now that Gay, Inc. has zeroed in on marriage equality. That singular focus on presumably monogamous matrimony can feel like a backlash to our more sexually experimental times, a backlash which is a silly notion because most HIV infections between men occur within the context of a primary relationship in which one or both partners do not know their HIV status. Both White and I are HIV positive, both long-term survivors. White says in his book "... in the 1970s, these questions of fidelity and couplehood didn't come up and we wouldn't exactly have known how to respond to them." Sexual etiquette assumed that "everyone would have multiple partners, that jealousy was definitely not cool" and that partners could always "annex a new atom." I was a serial dater, always amazed at how many guys in my area who hit on me and were involved in some sort of relationship. They seem to follow White's recounted NYC rule except their partners didn't know they had such an arrangement, or perhaps there was a mutual silence that zipped up the deal.

In that swirl of men, sex venues, and parties the city provided its creative class cheap rents. In the 1980s I paid $3.50 to enter The Everard Baths. "You used to be able to be a waiter two nights a week, support yourself the rest of the time, and you could go to your Herbert Berkoff class and learn how to be an actor. But now, no. That's the main reason why New York is dull these days. But I think the other reason is that a lot of the really interesting gay people died off in the 1980s," White said.

During those pre-Velvet Rope years it was "about the work" for most creative types, allowing almost anyone to meet almost anyone. In his *City Boy* review, author Daniel Mendelsohn writes in *The New York Review of Books*, "What's most pressingly at stake for him (White), in writing ostensibly about arts and letters, is the artists and the letters, the social and personal aspect of literary production." I've asked White what's wrong with focusing on the social and personal aspects of literary production—given his continuous entree to the city's creative class, I cannot imagine anyone not wanting to meet who he's met. White responded, "I believe that the fame of an artist or writer is mostly due to his legend, rather than his work. Look at Van Gogh, Rimbaud, Hemingway, Gertrude Stein. If we're honest about it, most of us respond to the extra-artistic image these people have."

White's own extra-artistic image comes across with ease. I learned immediately upon meeting White that even with his celebrity image preceding him he is without pretense. Although I'm not a starchy guy, I do rely on antiquated manners no longer taught. So off went a warm but respectfully formal email that White answered in less than 35 minutes. His simple lower case, one line note contained a date, time, location, and kudos on my writer's resume. We were strangers. Eventually, while turning a corner in his apartment building, not sure of my direction, White stuck his head out the door, beaming a huge smile. Once inside, he offered to make us a pot of tea with a blend sent from a friend he made while living in Paris. "And some dried fruit?" he asked. He made me feel like if I had said, "No thanks, but how about a grilled cheese sandwich," he would have made me one and asked how dark did I liked the bread grilled. I moved to his living room to set up a recorder, with him talking to me from the kitchen. His partner Michael scurried in and out with plastic baskets. "We're doing laundry today. If his passing through will be a bother, we can wait," White asked. It wasn't. When he brought out the tea and dried fruit and then sat down in his chair I realized he was just as excited as I was. My Q&A was next to me on the couch. White said he'd glanced at but hadn't read the questions. "I like these things to be fresh," he explained. Fumbling with the recorder, I finally got it working. "I'm sitting here in the apartment of Edmund Wilson..." I said, and then froze. "We'd both be in trouble if that were true." White's easy manner embodies what the city was like. In one of our interviews, he explained, "Fran Lebowitz used to say that everyone that read Andy Warhol's magazine *Interview* knew each other. It was such a small world, the downtown scene, that people all knew each other." Indeed. In 1978, when I was staying two blocks from Christopher Street on Charles Street with Elliot Cohan, brother of Martha Graham dancer Robert Cohan, and taking classes at Merce Cunningham's studio, Elliot asked if I'd like to meet the playwright whose work I'd found on his bookcase. Doric Wilson was walking towards us on Christopher Street during a Sunday promenade so crowded and ritualized that on both sides of the famed street men tried to walk casually, practically dick to butt in long lines that eventually ended up at the tip of Pier 45, abandoned, full of collapsed debris and holes through which men had fallen to their death in the water below.

Near the end of the Violet Quill interview, White says, "We may be the last generation of people who believed in the myth of the writer." Later he describes poet James Merrill's idea of "moral sculpture," the creative act of pretending that things are much more advanced than they are. Referring to his work with Dr. Charles Silverstein, co-author of *The Joy of Gay Sex*, White reveals with humility what many writers may not: "I created a kind of persona for myself who was much more comfortable with being gay than I actually was." He exposes perhaps his own myth and the idea others may have of him if only familiar with his novels.

Picano relates a similar experience with Silverstein when they worked on two later versions of *The Joy of Gay Sex*. That he found Silverstein "less comfortable with his gayness" than Picano was…" And that he actually developed more tolerance as we went along and got older." A myth broken? Remember too that Silverstein was one of the people behind the American Psychiatric Association removing homosexuality from its list of illnesses. White was prompted to explain that Silverstein, teaching a generation and beyond about gay sex, "was very inexperienced…He came out late and he went right into a relationship." Imagine that. In an era of sexual openness and experimentation often bacchanal, the man educating a generation of gay men was late to the party and likely monogamist. Silverstein not joyful? Perhaps not if joyful meant sexually prolific, as so many of us where in those years.

Back then Holleran, living in NYC then, was not exactly a dancer from the dance. He is rather shy and pleasantly reserved. When he had a firm chance to publish his most successful novel, *Dancer from the Dance*, he feared his parents might learn of his sexuality. So writer Eric Garber chose the pen name Andrew Holleran, not quite the fearless bon vivant who summered on Fire Island as did his characters drawn from the letters of a friend on which he based the book.

I do not note these divergences from the "myths" these writers may have accrued in order to be critical. I think each of these authors were brave to share their human inconsistencies. In a time when many think that if they can *remember* they are a historian, will we have the courage of White, Holleran, and Picano when we write down our history?

Even though *City Boy* is about New York City it symbolizes for gay men the collection of American cities to which gay soldiers moved post-World War II, having found one another in the confines of war. Later others decamped there in the heat of the 60s social and sexual revolution. Between June 23, 1960, when the Food and Drug Administration first approved oral contraceptives to June 5, 1981, when the Centers for Disease Control pronounced AIDS a disease, we experienced the only time in history when pregnancy could be prevented and STDs treated. Our collective memories of these years, and what younger men learn from reading our stories, will shape the narrative for many years to come.

"A novelist invariably has a strategic relationship to anyone he writes an essay about. I am drawn to a writer or photographer or painter because he or she actually was a friend and belonged to the same clan... or because they count as inspiring antecedents... I've always been intrigued by unjustly forgotten writers... and have written to bring their names back before the public, if only for an instant."

—from *Sacred Monsters*

SACRED MONSTERS

DONALD WEISE

"THERE ARE CERTAINLY people who call themselves 'gay novelists,' like Edmund White," Gore Vidal once said to me during an interview. "I think he's out of his mind. Why limit yourself any more than literature has limited you? In a world where people don't read, what are you going to make of a man who calls himself a gay novelist? What's that supposed to mean, that he's only going to write about cock?" I suppose everyone has his or her own definition of what constitutes a gay novelist, Vidal's being the most literal, but for me, Edmund White was the first gay novelist I read after coming out in college. Since I didn't know anyone who could show me a world of gay people I knew existed out there, I turned instead to literature for guidance. (Yes, I know, how very 20th century, but it *was* the 20th century.) I started with Ed's *A Boy's Own Story*—and I hated it. But don't take my word for it. Here's a passage from the book report I wrote to myself twenty-five years ago, the pages still tucked inside the novel: "White's little fairy is a poseur; a tiresome white kid whose ordeal over being gay is romanticized and dramatized all out of proportion...His character is exactly the kind of person I can't stand in real life, so why would I want to read about his so-called 'moral dilemma?'" Back then I went around holding forth like that. I was young, newly out, AIDS was everywhere, and I was angry at people, including Ed, apparently. The idea that years later I'd edit two of his essay collections and become one of his biggest fans was unimaginable at the time.

Happily for me, my feelings about Ed and his writing "matured" as I got older. Partly because I liked his other fiction but also because I'd read and admired essays he'd written for the *New York Times Book Review*, *Vanity Fair*, and the *New York Review of Books* among a handful of other publications. These were insightful and gossipy pieces on artists as varied as Jasper Johns, Robert Mapplethorpe, Jean Genet, and Ned Rorem. Ed, I discovered, is a cultural critic who can go deep with the best of them, yet at the same time be playful, racy, and drop the perfect nugget of gossip (more often than not sexual) into a serious discussion of French literature or modern photography. Much like the essays of Vidal, but without Vidal's self-conscious wit, condescension, and derision, Ed can take almost any topic, however grand, and discuss it as if it were no more complicated to navigate than the *TV Guide* crossword puzzle. In the hands of most writers, critical examinations of such heady authors as Foucault, Proust, or Nabokov turn into a literary death-march through the past. Not in Ed's case. Put another way, the size of a novelist's dick might be discussed prominently before a single work by the author is ever mentioned. To say this is my kind of writer is an understatement of the first order.

I first reached out to Ed about the possibility of working together on a new essay collection after publishing Vidal's book of essays, *Sexually Speaking*. It says something that I went from Vidal to Ed, my thinking being that Ed was outranked as a gay writer only by the Master. Or as Vidal once said of Ed the writer, "Edmund White can't wait for me to die so he can be King Fag." I approached the dauphin with a book proposal under the title *Arts and Letters*, as the common theme was artists and writers. I sent the table of contents to Ed at Princeton, dropped Vidal's name right and left in the cover letter since Ed wouldn't have ever heard of me, and without so much as checking my credentials, he said yes. If I'd come to appreciate Ed's work since reading *A Boy's Own Story*, I was now appreciating its author even more. Only I didn't see *Arts and Letters* to publication as it happened; I quit my job at the San Francisco press that was publishing it, deciding impulsively that I had to live in New York.

*

I was living in Manhattan only a few weeks when I emailed Ed to let him know that I was no longer in San Francisco but was now editing for a new publisher near his home in Chelsea. I asked if he was available for lunch so that we could finally meet in person. Although my email to him was out of the blue—for all he knew I was still in California, for all I knew he'd forgotten about me—Ed was immediately warm and welcoming. "Sure," he cooed. "How about you come by my place and ring my bell?" This not so subtle come on made me smile back then but never more so than right now, because, unknown to me at the time, I would become well acquainted with Ed's manner: shamelessly flirtatious and endlessly charming.

At lunch we talked a lot about me, something I wasn't used to with writers. Vidal, for one, never spoke a word to me that wasn't an answer or a directive handed to me as his editor. I was touched and flattered by Ed's attention. As one of his ex-boyfriends said to me, "When you meet Ed for the first time, and he turns that laser focus on you, where you feel like the most important person in the world because this important man thinks you're important, too, there's nothing like it." And there wasn't. Ed asked, "So, who all do you know in New York?" I said, "Just a friend from college." While I had known New Yorkers in publishing for years, I didn't know anyone well enough, say, to ask to a movie or spend the holidays with. That would come later, thanks largely to Ed. He named a handful of famous gay writers and editors whose names I recognized but had never met. When I said as much, he replied, "Well then, I'll throw a cocktail party and invite them over so you can meet everyone." Were this gesture alone all Ed had ever done for me, he would have my devotion for a lifetime. That this offer was only the beginning of a long list of generosities toward me must mean that he has my devotion for all eternity, because no one has ever been so consistently kind to me on such a large scale and never expected anything in return.

That kindness extended beyond just books and writers. Not long after I'd met him, Ed asked me to a talk he was giving at the prestigious Alliance Francaise, a midtown arts center devoted to French culture. He was to speak on Jean Genet, something he hadn't been called to do for some time and confessed to having to reread his own biography in order to recall the details from Genet's life. As you might expect, the finely-attired audience was full of French and French-speaking people. Sitting there alone, I felt underdressed, poor, and conspicuously out of place—not the first, or last, time that's happened. Ed's talk mercifully was in English, and he seemed to enjoy himself and the opulence of the evening. Once the talk was over and well-wishers ascended the stage to greet him, Ed spotted me in the crowd milling below the foot of the stage. He raised his hand as if to catch my attention and shouted above all the chatter, "Don't leave. We'll have dinner together." With that, everyone turned at once to regard me, a stranger—almost a kid, really—who'd been asked out by the guest speaker. His invitation was a real surprise, and I was flush with excitement over being singled out when clearly he knew some of these elegant people but chose to dine with me. I'd moved to New York in the hope of experiencing this kind of glamour, and here it was actually happening—dinner alone with one of my favorite authors. I felt like Cinderella being asked to the ball, and the cab to the restaurant downtown might as well have been the Prince's coach.

That first year in New York, when I was alone and single and still hadn't met all the people who would become my closest friends here, Ed and his partner, Michael Carroll, asked me over for dinner sometimes, the most memorable night being New Year's Eve, when Ed made lobster (until then I didn't know anyone who made lobster at home, but then I'd never met anyone like Ed). Someone had brought along a bootleg recording of Judy Garland dictating her memoirs, drunk ("I'm the mother of three beautiful children, goddammit! Liza, Lorna and… Joey."), that captivated everyone so much that we missed ringing in the New Year; only the celebratory shouts from across the street at midnight snapped us out of Garland's spell. Another evening Ed invited a group of us guys to come watch the HBO premiere of *Angels in America* on TV in the bedroom. We all climbed onto the bed or sat on the floor around it, at first anticipating an emotional night of viewing, but we began wisecracking and mocking the production once we realized the movie had little in common with our own firsthand experiences with HIV/AIDS. The show felt so safe, as if they'd filmed an AIDS movie for straight people. (I've since been told the actual play is nothing like that, and I don't imagine it is.) Ed didn't laugh or critique the movie along with the rest of us but made one memorable observation: "The problem with Tony's writing is his characters say exactly what they think." People pay for writing programs to glean that kind of insight into craft, but there it was, free, for anyone who listened.

In time, Ed proposed a second book of essays, *Sacred Monsters*, which would also showcase his articles on artists and writers. I felt more "at home" with this new book than I had with the first since not only was I now friends with Ed, and therefore relaxed in his presence and not out to impress, but I had personal involvement with some of these writings. His review of John Rechy's memoirs that appeared in the *New York Review of Books*, for example, was something I asked Ed to do as a favor because years back they'd published a homophobic review of *City of Night* titled "Fruit Salad," and anything Ed had to say would not only promote the book but help quell the lingering resentments anyone might still feel. The book covers everyone from John Cheever and Allen Ginsberg to E.M. Forster and David Hockney. Ed's piece on Edith Wharton, also published in the *New York Review of Books*, but not at my behest, is one of my favorites in the second collection, and I remember him working on it. I stopped by his place one afternoon while he was writing this lengthy review of Hermione Lee's new Wharton biography. Spread out all over the dining room table were oversized photo books containing sepia-toned images of New York City during Wharton's day; Fifth Avenue still dotted with mansions where Rockefeller Center now stands, the Plaza Hotel and Central Park across the street the only landmarks looking at all familiar to me. Ed didn't say so but I gathered that for him seeing pictures from the world Wharton lived in resulted in writing a more vivid review. I knew Vidal prepared for book reviews in this elaborate manner, sometimes reading a person's entire body of work before reviewing the author's new novel, but it hadn't occurred to me that Ed did that sort of preparation, too.

If Vidal is a frequent thread in this essay about Ed, it's because he once had played a part in both my life and Ed's but for different reasons. For me, Vidal was the first author I published, and I'm forever indebted to him for that. Ed wasn't as lucky. He wrote a play, *Terre Haute*, based loosely on Vidal's ongoing correspondence/friendship with Oklahoma City bomber Timothy McVeigh,

of whom Vidal was fond. I dropped in on Ed one evening only
to find him on the phone with Vidal, discussing the play. Once
the call ended, Ed came into the room and said, excitedly, "Gore
read and likes my play." He didn't need Vidal's approval to stage
the show (in part because the "Vidal" character is as much Ed
himself as it is Vidal), but having his cooperation was helpful.
However, that cooperation ended with the play's premiere, when
Terre Haute was well received. Suddenly Vidal objected, throwing
accusations of character assassination at Ed, in public and on record, and finally declaring a lawsuit. When I read that, I told Ed,
"But I was there the night you had him on the phone, when you
said he liked the play." Vidal later withdrew the lawsuit, but his
protests nonetheless marred an otherwise successful engagement.
Or maybe he actually helped promote the show, since no one
knew how to make headlines better than Vidal.

By now my friendship with Ed had reached a point where
there was nothing I wouldn't do for him. In fact, I welcomed any
opportunity to help should the occasion arise. When he was hos-
pitalized with a stroke several years ago, his partner, Michael, who
was there when the stroke happened and had been with Ed con-
tinuously since, phoned to ask if I'd come sit with him while he,
Michael, ran errands. There was only one answer for me, and
shortly thereafter I was at Ed's bedside keeping him company.
Despite the stroke, he was in surprisingly good spirits, though this
may have been put on for my benefit since he doesn't like being
a downer, ever. Or it may have been to mask his understandable
worry that he couldn't, at that time, move his legs or speak ordi-
narily. He asked apprehensively whether his speech had been
affected by the stroke, knowing that it had been but needing as-
surance. His speech wasn't nearly as bad as I'd anticipated when
I received news of the stroke, however, and I was grateful that
such a dignified person had been spared that. I quickly changed
topics as a way of taking his mind off things, and so started talking
about subjects he enjoyed most with me: men I was involved with
and gossip about other writers. As I spoke he dozed off for short
whiles only to wake up, turn to me suddenly, and almost look
apologetic, as if by falling asleep he was being a bad host. In some
way it felt like my life had come full circle: Years ago I'd sat next
to my grandfather's hospital bed, reading Ed's then-new book *Our
Paris* while my grandfather slept. Now here I was sitting next to

Ed's hospital bed, reading Andrew Holleran, as Ed slept. (Andrew, if you're reading this, beware the pattern taking shape.)

A social worker suddenly appeared and took down Ed's personal information for the move to another facility where months of physical therapy were to follow. She dutifully went down the list of questions, having no idea who he was, asking name, age, and address. When she came to occupation, Ed answered, without a moment's hesitation, "Freelance writer." I was astounded by his humility. To think of all his extraordinary accomplishments and yet, when you got down to it, Ed saw himself as no more than a freelance writer. I had to restrain myself from correcting him by telling the social worker, in a burst of pride, "He's the fucking most brilliant gay writer of all time!" Then again, maybe under the circumstances, "freelance writer" flew better with the largely straight healthcare professionals assisting Ed.

Recently, Ed and Michael hosted a party in their home for a young professor friend of theirs visiting from out of state. There were about twenty guests, comprised in part of the men who form the core of my innermost circle of friends. They ranged from people I'd met in New York as long as ten years ago and who have since become as close to me as family to more recent but no less cherished people, including boyfriends of friends who "married" into our circle. One such boyfriend took a seat next to me in the living room and asked how I'd met Ed and Michael. I shared an abbreviated version of this essay: how the first book of essays led to my friendship with Ed, which in turn led to friendships with friends of Ed's, which in turn opened the door to my new life in New York, and then to the second collection, *Sacred Monsters*. After all these years I often take everything for granted, but I sometimes need to remind myself that there was a time when I'd arrived in town and knew just that one college friend I'd mentioned to Ed over lunch. Looking around the room the night of the party, I marveled at how one book—and, more importantly, one man—had changed the course of my life. You don't publish books to make friends, but friendships develop if you're fortunate. On that count I've been fortunate in spades.

"I'd rather come back with a few transcendent memories than an album of snapshots."

—from *Jack Holmes and His Friend*

JACK HOLMES AND HIS FRIEND

JEROME ELLISON MURPHY

LIKE SO MANY a protagonist of heroic fantasy, Edmund White's Jack Holmes is endowed with a gift to face the trials of a perilous journey: in Jack's case, it's his enormous cock.

Jack's member, like a magical talisman, charms and awes those whom he encounters—individuals who covet, flee or resent its power, providing more insight into themselves than into a protagonist who in some more childish fantasy might remain a cipher, undefined, for projections of readerly subjectivity. But the demands of survival in New York chastise an unformed character, and as in any good adventure tale, this hero must confront situations in which his magic falters: "The guy didn't seem unduly impressed by Jack's huge penis, and Jack felt relieved but also slightly confused, like a movie star who finally finds a Caribbean island where no one recognizes him."

There are two cultural realities, the sexual and the racial, one explicit, one implicit, Edmund White evokes in *Jack Holmes*, a fable of bracing authenticity and delicious wit—one of his most breezily readable, yet most psychologically resonant works. Many readers, myself included, regard White's oeuvre as a national treasure. But here I confess. Overextended and exhausted, numbed by news media's ubiquitous overtures and the steady noise of internet discourse, looking for a good read, I was first drawn in by Bloomsbury's cover design: a pair of reclined male legs, crossed over a black and white cityscape background. While their air of sophisticated relaxation seemed to conjure strains of Gershwin to drift across these skyscrapers in grayscale, their indeterminate masculinity seemed evocative of a delicious tension between gay and straight sensuality (I had recently been re-savoring the angst of Guy Willard's coming-out story *Mirrors of Narcissus*). As it turned out, given the book's thematic arc, there was considerable irony in the allure of surface attributes.

This novel seemed poised to reflect *Us* in some representative, but teasingly erotic way: *Us* being gay men, or men period, or just Americans still grappling with relatively recent political and cultural upheaval. A gay man's relationship to straight men is one negotiation which, like his own coming out, never truly ends, despite whatever stance he's currently chosen. The novel fulfills this promise, but one of the reasons to return to *Jack Holmes* is that it does so in unexpectedly topical ways. Like the work of Sylvia Plath, one of my favorite poets, White's novel traces fault lines in the collective psyche of a period whose effects are still being felt, while engaging the timeless craving for fantasy in such a way as to deliver, as Ezra Pound called poetry, "the news that stays news."

Here that craving involves what White in *City Boy* referred to as "race and sex, the two great American obsessions." Sexual reality vies with sexual fantasy in the novel's narrative spotlight, but that light limns a surrounding darkness where corresponding racial fantasies and realities grapple, and as we will see, this shadow narrative is not so indistinct as it might seem.

It's the early sixties as Jack Holmes emerges self-invented from his mysteriously eccentric Detroit origins into a *bildungsroman* shaped by his desire to please both men and women, accommodating himself to perceived immediate needs. Meanwhile the nation awakens, chafing within a corset of decorum and archetype. Around this time (1961) Plath, in an artistic breakthrough, composes "In Plaster," describing a hairy yellow body yearning to break out of its cast:

> I shall never get out of this! There are two of me now:
> This new absolutely white person and the old yellow one,
> And the white person is certainly the superior one [...]

I gave her a soul, I bloomed out of her as a rose
Blooms out of a vase of not very valuable porcelain,
And it was I who attracted everybody's attention,
Not her whiteness and beauty, as I had at first supposed. [...]

She may be a saint, and I may be ugly and hairy,
But she'll soon find out that that doesn't matter a bit.
I'm collecting my strength; one day I shall manage without her...

The divided self, the "colored" soul of America inside a spot-less contour that conceals various physical, sexual, and racial realities, has already begun to show cracks. Having absorbed here-tofore accepted tropes, Jack maintains a stable of personas for expedient rotation, but New York is another story, bringing real-ity's firm hand to bear on his fairy-tale malleability: "Jack was stunned," during a job interview, "that his character, which felt like Play-Doh in his own hands, could be firmed up into such a tidy biscuit."

As in TV's *Mad Men*, a crisp, starched wardrobe of patriarchal tradition now finds itself subject to some unavoidable and messily organic realities. Its spotless uniforms, like Jackie O.'s dress, are now being sullied with blood and tears, unavoidable bodily excre-tions; American archetypes, previously smooth and sculptural as statues, disclose their unexpected pimples and hairs. A dawning disillusionment begins to find vivid local expression. The hetero-sexual Will Wright, object of Jack's decades-long infatuation, confesses after trimming his mistress's pubic bush: "There was an essentialist in me that didn't like the idea that I'd intervened and altered her toward a look I preferred. I had to squint morally and pretend that nature had trimmed her that way." It's as if one had expected a fanciful topiary to emerge perfectly shaped, without the disenchanting labor of pruning.

As social and sexual mores keep pace with the narrative's for-ward stride into the eighties, so that our protagonist navigates society as an acceptably "gay" figure rather than as an insidiously deviant "faggot," early diagnoses of AIDS intrude on a vision of sexual recklessness that is itself revealed as unsustainable fantasy. The "venereal filth" that repels Will in the homosexual lifestyle taints his own marital bed in the form of pubic lice he picks up from Italian heiress Pia, with whom he conducts an affair that for once makes his existence, like a work of art, dramatic. Nature's chaotic energy, White seems to suggest, is forever at odds with the human craving for clean Apollonian structure.

Rendering this cultural upheaval, led by urban bohemia that allowed for gay visibility, White encapsulates the turning point in one killer line: "Befriending a gay was like knowing a Negro—you didn't want too many, but one was chic." And here a reader, before indulging in retrospective amusement, might question just to what extent this dynamic has changed.

In *Jack Holmes*, White becomes our theater critic of cultural identity. As society shifts, archetypal roles must undergo investigation, and White's omniscient narrator wields the unsparing spotlight. "Jack knew that Howard, as a New York Jew, was studying him with amusement as a type, a Midwestern WASP ... Jack chuckled when he thought of how far he was from the conventional WASP of Howard's imagination." Alice, Jack's Greenwich Village roommate, "was from an old Southern family, though there was nothing of the debutante about her"; elsewhere Jack engages in sexual hijinks with "a guy of forty who'd mastered the preppy look without having learned the manner." Interrogation of artifice becomes the presiding motif as White shakes loose the dancers' disguises at a superficial society masque. This skill at dismantling social pageantry is one of the abiding delights of his fiction.

When Jack Holmes unmasks to his friend as an infatuated homosexual, the revelation elicits sympathetic (and not empathetic) disgust. Will's repulsion, made all the more painful to Jack by the gentility with which his friend's background demands this be handled, compels Jack to realize that "now he had to deal with the facts. In his fantasies he'd been playing with clouds; now he had to pick up solid boxes with sharp corners. Reality felt like a pitiful comedown."

Yet Jack persists in ascending this or that beanstalk into high clouds of fancy, however bruising the inevitable tumble. Reality thwarts each desired story arc, sometimes in hallucinatory ways. In a typical incident, after giving a young lover the key to his apartment, having (at last!) met someone close to his ideal, Jack finds imperfection distorting the fabric of this enchanted tapestry:

"Once Jack came in and found a little old crone with thick glasses and a hooked nose bent over a book, her nose almost touching the page. Jack drew back in alarm—but the crone turned out to be Rupert without his contacts in and without his head thrown back in his usual triumphant posture. The transformation from butt-boy to witch was so dramatic that ever after Jack found something factitious about Rupert's beauty."

With marvelous economy, White has sketched the essential dilemma of Jack's engagement with the world, that of the ideal versus the real. "Once" leads us into its own warped and certainly dubious "ever after." Three sentences trace a darkly comic fairy tale arc, in which the hero can only live happily by embracing, like Rimbaud at the end of *A Season in Hell,* some "gnarled reality." No fairy tale is without its crone, however much Jack—or we— may wish to extricate from its components the castle where a conventionally handsome prince will preside. Such delights are not easily won, and, in their very unlikelyness, are perhaps mirages. The mottled actuality Jack learns to accept in the form of a bald and portly older partner, embracing virtues that transcend the physical, is that of a tree—flexible, grounded, rooted and alive— versus that of a brittle architectural column, the stylized Platonic ideal, he must erect in thrall to Will Wright: a concept embodied in the phallus Jack hornily imagines as the "hard pure white bone of [Will's] desire." How telling that despite his own superlative endowment, over which countless bedmates salivate, Jack still craves this imagined avatar of masculine, and racialized, purity.

What is it precisely that draws Jack to Will, whose acne scars mar a patrician profile? Is it the promise of a securely untroubled manhood, an identity both fabulous and grounded? We find a clue in how deliberately White emphasizes the motif of "blue-bloodedness" in various descriptions of Will. Will's prominent and sometimes blue nose, "blue-white stomach," and even his (long-awaited) penis with its ropy blue vein, along with the typical blueness of his shirts, all evoke a supreme genetic inheritance unavailable to Jack, in flight from his own undistinguished status as a "Midwestern nobody."

This aspect of Will's magnetism finds voice in a lament made by heiress Alex Newton as her marriage to Will unravels. "I thought my husband might not have made Ivy, but that was okay; he was a modest, soft-spoken, true-blue knight, a knight of the Round Table, and I his Guinevere." For Alex too, despite the fact that she belongs to Will's own class (in fact financially outranks him) Will represents the prince that childhood stories promise the princess: an emissary of that transcendent realm where chaotic manifestations of entropy shall nevermore interfere with desires.

Outside of fantasy, chaos will likely undo such fairy tales, as it did the nation's own version of Camelot. Acne outbreaks aside, this "scion of Charlottesville," he of the horses and fox hunts, is lanky, untidy, emotionally withholding, at times underhanded, and—crucially for his mirror-like relationship to Jack—in some core way incomplete. He envies Jack's sexual license and his inherently fascinating status as a sexual deviant; Jack envies Will's unquestioned position in society as a masculine heterosexual of good breeding. About the same height, both good-looking and able to be mistaken for members of the same social class, Jack and Will project on one another their respective dreams of domesticity and rebellion. Only between them, they intuit, might they complete the circuit of a total personality: but this endeavor must fail, as neither one of them is entirely that which their typecasting would imply. Hence the hilarity, mingled with heartbreak, that ensues, as though the two were running a three-legged race.

Relishing this dynamic, White christens his characters with an impish sense of irony. Jack, as his name implies, is sexual, priapic, the invitingly undefined protagonist of his own fairytale (wasting no time in climbing beanstalks all over town—or rather alluring a parade of lascivious admirers to climb onto his). His name suggests a parallel with "Jack" Kennedy, making this tale of illusion and disillusion resonant with the larger historical context (in one beautifully ironic scene, Will, a Catholic, mourns Kennedy's assassination while namesake Jack pretends to feel something). One could argue for the surname Holmes as an ironic echo of "homes," as our restless Jack, estranged from his family, searches for his own secure station, in contrast to breadwinner Will, with his nuclear family unit and upstate homestead.

Alas, poor Will Wright perpetually "will write," ever digesting his experiences into ideas for fiction, with a creative impulse that remains dejectedly dormant after a single unflattering review (White has a blast skewering Will's premature preening as a feted man of letters). Will, his name so associatively chosen, is the ostensible Apollonian figure, with a desire for both stability and advancement, belied by the inability to urge himself into artistic production—or to finally resist base physical urges, despite his genteel persona circumscribed by family tradition. With all of his first-world advantages, just how free is our Will? Then the novel's title, suggestive in its simplicity of children's literature (*Frog and Toad are Friends* come to mind), seems to evoke the tug-of-war between immature wish and adult resignation.

Regardless of whether these gestures—or jests—appeal to a particular reader, only a writer brilliantly alert to associative echo could so skillfully walk the velvet tightrope between insinuation and outright camp. Edmund White walks such tightropes again and again. "A week later he had a brief meeting with an old Austrian who had carefully brushed gray hair like wings under which the egg of his baldness was nesting," White observes, and hasn't yet finished the sentence. To fold multiple images into an analogy that works with such tactility and suggestive logic is a feat: here, White makes it look effortless.

I savor too the novel's forensic coolness, revealing now Will's acne scars and now Pia's overgrown pubic hairs. White's overhead lamp swings a merciless halogen glow across these characters' psyches and physiques. Into every unflattering crevice probes that trademark honesty, that serrating lack of sentiment. If, as Graham Greene said, there is a splinter of ice in the heart of a writer, White's writerly heart might just contain the full cube, of ample size for chilling a top-shelf narrative cocktail. He can be as pitiless as D.H. Lawrence in exposing animosities simmering below the surfaces of daily interaction (and certainly as pitiless in depicting post-coital repulsion).

Back to Sylvia Plath for a moment, who could have used one of those cocktails, after spending a disastrous humid summer in New York sweating through her meticulously prepared wardrobe in a sojourn that led to the breakdown depicted in *The Bell Jar*; and not long after describing the aforementioned white plaster cast, would go on to write in "Berck-Plage": "The nurses in their wingcaps are no longer so beautiful: they are browning, like touched gardenias." Back to this idea of the *Mad Men*-era uniform, starched and stylized, finding itself sullied by sinister organic processes. Let's expose at higher contrast this imagery of mottling, this browning, as of the Platonic apple-flesh, of a flawless American whiteness.

Whites' whites: are they racially offensive? With their casually voiced dismissals of various racialized Others, against a background of aspirational Eurocentrism? I suppose this depends on the view from where you're sitting. And we know that when it comes to seats, historically, economically, socially, some may inherit thrones, others stools, and that a stool may well resemble a throne to somebody with no seat at all. Where I currently sit, surveying this post-Toni Morrison American literary landscape, I find less offense in White's depictions than an intriguing, perhaps quite useful, dissection of Whiteness: its strategies first of delineation, then of enforcement. The ruthless laser-eye with which White scans his characters' physical imperfections, their at times sordid self-interest, their outdated notions of gender and sexuality, he also brings to bear on their racial attitudes. This merciless honesty is all of a piece.

Skewering his own racialized notions after an encounter with his lustful Italian mistress, Will Wright muses: "Idea for story: naïve white man thinks of all orgasmic women as Negro until he meets Italian heiress." Yet a hundred pages later, when Jack Holmes questions whether women really like sex, Will readily answers: "Some do. Black women do, I think." We wince with the recognition that, like so many other fantasy tropes, that of the Negro as illicitly sensual, as bestially uninhibited—as bodily versus cognitive—dies unwillingly.

It's then no surprise when Will's mistress Pia concludes, despite having taken various lovers, that the source of a horrific pubic lice infestation must have been "that black delivery boy from Bloomie's." This culprit is presented in stark contrast to Will's original suspect, Oliver, about whom Pia asserts: "Heavens, no. Poor Oliver, he's so terribly British. He'd die with shame." One wonders what the black boy (who is no longer named, for now his de-personalization is crucial) would be expected to feel, if not shame. But the answer is obvious. His feelings are irrelevant, not merely because he is a supporting player, but because he serves here as a necessary counterpoint. He symbolizes illicitness, a taint and mottle on the Platonic ideal of whiteness which these characters regard as sometimes oppressive, but to which they also aspire: a never-quite-attainable position of superiority, reinforced in the text's references to blue-white physique, like a gallery of gleaming Greek torsos.

Only psychotherapy might resolve such neuroses. Yet as his therapy session ends, Jack's sardonic Dr. Adams is "once again forced to stand, like an English monarch dismissing an African prince who hasn't quite grasped that his audience is over." The idea of the African as relatively low status is important in animating this analogy of condescension, and as Westerners our familiarity with that role allows us to overlook its remarkable specificity. But a reader who pauses here might be struck by this tableau's precise staging; see how deliberately far it has placed us from any scenario in which a British or American party might request an audience with African royalty. This little fairy tale is the underbelly of Camelot—debased blackness forming the necessary soil on which to build that castle gleaming just out of reach.

Such gestures are insistent enough in *Jack Holmes*, especially in Will's first-person narration, to invite some comparison to *The Great Gatsby*'s Nick Carraway, with his uneasy complicity in notions of racial hierarchy, but here one particular passage unlocks this conflict's ornate puzzle box. It does so with the same key unlocking the novel's love triangle, and its members' relation to their social milieu: the exposure of a perilous pretense.

This passage describes the Serengeti excursion Will makes with his wife Alex, ostensibly to re-establish the domestic equilibrium upset by his infidelity. Indeed, F. Scott Fitzgerald explicitly enters the scene as the relative age of their fellow travelers restores Will and Alex, by contrast, to a state of glamorous youth:

> We were once again the enviable young couple, American aristocrats [...] I allowed as to how I'd published a novel, and the people from Cleveland I'd confided in told the others, and soon their nicknames for us were Scott and Zelda. We tried to ignore the warning those names suggested of alcoholic defeat and madness and enjoy their more glamorous associations [...] Maybe because the other members of the safari saw us as so princely, so adorable, we tried to live up to their perceptions. Alex looked smart in her dark safari suit [...] She bought an absurdly colonial pith helmet that everyone admired, though its associations made the progressive Cleveland lady uneasy. Alex was relaxed and warm with the black servants [...]

In their excursion to "Africa," which is necessarily more a concept than an actual continent, Will and Alex are given license to masquerade, which has an aphrodisiac effect on them. Of course it does: they've now entered the very cradle of illicit black sensuality, of bestial instinct, in which they can only preserve their own status by proportional signifiers of Whiteness. Will is no more interested in the darker implications of this racial masquerade than he is in those of the Scott and Zelda personas. That White describes the wardrobe at some length (Alex's "carefully tailored jacket sporting huge external pockets she was careful to keep empty and flat") signals its function as costume, carefully chosen, and that this pretense is as dangerous, and as flimsy, as any of the other identities whose masks suddenly slip in these pages. The message is clear: Whiteness—especially in its need for props of flattened, subordinate blackness—is one more precarious fairy tale, folks.

Unsavory as such passages may or may not be, they support Toni Morrison's conception in *Playing in the Dark* of voiceless blackness as a crucial accessory to white identity as enacted in American literature. Literary whiteness, so clearly exemplified in the classic works of such writers as Hemingway, Twain and Cather, can't exist without it. Yet the anxious delineation of identity, whether in life or art, the impulse to define oneself against the other, the way straight adolescents call each another fag, is hardly restricted to Whiteness, though it has been manifested with gruesome familiarity to us in that particular vein. And so to fully answer the question of offensiveness is to ask—not without a shudder—whether the denomination of any cultural identity, especially at its contested outer boundaries, is not always engaged in the somewhat de-humanizing process of othering.

How, then, could those perpendicularly positioned "others" of gay and straight masculinity align? How could they establish, then sustain, any friendship? In one sentence, late in *Jack Holmes and His Friend,* Edmund White articulates the essential dynamic of gay/straight male camaraderie: "There were so few safe ritual male topics available to us that we ended up saying things that were real and personal."

In time, Will and Jack chafe inside their respective performances, as inside plaster casts, and it is the conversation each has with himself—when the ossified rituals fail—which seeks authentic voice. Having embraced (however imperfectly) the shadow aspects of themselves they once sought in each other, they become individuals of independent gravitation. Our last glimpse of Jack shows him smiling, nodding, "toward no one in particular." Jack is finally freed from his need for an audience, having set aside that magic mirror of idealized reflection in others' eyes. Pinocchio becomes a real boy. More to the point, Jack is no longer a protagonist, and no longer needs us, his readers.

Meanwhile, out here in real life, construing such ungainly and unshapely experience, we all still need one other. If we desire soaring castles, somebody has to lay the bricks. If we desire whimsical topiaries, someone has to trim them. As the apple of American idealism grew overripe, growing spots like that acne outbreak on Will Wright's face, its consumers had to ask what other fruits this tree might bear, what soil would nurture such divergent roots. Now we've got to get ourselves, in Joni Mitchell's phrase, back to the garden. As American identity further atomizes, as we become a nation of Others, there may be for us, as for Will and Jack, so few safe "ritual topics" available that we end up saying things more real and personal than ever before.

"For me a current lover has always been like whatever current book I'm writing—an obsessive project orienting all my thoughts."

—from *Inside a Pearl*

INSIDE A PEARL

ALYSIA ABBOTT

I WAS EIGHTEEN years old and living in Paris when I first heard of Edmund White. My father, an openly gay San Francisco-based writer, wrote me about White in a letter and instructed me to bring some books to his apartment on Île St. Louis. "Edmund used to teach at Columbia University—knows Susan Sontag—used to be a *Time* magazine editor. He's gay but raised a teenage nephew—a *very* nice, charming, funny person who it would be good for you to know for your writing career. He probably knows interesting French writers too!" In that summer of 1989, I was living abroad for the first time, spending my days working in a law office and my evenings alone in a dormitory for foreign girls on work visas. I was looking for a kind of guide, a friend, anyone to help illuminate the dark alleys of my solitude. Dad's letters were my only comfort. But he couldn't remember Ed's phone number, only his address, and when I made my way over to the apartment on a bright Sunday morning, no one answered the door. I rang several times before despondently walking back to the Metro, deciding it was not meant to be.

That same summer of 1989, in between reports of my father's rotating cast of roommates and our gossipy mutual friends at Café Flore, he wrote about his falling T-cell counts. Three years later he died in San Francisco with me at his bedside. The following spring I returned to Paris to scatter his ashes from a gilded cardboard box into the Seine, just steps away from Ed White's old apartment on Île St. Louis.

In 1994, I was living in New York, still adrift and grieving my father, but now in a community of college friends who knew nothing of the AIDS epidemic still raging. That's when I learned that Edmund White was also in mourning. His lover, a married French architect named Hubert Sorin, had just died of AIDS, at age 32. But before his death the two collaborated on a book celebrating their neighborhood of characters, *Our Paris*. Hubert illustrated White's vivid and witty descriptions with his own *bandes-dessines* (comics). Ed has said that in producing *Our Paris*, he felt like Scheherazade in *Arabian Nights*, determined to keep spinning stories as a race against death. Instead of doing so to save his own life, Ed kept telling stories to prolong the life of his beloved.

With the publication of this new book, Ed returned to New York City to read in a West Village bookstore, and once I heard about the event I was determined to meet him. At 23, I knew a little more about the world and of Ed White. I'd purchased his award-winning biography of Jean Genet, and passed his collection of essays, *The Burning Library*, eagerly amongst my literary friends. I approached him in the signing line following the reading. The literary lion was swarmed with people. Would he know who I was? Would he care? When I introduced myself, his eyes softened. He took my hand. Yes, he remembered. Dad wrote him about me and he was sorry to have missed my visit. Ed signed my copy of *Our Paris*, "In loving memory," and scribbled the phone number for his Paris apartment on Rue Faubourg, where he had lived with Hubert and now lived with his new boyfriend, Michael Carroll.

I happened to be going to Paris that fall and, feeling bold, called Ed. I dropped in with a friend late in the afternoon just as Ed was just finishing up some exercises with a private instructor, a "professeur de fitness." I waited for him to change as Michael mixed cocktails and served crackers. Sitting in his living room, talking about *Our Paris*, slightly buzzed, I professed my inchoate desire to write a tribute to my father. But inside I was trembling. Here was the celebrated Edmund White, in the very apartment I'd just read about, and here was me, with this vague idea of a dream of a book, a book I dearly wanted to write, holding onto it like a beacon of light that carried me through my grief. Who did

I think I was kidding? I was no writer, not yet. I had no idea where to even begin. But Ed was supportive. He recommended I read *Cheever's Letters* edited by Cheever's daughter. He told me he'd introduce me to some friends in New York.

I clung to the memories of that conversation and to the works of Edmund White after I returned to NYC and struggled with how to best to memorialize my relationship with my dad. I felt, and continue to feel, a familiar comfort nestled inside Ed's pages. Ed White has been called a "triathalete" of prose letters: a master novelist, biographer, and memoirist. I've read many of his books and essays but have always most connected to his autobiographical work. This is not only because, identifying as a memoirist, I love to study how different writers tackle the puzzle of self, but because the worlds that Ed describes are themselves so fascinating and are described with such loving detail and wit. Reading his works is to travel through history with the most generous and charming of companions. His books also provide me a way to better understand my father, what it meant to be closeted in the Midwest in the 1960s and then sexually unleashed in a coastal city after Stonewall. Photos of Ed at his Michigan boarding school as a young man, in glasses and crew cut, remind me of pictures of my own dad in Nebraska, stiff and smart and a little too sensitive to survive the plains in the McCarthy era.

Ed White was a more prolific and successful writer than my father. More readable too. My dad was drawn to an experimental post-modern style while Ed's work, despite its many sex scenes, is grounded in the classic 19th century novel form. And yet through Ed's writing, more than any other literary works I've come across, I feel able to understand my dad's aspirations, his sexual awakening and eagerness for adventure, his desire to mix in a world of French intellectuals and fantastic characters. Ed White lived the life my dad would have loved to live and, crucially, a life that Ed continues to live.

Though living with HIV, Edmund White has a rare non-progressing strand of the virus. He's won the lottery of sorts but in doing so has had to painfully watch scores of friends and lovers die before him, including very young lovers like 32-year-old Hubert. There's a particular guilt known by survivors of the AIDS epidemic, especially known to those who see no reason why they were spared. Though Ed moved to Paris in 1983 to escape the

338 · CRASHING CATHEDRALS

specter of AIDS that haunted New York in that era, grief runs
through Ed's Paris books, especially *Inside a Pearl: My Years in
Paris*, which he'd published in 2014. Like many of his books *Pearl*
is a story about friendship but as in many of his books, friendship
is tied to loss. "By some magical fetishism," he writes near the
book's end, "I sometimes think that if I dialed old phone numbers
of friends, long since dead, they'd answer."

Hubert, who illustrated *Our Paris*, and inspired the fictional Julien in *A Married Man*, is plainly himself on the page in *Inside a
Pearl*. "When my lover Hubert Sorin was dying of AIDS," White
writes, "he was always trying to fix me up—posthumously, as it
were—with the cute busboy at the hotel." In writing me that letter
in 1989 I wonder, now, if my dad wasn't also trying to set me
up—posthumously—with the successful writer around the corner, a gay father figure. (Dad was always pushing me as a writer,
even referring to my "writing career" at 18—when I'd yet to publish anything outside of my freshman comp notebook.)
Unconsciously I appointed Ed to that role. I've since learned he's
played mentor to many young writers, including Rakesh Satyal
and Andrew Sean Greer. Not only is he a winner of numerous
international literary awards but he's one of our most important
living LGBTQ pioneers. He took part in the 1969 Stonewall Riots, cofounded the Violet Quill and Gay Men's Health Crisis.
Through his autobiographical fiction and copious memoir writing
Edmund White is the preeminent keeper of our collective
memory.

I write "our" memory, but as a straight woman I know the
collective memory doesn't really belong to me. Yet as a woman
who was raised alone by a gay man in the 70s and 80s, a man who
died of AIDS at the height of the epidemic in the 90s, I continue
to feel a powerful kinship with the LGBTQ community. This is
perhaps another reason Ed's work resonates so much with me.
Though his work depicts the intricacies and desire-driven rituals
of gay life in the 20th century, he also makes room for the straight
women in his life.

Inside a Pearl is an ode to Ed's years in Paris, a city so cold, grey
and misty it's like living "inside a pearl," and also an ode to his
friendship with Marie-Claude de Brunhoff. An illustration of Ed

and "MC" (as she's called) graces the cover of the hardback edition and in the memoir's opening line he reveals he discovered France through her. Nevertheless, he writes of being initially suspicious of MC's flirtatiousness. "Hadn't she been told that I was the coauthor of *The Joy of Gay Sex* and impervious to her allure?" He then goes on to explain how in France especially "straight and gay women never shied away from taking a gay man's arm." Later in the book when MC's husband, the son of Babar creator Jean de Brunhoff, leaves her for a younger woman, Ed comes to her side, providing her companionship and comfort when she needs it most. He describes their relationship as a sort of ideal in the essay "Straight Women, Gay Men," written in 1991 and published in *The Burning Library*. "The 19th century German philosopher Hegel thought that the highest human love is that of brother for sister, since it blends the reciprocity of two genders into a tender, sexless relationship in which neither partner has a motive. By that definition a gay male-straight female friendship approaches those disinterested heights."

I've had similar thoughts regarding my relationship with Dad. Because he was a gay man who populated his life with male friends and lovers, I felt confident that I'd always be the most important woman in his life. And though I was left alone many nights he spent seeking companionship in San Francisco's gay bars and clubs, I also suspected that, despite these efforts, our relationship was his only constant, and that I'd be the one looking after him and tending to him, the way a girlfriend or wife might, as I in fact did in his final months.

I wasn't aware of these parallels when I first encountered Edmund White in my 20s. In 1998, 27 and working at the New York Public Library, I ran into Ed and Michael at a Nabokov event at the library. I invited him to take part in a reading I wanted to organize for the anniversary of my father's death at the now defunct A Different Light bookstore in New York. I'd edited the letters my father and I wrote each other in college, starting when I was a freshman at NYU and ending when I graduated early to move back home. I proposed that we might "perform" the letters together, with Ed playing the role of Dad, a 40-something gay man making his way through life as a single under-employed writer in the city and me playing myself, a self-centered but still loving daughter exploring herself and Europe for the first time.

We met for sushi at a restaurant in Chelsea near the apartment he shared with Michael to go over our lines. Taking place as it did on World AIDS Day 1999 (my father died December 2nd) the reading was for me a profoundly powerful evening and the most satisfying way to close out the century. But in retrospect the night is most notable for what took place afterwards.

The downstairs of A Different Light was stuffy and hot, packed full of young men, who after filling up the seats sat along the floor. There were fans of Ed White, but also my friends, friends of friends, and a handful of work colleagues. As different folks approached our table to say hello, or get a book of Ed's signed, he would whisper to me, and discretely point. "That one's good looking… He's cute. Oh, look at HIM!" like someone trying to choose their favorite pastry in a bakery window.

I would discover an echo of this scene in the pages of *Inside a Pearl*. "MC liked to think of us as the scandalous couple in *Les Liaisons Dangereuses*, calling herself Madame de Merteuil and me Valmont. Once we went to hear Hubert Selby Jr. read at the Village Voice bookshop… MC nudged me in the ribs and indicated an extremely handsome redhead wearing designer clothes: 'There's one for you!'"

At the time of our A Different Light event I was 28 going on 29 and in a stunted stage of romantic development. I'd spent the majority of my 20s chasing after beautiful but unavailable young men, and one in particular who played the role of Jordan Catalano to my Angela Chase, (as depicted in the 90s teen drama *My So-Called Life*). I was so focused on which boys might like me, and what I needed to do to *get* those boys to like me, that I neglected to consider who I was attracted to, and that desire itself could be empowering.

As I was finishing up with a friend congratulating me on the night, Ed pointed out a tall, shaggy young man approaching our table. Jeff Howe and I had met a couple of times. He'd gone out of his way to introduce and reintroduce himself to me at various functions, but it never went any farther than that. "HE'S cute," Ed gushed and I thought to myself, *he IS cute*. I asked Jeff out the next week, the first and only time I've ever asked a man out on a date. And today we're married. Naturally it'd take an older gay man to school me on how to desire men.

Ed helped me romantically but, more crucially, he nudged me along my path as a writer and memoirist. At my request he generously wrote me letters of recommendation to graduate school, helping me get into the New School's MFA program, where I wrote the beginnings of what would be my 2013 memoir, *Fairyland*. As part of my thesis on the power of place in literature I carefully reread Ed's Paris books: *Our Paris* and *The Married Man*, a fictionalized account of his relationship with Hubert, which he published in 2000. In *The Married Man* one metaphor in particular stayed with me. AIDS is like a hungry lion following behind you. You dare not turn around to look, but you can hear the movement of his heavy paws. You can feel his hot breath on your neck at all times.

I complimented Ed on this line. "Oh! I stole that from Balzac," he said, reminding me that so much of the art of writing is the art of theft. So I borrowed his image in my own work-in-progress. Though the lion never made it to the published version of the memoir, considering AIDS as a carnivorous predator helped me to understand and articulate that particular menace inspired by loving someone afflicted with a terminal illness.

When I was scouting for esteemed writers who could blurb *Fairyland*, I reached out to Ed through Michael, and he generously complied. When I read his opening words, "A vivid, sensitively written account of a complex but always loving relationship," I felt a surge of contentment. If the writer my father so admired, admired the book I wrote about my father, then I must have done something right.

As I write this essay, it's the summer of 2018 and I'm sorry to note that I've not seen Ed in years. Both of us have changed in the last three decades. I live in Cambridge with two children and don't get to New York as much as I'd like. After a heart attack in 2014, Edmund isn't as agile as he once was. Yet he continues to publish books every year or two and I feel, as much as I feel anything, that we need him in our culture more than ever. Why? He answers that question in the final pages of *Inside a Pearl*: "[I'm] alive in order to—well, to teach, to trick, to write, to memorialize, to be a faithful scribe, to record the loss of my dead."

"What did they say about Helen of Troy? That her face launched a thousand ships? That's you, you're that beautiful. A thousand ships."

—from *Our Young Man*

OUR YOUNG MAN

RICK WHITAKER

EDMUND WHITE'S LATEST novel, *Our Young Man*, is a French-American fantasy inspired by Oscar Wilde's *Picture of Dorian Gray* and Alphonse Daudet's *Sapho*. The hero (who is not at all heroic), Guy, is a wildly successful French fashion model who arrives in New York just before AIDS does at the beginning of the 1980s. His seductive talent is for looking young and staying beautiful—even after he's no longer young, and even when he uses a lot of cocaine to keep thin. He easily earns a lot of money, and some rich older men fall for him and give him an apartment, a car, a house on Fire Island. His first lover, a young Spanish art forger, ends up in prison for his Dalís, and his second, a young blond with a twin, ends up going to South America alone, Guy having decided at the last minute to stay put in Manhattan. It is not the kind of novel that turns out a neat moral, or even a dominant theme. The characters do not learn any important lessons from their choices; they have no epiphanies. After the story ends, life just goes on. What we get, instead of gravitas, is an entertaining masterpiece of staying on the surface, not unlike the novels of Wilde and Daudet.

Daudet's 1884 novel *Sapho*, upon which White's novel is loosely based (it was "a springboard," he says), tells the story of Fanny Legrand, a beautiful muse and model in Paris. Long before the action of Daudet's novel begins, she posed for a sculpture which became a French favorite and was often reproduced. When the novel opens, Fanny is seducing young Jean Gaussin, whose father had a copy of the sculpture on his desk. Jean's uncanny familiarity with Fanny's semi-naked body, however, is revealed to him only later—when it's too late. At first, he is simply seduced by a woman who is pretty and seems young.

In an unsigned 1885 review in *The Nation*, a critic says of Daudet, "He is realistic without being systematically vulgar; he does not absolutely prefer odious, hideous, loathsome subjects and characters; he is not a pessimist, and there is in him an irrepressible touch of the gay, cheerful, optimist South." [*The Nation* Number 1072, Jan 14, 1886]. Edmund White is from Ohio, but the same could nevertheless be said of him as a novelist, especially in *Our Young Man,* which is remarkably free of the slightest hint of schadenfreude or bitterness.

Edmund White's gallivanting Guy is photographed nude when he really is young by a Parisian photographer who, unbeknownst to Guy, sends the photos to a New York editor at *Blue Boy* magazine who prints them in the early 1970s, long before Guy comes to America. Later, when he's in his 40s but still looks 25, his true age is revealed to his boyfriend, young Kevin, when Kevin remembers having seen (and used) the images of Guy in *Blue Boy* when he was 12.

I have read *Our Young Man* in manuscript, courtesy of its author, a friend. It was published by Bloomsbury in 2016. On a personal note: Ed and I read our new work aloud to one another regularly, and I heard him read parts of *Our Young Man* while he was writing it, especially during the summer of 2013 when I spent a week in Maine with Ed and Michael Carroll, his husband. I will surely always associate the tone of this novel with the laughing, happy sound of Ed's voice, one of the most companionable, warmly musical speaking voices I have known. His voice corresponds to his personality, which is irresistibly genial, sincerely friendly, and almost miraculously elegant in its bearing of Ed's erudition, wisdom, and loving kindness. In many years of close friendship, I have never once seen Ed rude, condescending, cruel, stingy, dismissive, or unpleasant. *Our Young Man* is very much like the cuddlesome titan who dashed it off.

*

White, of course, is a master of the adorable gay phrase, the bon mot, and the expression of what a certain type of gay man might think but not say. Here in *Our Young Man*, Guy is fucking beautiful young Kevin for the first time. "He was taking Kevin's cherry! The words made him harder and made him feel privileged, masterful, married. He thought how many men would pay unlimited amounts to have this inaugurating experience with this boy. He didn't want to feel like a middle-aged pedophile, he didn't even want to think all this would make a good porn film. He wanted every thrust, every second, to be laden with tenderness, a salute from him to Kevin, a deep recognition. He wanted Kevin to like what was being done to him, to push back for another joyous millimeter of penetration. He didn't want him to label it Guy's First Fuck or Kevin's First Time. He didn't want the idea and the label to crowd out the sensation or to sharpen it; he wanted it to be pure sex, undramatized."

Part of the charming comedy of White's novel is its funny difference from Daudet's 19th century novel with its period shyness about sex. Though sex is certainly at the heart of Daudet's story, it is barely mentioned. But while fucking Kevin again later, the high-fashion jetsetting (but unjaded) model Guy sees their reflections in a mirror. "Suddenly nothing in the world seemed to Guy more glamorous than homosexuality, as romantic as heady white gardenias nested in polished green leaves. 'Can I come in you?' Guy asks."

White's narrator relishes intimate experience along with sex. When Guy and Kevin shower together after their first time in bed, White describes how they "rotated in the narrow tub under the showerhead; whoever wasn't under the water soaped up, stood with legs ajar to wash his own crack, took the blasts full in the face, lifted his arms to clean his hairless pits."

Our Young Man, which was written on either side of a major heart attack and open-heart surgery, is a lighthearted novel, filled with jokes and wit. White, who has taught at Princeton for many years, has Guy fellating Kevin in the shower. Kevin offers to reciprocate, saying it's only fair if they do. "Only Princeton boys care about fairness," Guy said. When Kevin, his first time on Fire Island, asks Guy if everyone there is always so friendly and in such

348 · CRASHING CATHEDRALS

a good mood, Guy says, "They're drunk now, and optimistic, but they will soon be squabbling over household expenses and hoping they'll find love later in the Meat Rack. They'll be arguing, 'Why did you buy that expensive leg of lamb?' And they become especially cross at the beginning of September when they realize the season is over and they've danced their tushes off and fucked a lot in the bushes, but, hey, they haven't bagged a beau for the winter and they've maxed out their credit cards."

Chapter One of *Our Young Man* ends with perhaps White's most hilarious scene ever. On Fire Island, Guy meets Edouard, a French baron with a taste for beautiful young men and also pain, leather, and humiliation. "They were introduced and the baron, ugly as a commissar, held on to Guy's hand for an uncomfortably long interval." Guy visits the baron's yacht for orgies and is invited for dinner à deux. "The butler called Guy 'Monsieur' and the baron 'Monsieur le Baron.'" Edouard points out to Guy a badly painted portrait of his mother. "The painter had shown more interest in the candy-striped silk dress with its frothy lace bodice than in the subject's face, which looked fairly generic. 'She was a saint—but a powerhouse, too. I've tried to follow her example by surrounding myself with beauty and sensitivity.' He winked. His newly installed hair was dyed a Death-in-Venice black." I won't spoil the reader's pleasure by describing the filthy ending of Chapter One. But it's a classic of gay fiction, as is *Our Young Man* altogether.

Like every bookish gay man of my generation (I was born in 1968), I have waited impatiently for each of Edmund White's new books to appear, and read them instantly and repeatedly with a singular kind of pleasure. For me, Edmund White has always been not just the head of the gay-literature pack, but also a leading figure in American letters whose essays have been of equal importance to his fiction. He is that to which one aspired when I was younger; now he is simply the best there is, the most eloquent, the hardest-working, and the most intellectually attractive. The fact that he is aging and will presumably not live forever is suggestive, for me, privately, of something sadly looming in my mind: the end of the age of gay sensibility. I hope, but doubt, that it will outlive Edmund White. If it does, it will be due in no small part to the memory of him we have on account of his ravishingly good books.

*

White has taught generations of gay men how to write honestly, without shame, to tell with grace and courage the true stories of our own lives. As a writer, activist, intellectual, teacher, and friend, Edmund White continues halfway through his 70s to exemplify the very best of literary culture. He is the most indispensable gay writer in America—read, admired, and loved by so many.

"We never read the same book twice. But each time it is our book, locked in our innermost heart as we move and change through time."

—from *The Unpunished Vice*

THE UNPUNISHED VICE:

A LIFE OF READING

TOM CARDAMONE

OF COURSE, IN the time it took to compile these appreciations of Ed's work, he produced another book.

What an astounding volume, as if Ed overheard our joyous conversation of *his* work and expanded on it upwards and outwards. As the consummate memoirist, you would think he had left no page unturned, but then this diamond surfaces, *The Unpunished Vice: A Life of Reading.* Here is a multi-faceted account of superlative literary reflection, borne from the earthquake (lifequake?) of a heart attack. Here we have memories and discourse on a lifetime of books read, the texts that have influenced White's art and thinking—books savored, books turned over again and again as new aspects reveal themselves, and most important: the people, the friends and colleagues who delivered these books into his life.

Edmund White suffered a heart attack in 2014, which left him for the first time in his life uninterested in reading or writing. Surreal daydreams swirled up to fill this void, and when this drought broke, he finished work on the novel *Our Young Man* (it was halfway done before the heart attack) and in reading again, he began to consider the habits and desires that had filled his shelves with books. Readers of his previous biographical (both fiction and nonfiction) works will run into a familiar cast: his somewhat wacky mom gifting the young White a biography of Nijinsky, his close friends in young adulthood, Marilyn and Charles, swaying his impressionable taste with books and literary conversations. Boyfriends and crushes appear; his husband, Michael Carroll, once a young lover from *Inside a Pearl*, is now a published peer with clashing tastes and convictions. As White narrates coming into his own as a writer, *The Unpunished Vice* grows into a veritable avalanche of interesting books and talented folk: the early admiration of Nabokov, the friendship of John Irving and Joyce Carol Oates, just to name a few, are all described here with wit and candor. *The Unpunished Vice* itself is dedicated to Rick Whitaker, a favorite author of mine who wrote about *Our Young Man* in the previous chapter, and whose friendship is lovingly, rakishly detailed.

White visits his own books with the lightest of finger taps. Only when a solid correlation in another text, a stylistic point learned or a moment of inspiration, presents itself are we treated to the germinations of his own work, and then often with just a sentence or two. These moments, though fantastic, fall outside the thesis of tackling a life of reading, and those interested can find satisfaction elsewhere in White's work, the Genet chapter in *My Lives*, for example, or specific author monographs in *Arts and Letters* and *The Burning Library* that Kevin and Charlie talked about earlier.

As a memoir, *The Unpunished Vice* also serves as an important document chronicling gay literary history (more on that later). The characteristically generous dollops of advice also place this book on the books-for-writers shelf.

"I like to read great books not because I'm hoping to imitate them but because I want to remind myself how good you have to be to be any good at all. We won't be read in the light of other writers in our zip code or decade but as we compare to Proust, Joyce, and Nabokov. History has set the bar very high, and one must jump over it, not do the limbo under it."

So simple it could be printed and taped up on the wall as permanent advice to an aspiring writer. And then there are the frightfully inspiring observations:

> I think in fiction we admire energy more than virtue—even in an energetic paranoid, like Kinbote in *Pale Fire*, who takes all the unbleached floss of experience and weaves it into a tight, gleaming knot. There is an energy, a force, in paranoia; the paranoid might be called a completist. He reassures us that creation follows a design, that things aren't running down through entropy.

Don't expect doctrine, but fluidity here. The running commentary on what makes a viable novel, and the conversation with himself as he reviews a lifetime of reading, is breezy and affirmative. And breezy is a compliment to his style, attesting to how enjoyable the ride is—the knowledge shared is just so artfully compact. The titles that pour forth not only invite you to recall your own favorites, but more than once I dropped something into my amazon.com queue or checked online to see if it was currently available at the Strand. Expect to fall outside of your comfort zone here and there. I was lost when he discussed Russian novelists, not having covered much ground there. Conversely, I was relieved to see my opinions of 20th century Japanese literature justified (though I enjoy Mishima's novel-length suicide notes and White doesn't).

I would like to politely chastise the reviewer elsewhere who complained that Ed spends too many compliments on literary friends in this book. Actually, the commentary on literary relationships elevates *The Unpunished Vice*. The stories of nourishing artistic and intellectual camaraderie make the gift of a particular book all the more meaningful, the lessons learned applicable to life, not just the trade of telling tales. Recounting these connections provides an important history of gay literary output, the intersections of which won't be found anywhere else.

First and foremost, ours is a history of friendship.

For well over twenty years, I have committed myself to reading one author biography a year to better source the secret to being a successful writer (and the answer is a rather dull one, my friends: talent + time management). These biographies however, big and small, all share a singular failing: they never fully plot out the reading life that makes a writer. Sure, the drama of relationships, the pathologies found in bottles of liquor and the like lend themselves to much more theatrical reading than, say, a list of books. Still, these wholly unique libraries should be cataloged for a deeper understanding of influence, of development, those secret competitions and thirsts that form a successful writing career. I've only encountered one such book, Thomas Wight's estimable *Built of Books*, a celebration of Oscar Wilde's reading habits. Surely there are others. Though it's worth noting that White clarifies my thesis toward the end of *The Unpunished Vice* by warning us not to judge a writer by his library, as favorites are passed to friends and shelves fill up with books to blurb and review. And I can attest to this, having been invited to Ed and Michael's apartment to discuss this project. I had only seen, but had never spoken to, Ed at a reading and the Lammies, so I was nervous (and secreted one of those small airplane bottles of whiskey in my bag in case I needed a nip), and of course they were gracious and encouraging, answering my questions and making suggestions. As my eyes drifted over to the voluminous, overstuffed bookshelf, stacks of proofs with tear sheets jutting out, I felt Ed eagerly follow my gaze. I swear I know he was thinking, "What can I send home with this guy?"

Early on in *The Unpunished Vice*, Ed quotes his younger self's Wildean pronouncement, "I may never be so well known as John Updike, but to my few readers I'm indispensable." Well that's certainly changed, as attested by the PEN/Saul Bellow Award for Achievement in American Fiction that was bestowed on him in 2018; Edmund White now is every bit as well-known as Updike or any of his contemporaries in American letters. *The Unpunished Vice* is an exquisite, winding staircase though the rich and varied library of an important writer's readings, one that, like the very best books, delivers the reader to secret but familiar chambers seemingly—if only—without end.

CONTRIBUTOR BIOGRAPHIES

ALYSIA ABBOTT is the author of *Fairyland, a Memoir of My Father*, a recipient of the Madame Figaro Prix Heroine and the ALA Stonewall Award. Named a New York Times Editors Pick and one of the best books of the year by *the SF Chronicle* and Shelf Awareness, it was also finalist for the 2014 Lambda Literary Award and a Goodreads Choice Award. It has been published in the United States, the UK, France, Poland ,and Spain; translations are forthcoming in Brazil, and Italy. Her writing has been published in *TriQuarterly*, *Lit Hub*, *Out*, *The Boston Globe*, *The NYTBR*, *Vogue*, and elsewhere. The recipient of a fellowship from Ragdale Foundation and an MFA in creative nonfiction from the New School, Abbott teaches the Memoir Incubator Program at *Grub-Street*.

BRIAN ALESSANDRO is the owner and editor-in-chief of *The New Engagement (TNE)*, a literary journal with a fast-growing social media following, and over 14,000 monthly page views and 5,000 monthly users of the online edition. TNE is currently publishing original work by several well-known authors, including Edmund White (his first poem in sixteen years), Pulitzer Prize and National Book Award-winning poet Richard Howard, Murzban F. Shroff, MG Stephens, Seamus Scanlon, Nadia Ibrashi, and Sue Kaufman Award-winner Michael Carroll, whose memoir explores his marriage to White, in their bi-annual print issues. They have also been included in the *EBSCOhost* humanities section available to college and university libraries and in the *Poets & Writers literary* magazines database .*TNE* was recently featured in the *LGBTQ Writers Caucus* for the AWP and has been profiled by Carroll in *Lambda Literary*.

Brian's first novel, *The Unmentionable Mann*, was published by Cairn Press in September 2015, and received favorable reviews from the *Huffington Post, Examiner.com, The Leaf*, and was excerpted in *Bloom*, the Edmund White-advised LGBTQ literary journal. The book was also featured at the 2016 Tucson Festival of Books and nominated for an Independent Book Publisher Association (IBPA) award for Best New Voice. Brian is also the writer and director of the feature film, *Afghan Hound*, which co-stars Matt McGorry, and has been screened at the Left Forum and The Institute for Contemporary Psychotherapy as part of its trauma training series.

Additionally, *HiConcept Magazine* recently nominated his short stories ,*Mandarin Slang* and *The Commands of Class and Carnage*, for Pushcart Prizes. Brian holds a master of arts in clinical psychology from Columbia University, and has taught the subject, along with English literature, at the high school and college levels for 13 years. Brian is currently adapting White's 1982 classic, *A Boy's Own Story*, into a graphic novel for Deep End Productions and Top Shelf Productions with Carroll, and developing a cable series entitled *The Disembodied* with Jonathan Caouette) *Tarnation*) and Daniel Dreifuss (the Academy Award-nominated *No*).

DAVID BERGMAN is the author or editor of over a dozen books. His study *Gaiety Transfigured: Gay Self-Representation in American Poetry* was selected as an Outstanding Book of the Year by *Choice* and Gustavius Meyers Center for Human Rights. He is also author of *The Violet Hour: The Violet Quill and the Making of Gay Culture*, a book, which according to Richard Canning, "confirms its author's preeminence among contemporary critics of gay male literature." Bergman is also the editor of John Ashbery's *Reported Sightings* and Edmund White's *The Burning Library* as well as of *Gay American Autobiography*. A poet whose work has appeared in *Poetry, American Scholar, New Republic,* and *Yale Review*, his first book *Cracking the Code* won the George Elliston Prize for poetry. His

EDMUND WHITE BY THE BOOK · 359

latest book of poetry is *Fortunate Light*. His latest work of criticism, *The Poetry of Disturbance*. He is a professor emeritus of English at Towson University outside of Baltimore.

RICHARD CANNING is Professor of British and American Literature at the University of Northampton. He has interviewed Edmund White many times, most extensively in his first book, *Gay Fiction Speaks: Conversations with Gay Novelists* (New York/London: Columbia University Press, 2000). Its successor *Hear Us Out* (New York/London: Columbia University Press, 2004) won a 2005 Editors Choice Lambda Literary Award. Canning is author or editor of seven other books, and is completing a critical biography of Ronald Firbank for Harvard University Press.

TOM CARDAMONE is the author of the Lambda Literary Award-winning speculative novella *Green Thumb* and the erotic fantasy novels *The Lurid Sea* and *The Werewolves of Central Park* as well as the novella *Pacific Rimming*. So far he has cobbled together two short story collections, *Night Sweats: Tales of Homosexual Wonder and Woe* and *Pumpkin Teeth*, which was a finalist for the Lambda Literary Award and a Black Quill Award. Additionally, he has edited *The Lost Library: Gay Fiction Rediscovered* and the anthology *Lavender Menace: Tales of Queer Villainy!*, which was nominated for the Over The Rainbow List by the LGBT Round Table of the American Library Association. His short stories have appeared in numerous anthologies and magazines, some of which have been collected on his website www.pumpkinteeth.net.

MICHAEL CARROLL has been married to Edmund White since 2013. They met in Paris in 1995, the year White's collection *Skinned Alive* was published. He is the author of *Little Reef and Other Stories*, winner of the 2015 Sue Kaufman Prize for First Fiction from the American Academy of Arts and Letters. With Brian Alessandro he is the co author of the upcoming Edmund White's *A Boy's Own Story: A Graphic Novel*. His collection *Stella Maris: Key West Stories* will appear from Turtle Point Press later in 2019."

PHILIP CLARK is co-editor of the anthology *Persistent Voices: Poetry by Writers Lost to AIDS* (Alyson, 2009) and of *In the Empire of the Air: The Poems of Donald Britton* (Nightboat, 2016). His essays and reviews about gay and lesbian literature, history, and art have appeared in numerous journals and books, including *1960s Gay Pulp Fiction: The Misplaced Heritage* and *The Oxford Companion to the Photograph*. He is the recipient of a MacDowell Fellowship to complete a biography of H. Lynn Womack, a Washington D.C.-based publisher and First Amendment pioneer in operation from the late 1950s to the early 1970s.

PHILIP F. CLARK is the author of *The Carnival of Affection: Poems*, published by Sibling Rivalry Press, 2017. He is currently an Adjunct Assistant Professor in English and Poetry at City College, New York, where he received his MFA in Creative Writing/Poetry, in 2016. His poems, essays, and interviews have been published in *Assaracus Journal of Gay Poetry*, *Lambda Literary*, *Poetry in Performance*, *The Conversant*, *Atomic Micro Press*, and most recently in *Transition: Poems in the Aftermath*, published by Indolent Books. His poetry blog is The Poet's Grin, at https://philipfclark.wordpress.com

ROBERT GLÜCK is a poet, fiction writer, editor, and New Narrative theorist who has served as director of San Francisco State University's Poetry Center, co-director of Small Press Traffic Literary Center, and associate editor at Lapis Press. His books include two novels, *Jack the Modernist* and *Margery Kempe*, two books of stories, *Elements* and *Denny Smith*, a book of poems and short prose, *Reader*, and with Kathleen Fraser, a book of prose poems, *In Commemoration of the Visit*. With Bruce Boone, Glück translated La Fontaine for a book of that name. With Camille Roy, Mary Berger, and Gail Scott, he edited *Biting their Error: Writers on Narrative*. Glück prefaced *Between Life and Death*, a book of Franks Moore's paintings, and he made a film *Aliengnosis* with Dean Smith. Most recently, Glück published *Communal Nude: Collected Essays, and Parables*, an editioned artist book with Cuban artists Jose Angel Toirac and Meira Marrero Diaz. In 2019, Margery

Kempe will be republished by New York Review of Books Classics. Glück lives "high on a hill" in San Francisco.

ALLAN GURGANUS's fiction has been translated into sixteen languages. Books include *Oldest Living Confederate Widow Tells All*, *White People*, *Plays Well with Others*, *The Practical Heart* and most recently *Local Souls* and *Decoy*. Gurganus's essays are seen on the Op-Ed page of the *New York Times* and in *The New York Review of Books*. A finalist for the Pen-Faulkner Prize, he has been awarded the Los Angeles Times Book Prize, the American Academy's Sue Kaufman Prize for best first novel, a Guggenheim Fellowship, the Lambda Literary Award and the National Magazine Prize. Film adaptations of Gurganus's work have won four Emmys. A Fellow of the American Academy of Arts and Letters, Gurganus cofounded Writers Against Jesse Helms. His novel *The Erotic History of a Country Baptist Church* will be published by Liveright-Norton.

TREBOR HEALEY is the recipient of a Lambda Literary award, two Publishing Triangle awards and a Violet Quill award. He is the author of three novels, a book of poetry and three collections of stories. He co-edited the anthologies *Beyond Definition* and *Queer & Catholic*. www.treborhealey.com.

WAYNE HOFFMAN is the author of the novels *Hard*, *Sweet Like Sugar*, and *An Older Man*, and his stories have appeared in *Fresh Men 2*, *Best Gay Stories 2010*, *Mama's Boy*, and other anthologies. He is executive editor of *Tablet* magazine, and his cultural reporting has appeared in the *Wall Street Journal*, *Washington Post*, *Village Voice*, *The Nation*, and elsewhere.

ALDEN JONES's travel memoir, *The Blind Masseuse: A Traveler's Memoir from Costa Rica to Cambodia*, was published by the University of Wisconsin Press. *The Blind Masseuse* explores the ethics of traveling as an American abroad and was named Recommended Reading by PEN American Center and a Top Ten Travel Titles of 2013 by *Publishers Weekly*. Her story collection, *Unaccompanied*

Minors, won the 2013 New American Fiction Prize and was named by the Star-Ledger's Jacqueline Cutler as one of the "Ten Best Books of 2014 by New Jersey Authors." She teaches creative writing at Emerson College and in the Newport MFA program, and is the co-director of the Cuba Writers Program.

KEVIN KILLIAN has written three novels, *Shy* (1989), *Arctic Summer* (1997), and *Spreadeagle* (2012), a book of memoirs, *Bedrooms Have Windows* (1990), and three books of stories, *Little Men* (1996), *I Cry Like a Baby* (2001), and *Impossible Princess* (2009). He has also written three books of poetry, *Argento Series* (2001), *Action Kylie* (2008), and *Tweaky Village* (2014). Killian is a leading figure of the so-called "New Narrative" movement, a loosely organized group of writers with a common project: the infusion of prose fiction with the theoretical insights of experimental poetry in our time. New projects include *Screen Tests*, an edition of Killian's film writing, *Nude*, a book in collaboration with New York-based artist Ugo Rondinone, and a book of Killian's intimate photographs, *Tagged*, released in January 2013.

SHEILA KOHLER is a South African author now living in the United States and the author of ten novels (including *Cracks* which was adapted into a 2009 film of the same name), and three short story collections. Her writing has appeared in the *New York Times*, *O Magazine* and included in the *Best American Short Stories*. She has twice won an O. Henry Prize. She's the author of the recent memoir *Once We Were Sisters*.

KATHE KOJA is a writer, performer, director and independent producer whose work crosses and recombines genres. Her novels have been multiply translated and optioned for film. She creates performative events, solo and with an ensemble of artists, with her company Loudermilk Productions LLC.

ZACHARY LAZAR is the author of three novels and the memoir *Evening's Empire: The Story of My Father's Murder*. It was selected as a Best Book of 2009 by the *Chicago Tribune*. He earned an AB degree in Comparative Literature from Brown University (1990) and MFA from the University of Iowa Writer's Workshop (1993). In 2015, he was the third recipient of the John Updike Award from the American Academy of Arts and Letters.

DAVID McCONNELL is the author of, among other books, the acclaimed novel, *The Silver Hearted*, 2010. His short fiction and journalism have appeared widely in magazines and anthologies, including *The Literary Review* (UK), *Granta*, *Prospect Magazine* (UK), and *The Paris Review*. His most recent work, the narrative non-fiction *American Honor Killings, Desire and Rage among Men* (Akashic, March, 2013) has garnered widespread accolades. He lives in New York City. He was co–chair of the Lambda Literary Foundation from 2009-2011. A novel is forthcoming.

JEROME ELLISON MURPHY earned his MFA from the Creative Writing Program at New York University, where he currently serves as Undergraduate Programs Manager .He currently co-curates the Bespoke readings series at Bureau of General Services Queer Division bookstore, and is a frequent participant in the Emotive Fruition performance series curated by Thomas Dooley. He has also served on the board of Lambda Literary Foundation, the world's foremost non-profit supporting LGBT literature. His critical writing has appeared in *LA Review of Books*, *Publishers Weekly*, *The Brooklyn Rail*, *Lambda Literary Review*, and *American Poets*, while his poetry appears in *Narrative Magazine*, *LitHub*, *The Awl*, NPR's *RadioLab*, *Spunk*, *Bellevue Literary Review*, and on the ceiling as you lie awake at 4 a.m. See more at jemwords.com.

ANGELO NIKOLOPOULOS is the author of *Obscenely Yours*. His poems have appeared in *Best American Poetry*, *Best New Poets*, *Boston Review*, *Fence*, *The Los Angeles Review*, *PANK*, *Tin House*, and elsewhere. He teaches Creative Writing at New York University.

FRANK PIZZOLI has interviewed Edmund White two times for *Lambda Literary Review* and once with Felice Picano and Andrew Holleran as surviving members of The Violet Quill. has written for *The Brooklyn Rail*, *Gay & Lesbian Review Worldwide*, and *Windy City Times*. His work has also appeared in *The Huffington Post*, *White Crane Review*, and *POZ*. He is founding publisher and editor of *Central Voice* newspaper.

LEO RACICOT is an award-winning poet and essay-memoirist. He is currently working on a new biography of Edmund White and is Mr. White's official bibliographer. Leo lives in Lowell, Massachusetts.

NICHOLAS F. RADEL is Professor of English at Furman University, Greenville, South Carolina. Co-editor of *The Puritan Origins of American Sex*, Radel is the author of articles on American literature and drama, including essays and encyclopedia entries on Edmund White's works. His most recent book is *Understanding Edmund White*.

JERRY ROSCO has contributed stories and articles to anthologies, journals and magazines, including *Chicago Review*, *Literary Review*, and anthologies *What Love Is* and *Speak My Language*. He is author of the biography *Glenway Wescott Personally*, an ALA Stonewall Honor Book about the 1920s expatriate novelist. He has also edited two volumes of Wescott journals, *Continual Lessons* and the Lambda Literary Award winning *A Heaven of Words*.

SARAH SCHULMAN is the author of 16 books, as well as plays and film. Her interview with Edmund was reprinted in her book *The Gentrification of the Mind: Witness to a Lost Imagination*.

TIM TEEMAN is a multi-award-winning Senior Editor and Writer at the *Daily Beast*, overseeing the site's arts, culture, LGBT, style, and media coverage. He also writes across the site on many different topics. Tim has won two New York Press Club awards and three Los Angeles Press Club National Arts and Entertainment Journalism awards for his *Daily Beast* writing, as well as an NLGJA award for profile writing, and been honored in the NLGJA's journalist of the year and interviewer of the year categories. Tim's first book, *In Bed With Gore Vidal: The Private World of an American Master*, was a #1 Amazon bestseller, and nominated for a Lambda Literary Award. Tim previously worked for *The Times* of London for fourteen years, as Arts and Entertainment Editor, and US Correspondent (a position which brought him to New York). He edited the UK's LGBT newspaper, *The Pink Paper*. He has also written for publications including the *New York Times*, *Town and Country*, *The Observer* (UK), and *Attitude*.

LYNNE TILLMAN is a novelist, short story writer, and cultural critic. She is currently Professor/Writer-in-Residence in the Department of English at the University at Albany and teaches at the School of Visual Arts' Art Criticism and Writing MFA Program. Tillman is the author of five novels, three collections of short stories, one collection of essays, and two other nonfiction books.

IAN RAFAEL TITUS has written fiction and poetry for *Velvet Mafia*, *Into the Abyss*, *Frozen Tears II* and *III*, and *Visionary Tongue*, a writers' workshop fanzine established by author Storm Constantine and Eloise Coquio. His essay on Melvin Dixon's novel *Vanishing Rooms* appears in *The Lost Library: Gay Fiction Rediscovered*.

COLM TÓIBÍN is an Irish writer who has worked as a journalist before achieving fame as a fiction writer. His works often depict Irish society and explore themes of creativity and homosexuality. His most famous novels include *The Blackwater Lightship* and *The Master*. He is the Irene and Sidney B. Silverman Professor of English and Comparative Literature at Columbia.

CHARLIE VÁZQUEZ is the author of the novel *Contraband* (Rebel Satori, 2010), several short stories and poetry, as well as having edited two anthologies of Latino literature: *The Best of PANIC!*) Fire King, 2010), which was based on his breakthrough East Village reading series (2008-2011), and *From Macho to Mariposa* (Lethe, 2011) with author and cultural producer Charles Rice-González. He's the former New York City coordinator for Puerto Rico's "Festival de la Palabra", and was awarded a Commendation for his work in the Latino writing community by New York City Comptroller Scott M. Stringer in 2014. He's appeared on several TV and radio shows in the United States, Puerto Rico, Canada and Mexico, as well as at universities and cultural institutions. He works as an arts administrator with a focus on programs for people-of-color and immigrants in the Bronx.

WILLIAM STERLING WALKER is a New Orleans native who writes and makes art in Brooklyn. He is the author of a collection of stories, *Desire: Tales of New Orleans*, published by Chelsea Station Editions, which was nominated for the Lambda Literary Foundation's 2012 LGBT Debut Fiction Award. His short stories have been anthologized in *With: New Gay Fiction*, edited by Jameson Currier, *Best Gay Stories 2013*, edited by Steve Berman, *Best American Gay Fiction, Vol. 2*, edited by Brian Bouldrey and *Fresh Men*, edited by Don Weise and selected by Edmund White. A memoir of his coming out appeared in the Lambda Literary Award-winning anthology, *Boys Like Us: Gay Writers Tell Their Coming Out Stories*, edited by Patrick Merla. He wrote the biographical entries on poet James Merrill and film director Douglas Sirk for *The Scribner Encyclopedia of American Lives*. He has written for many publications, including the *Boston Book Review* and *Publisher's Weekly*. He has shown his collages in group shows in New York and Connecticut, including a show of artist couples at the Brooklyn Public Library curated by Lynn Saville. Mr. Walker earned a Bachelor of Arts degree in English from The University of New Orleans and a Masters Degree in Fine Arts in Creative Writing from Brooklyn College.

DONALD WEISE has twenty years' publishing experience, the majority of which has been devoted to LGBT literature. He's editorial director of Magnus Books and has served as Publisher of

Alyson Books and Senior Editor at Carroll & Graf Publishers. Don was named by *Publishers Weekly* as an industry "Change Maker" and listed among *Out Magazine*'s "100 Most Intriguing Gay Men and Lesbians" of the year. He's also the author of the award-winning books *Black Like Us: A Century of Lesbian, Gay & Bisexual Fiction, Time on Two Crosses: The Collected Writings of Bayard Rustin, The Huey P. Newton Reader, Sexually Speaking: Collected Essays of Gore Vidal,* and *Fresh Men: New Voices in Gay Fiction.* He lives in New York City.

RICK WHITAKER is author of *Assuming the Position: A Memoir of Hustling, The First Time I Met Frank O'Hara: Reading Gay American Writers,* and *An Honest Ghost,* a novel published by Jaded Ibis Press in 2013. He works at Columbia University's Italian Academy for Advanced Studies.

ACKNOWLEDGEMENTS

MY DEEPEST APPRECIATION to the writers herein who made this book happen. Special thanks to Christopher Stoddard and Jerry Rosco for seeing it through. Thank you, Lincoln Perry, for the use of your photograph of your bust of Edmund White. Thank you to booksellers and librarians everywhere; you are the celestial beekeepers of our dreams and rediscovered truths. Love and thanks to my Leo, for holding my hand when the plane takes off.

ACKNOWLEDGEMENTS

NO SPECIAL APPRECIATION to ...

BOOKS BY ITNA

Urban Gothic: The Complete Stories
Bruce Benderson

Settlers Landing
Travis Jeppesen

Bruno's Conversion
Tsipi Keller

The Beads
David McConnell

The Virtuous Ones
Christopher Stoddard

After David
Catherine Texier